T0384019

Scaling Responsible AI

Scaling Responsible AI

From Enthusiasm to Execution

Noelle Russell

WILEY

To Warren Russell—my husband, high school sweetheart, and best friend. You are the ultimate "Hype Man," and your unwavering support, love, and gentle pressure to pursue my own greatness made this book possible.

About the Author

Noelle Russell is a multi-award-winning technologist, entrepreneur, and global keynote speaker with over 20 years of experience in IT, specializing in data, cloud, conversational AI, and generative AI. She is the founder and CEO of the AI Leadership Institute, a platform dedicated to empowering companies and individuals to embrace AI responsibly and at scale. Her educational framework—"from the boardroom to the whiteboard to the keyboard"—bridges the gap between executive education, technical leadership, and workforce enablement.

Noelle's career journey has seen her lead groundbreaking AI initiatives at NPR, Microsoft, IBM, AWS, and Amazon Alexa. Her work has spanned the development of responsible AI solutions across 30 industries and business functions, and she has become a trusted advisor for organizations navigating the transformative power of AI. In recognition of her impact, Noelle has received numerous accolades, including the Microsoft Most Valuable Professional (MVP) award for Artificial Intelligence for three consecutive years and VentureBeat's Women in AI Responsibility and Ethics award.

As a passionate advocate for inclusive innovation and AI literacy, Noelle founded the "I ❤ AI" community, creating a space for learning, collaboration, and advancing AI for good. Her groundbreaking projects include JusticeGPT, a tool designed to provide advocacy resources, and the AI Startup Accelerator, which helps entrepreneurs launch and scale AI-powered businesses.

Noelle's thought leadership extends beyond technology; she is the author of several works, including her forthcoming book *The Lamplighter Effect*, which outlines 12 leadership principles for thriving in the era of AI. She also hosts the podcast "Good Morning, AI," where she spotlights female AI leaders and explores the potential and challenges of AI in today's world.

Noelle's life philosophy is rooted in empowering others to achieve success through innovation and resilience. From her early days on the Amazon Alexa team, with no prior experience in AI, to becoming a sought-after leader in the field, her journey reflects the power of persistence and vision. When she's not building the future of AI, Noelle enjoys spending time with her husband and six children, mentoring aspiring leaders, and advancing opportunities for women and girls in technology.

Acknowledgments

First and foremost, I want to express my deepest gratitude to my parents, Alicia Cirino and Irving Robinson, who instilled in me the values of continuous learning and the love of science fiction.

To my children, Ben, Max, Jacob, Joslyn, Mia, and Sage, thank you for your unwavering support and patience. Writing this book required countless hours of focus and dedication, and I am forever grateful for the time and space you gave me to bring this vision to life. Your love and understanding made this journey possible.

To the incredible members of my I ❤ AI community, you are the heartbeat that keeps me inspired and moving forward in the ever-evolving world of AI. Your passion and curiosity drive me to push boundaries and continue exploring new possibilities.

To the founding members of the AI Leadership Institute, thank you for believing in this mission from the very beginning. Your contributions and insights have helped shape a platform that empowers leaders to harness the transformative power of AI responsibly.

To my clients, who entrusted me to build responsible AI solutions across 30 industries and countless business functions, your trust and collaboration have been instrumental in bringing meaningful innovation to life. Thank you for allowing me to be part of your journey toward creating a better future.

Finally, I want to thank every manager, leader, and colleague who told me "No." Those moments taught me resilience and the power to turn obstacles into opportunities. You inspired me to transform "No" into "Let's go." This book is as much a reflection of those lessons as it is of my successes.

This work is a culmination of the support, inspiration, and challenges I've encountered along the way. Thank you all for being part of this journey.

—Noelle Russell

Contents

Introduction

People often ask me how I got started in the technology industry. I think back and remember with a smile that I got started in technology during a time when we all thought the world was going to end. Y2K.

I spent the first 12 years of my career at IBM, entrenched in FORTRAN, Smalltalk, and Java. I taught hundreds of thousands of engineers and system administrators how to go from mainframe to client server, from client server to web/mobile, mobile to cloud, cloud to big data, big data to AI. I have always been on the bleeding edge.

Eventually, my career in the tech industry led me to Amazon, where I found myself at the forefront of innovation, leading a team at Amazon Web Services (AWS). Then, in 2014, an email from Jeff Bezos sparked a new chapter in my journey. The vision was to build the *Star Trek* computer, and I felt an immediate pull to be part of that journey.

As a caregiver to my dad and a mother of six, my oldest child with Down Syndrome, I was searching for a way to use technology to make the world more accessible to the people I love most. When given a chance to help build something that would allow me to use my voice to change the world, I jumped at the opportunity.

On joining the Alexa team, I immersed myself in creating over 100 Alexa skills in the first year, each reflecting my unique perspective as a woman, a Latina, a mother, and a caregiver. I have over 25,000 five-star reviews and have created new categories on what initially was seen as a kitchen device. I saw more.

In a team dominated by men, I stood as the only woman, the only Latina, and the only mom. Throughout my experiences, I strove to build applications that would go beyond the conventional and help caregivers, empower individuals, and foster personal growth.

This journey led me to understand the profound impact that technology, specifically artificial intelligence (AI), can have in enriching lives. It became my mission to harness this technology to create an inclusive and supportive environment, not just for my son but for countless others who would benefit from its potential.

As I immersed myself in the world of AI and innovation, I encountered both triumphs and challenges. One of the most significant hurdles I faced was the lack of representation of women and people of color in the tech industry. I had to navigate spaces where I often felt like an outlier, continually proving my worth and capabilities in a male-dominated environment. However, rather than succumbing to the pressure, I used these experiences to fuel my passion for creating positive change within the industry.

In my pursuit to advocate for inclusive innovation, I became involved in initiatives aimed at empowering women and underrepresented groups in technology. I mentored aspiring technologists, sharing my own journey and encouraging them to pursue their goals with determination and resilience. Through this work, I sought to build a community where everyone, regardless of their background, could thrive and contribute to the innovation that drives our world forward. The AI Leadership Institute was born.

This intricate intersection of technology, my core values, and advocacy shaped my identity and purpose in profound ways. It fueled my creativity and commitment to effecting positive change, not only for my own family but for communities worldwide. My journey with technology and innovation became a testament to the transformative potential of embracing diverse perspectives and harnessing technology to elevate humanity.

After Amazon, I was recruited to join the team at Microsoft to help launch a new world of democratized AI through Azure AI services. During my tenure there, I influenced over $1 billion in Azure AI sales to the top worldwide brands looking to implement AI solutions, and this was all before 2018.

One thing I learned at Microsoft, Amazon, and IBM is that although it is important to have good technology, *you must have responsible leadership to match*. Many organizations that invested in AI from 2014 to 2020 struggled to deploy those ideas to production.

This book explores what I saw working and not working in the world of AI at the companies I helped along the way. From playground to production, there are steps the successful have taken, and I want to share those ideas with you. This book will outline the frameworks, checklists, and resources I have used to help advise organizations just like yours.

Artificial intelligence, in the early stages, is a lot like a baby tiger. Through the course of this book, we will tame that tiger into a solution that is safe and responsible and that serves everyone.

What Does This Book Cover?

Artificial intelligence has moved beyond the realm of hype and headlines, becoming an integral force shaping industries, economies, and societies. Yet, with great power comes the need for great responsibility. *Scaling Responsible AI: From Enthusiasm to Execution* is a definitive guide for leaders, innovators, and practitioners navigating the complexities of building and deploying AI at scale.

This book bridges the gap between the excitement of AI's potential and the disciplined execution required to harness it responsibly. With frameworks like LEAD AI and SECURE AI, practical strategies for scaling, and thoughtful discussions on ethics, governance, and fairness, this book equips readers with the tools to build AI systems that are innovative, impactful, and inclusive. Whether you're grappling with the challenges of ideation, implementation, or long-term resilience, this book provides the insights and lessons needed to lead the AI transformation with confidence and clarity.

Chapter 1: Lead AI: A Framework for Building Responsible AI In this first chapter, explore the pillars of the LEAD AI framework—a roadmap encompassing Leadership, Ethical foundations, AI governance, Designing for inclusivity, AI strategy, and Implementation—to lay the groundwork for developing artificial intelligence that is helpful, honest, and harmless.

Chapter 2: The Hype of AI: Capturing the Excitement Explore both the thrilling possibilities and the sobering realities of AI's rapid emergence through analogies like the darling yet dangerous baby tiger, highlighting the importance of responsible and ethical development amid the hype.

Chapter 3: Building the AI Sandbox: Safe, Responsible Spaces for Innovation Discover how to construct a controlled playground for AI experimentation, from establishing ethical policies and identifying low-risk use cases to aligning innovations with core values and scaling solutions responsibly.

Chapter 4: From Ideation to Action: Setting Up for Successful Business Outcomes Journey from vision to implementation as we explore strategies for aligning AI with business values, pushing boundaries responsibly, evaluating risks, finding the right complexity level, and ultimately delighting users with remarkable solutions.

Chapter 5: From Playground to Production: Embracing the Challenges Traverse the details of transitioning from concept to implementation as we tackle infrastructure needs, team dynamics, data challenges, balancing iteration speed with steady progress, and ultimately planning for the long-term sustainability of AI solutions.

Chapter 6: Beyond the Prototype: What Happens After POC? Transition from prototype to production pilot as we tackle shifting mindsets, visualization, scalability, continuous improvement, and balancing short-term wins with a long-term vision to successfully scale AI solutions and prepare for future challenges.

Chapter 7: SECURE AI: A Framework for Deploying Responsible AI Explore the SECURE AI framework spanning security, ethics, compliance, bias mitigation, Red Teaming, explainability, accountability, and iteration to responsibly evaluate, develop, and deploy artificial intelligence.

Chapter 8: Architecting AI: Designing for Scale and Security Master the intricacies of architecting enterprise-grade AI through strategies for security, scalability, evaluating options, and responsible implementation across the full development lifecycle.

Chapter 9: Why Change Is the Only Constant in AI Navigate the ever-shifting landscape of AI by embracing uncertainty, fostering resilience, encouraging diverse perspectives, prioritizing continuous learning, and crafting a forward-thinking mindset.

Chapter 10: Model Evaluation and Selection: Ensuring Accuracy and Performance Demystify the complexities of responsible model management, from leveraging open-source AI and maintaining integrity to ensuring fairness, planning updates, utilizing top tools, and proactively preparing for future changes.

Chapter 11: Bias and Fairness: Building AI That Serves Everyone Confront how bias manifests in AI systems and explore strategies to detect unfairness, increase transparency, mitigate harm, comply with evolving regulations, and ultimately build inclusive AI that serves all equitably.

Chapter 12: Responsible AI at Scale: Growth, Governance, and Resilience Illuminate the nuances of scaling AI ethically and securely through robust governance frameworks, regulatory navigation, handling disruptions, and ultimately cultivating organizational resilience and adaptability.

Chapter 13: Looking Back: Lessons Learned and Insights Gained Reflect on lessons learned, gain wisdom from AI experts, and explore strategies like embracing collaborative ecosystems, driving accessibility, and preparing proactively to chart an ethical and inclusive path forward.

Chapter 14: The Future of AI Leadership: Transforming Potential into Power Explore the emerging imperatives for a new breed of bold, ethical leaders who can harness AI's world-altering power responsibly, inspire confidence amid complexity, and ultimately chart a course toward an AI future aligned with human values.

Chapter 15: AI's Impact and Intention: Envisioning a World Transformed As we stand at the dawn of an AI-transformed world, this journey illuminates the path forward through key insights–collaborate cross-functionally, implement responsibly, architect intentionally, iterate with agility, evaluate comprehensively, and lead ethically–to harness AI's immense potential while building an equitable future that uplifts humanity.

Additional Resources

Throughout the book, you'll find sidebars that will provide more information that might aid your understanding of AI. Keep your eyes peeled for the following:

A note indicates information that's useful or interesting, but somewhat peripheral to the main text. A note might be information that you might find relevant as you learn about AI.

Warnings describe potential pitfalls or dangers. Be mindful of this information as you travel the AI landscape.

A tip provides information that can save you time or frustration and that may not be entirely obvious.

Real-World Scenario

A real-world scenario is a type of sidebar that describes a task or example that's particularly grounded in the real world. This may be a situation I or somebody I know has encountered, or it may be advice on how to work around problems that are common in real, working AI environments.

Reflection Questions

The reflection questions, which are found at the end of each chapter, are designed to help you deeply engage with the key concepts presented. It is your opportunity to pause, think critically, and consider how the ideas that have been discussed can be applied to your own leadership journey. By reflecting on these questions, you'll be able to better understand the text, identify areas for personal growth, and translate theoretical knowledge into practical action. To help you get the most out of reading the material, I suggest you use these questions in the following ways:

Set aside quiet time. Find a quiet space where you can focus without interruptions. Reflection is most effective when you can think deeply and without distractions.

Read each question carefully. Take a moment to fully understand each reflection question. There's no need to rush—let the question sink in.

Write down your thoughts. Consider keeping a journal where you can write down your reflections. Writing helps solidify your thoughts and enables you to revisit them later.

Be honest with yourself. Reflect on your experiences and thoughts candidly. This process is for your personal growth, so it's important to be truthful in your answers.

Take action. After reflecting, think about how you can apply these insights in your daily leadership practices. Identify specific actions you can take to improve and grow.

By following these simple instructions, you'll maximize the benefits of the reflection process and more effectively integrate the chapter's lessons into your leadership approach.

How to Contact the Publisher or the Author

If you would like to contact the author, please do so at:
786-509-4209
noelle@aileadershipinstitute.com

Ready to transform your organization with Responsible AI? We've developed a comprehensive framework that brings this book's concepts to life – covering everything from strategic planning and policy design to team structuring and security protocols. Take the next step in your AI journey with our detailed, step-by-step implementation guide, available at no cost at https://responsibleaibook.com.

If you believe you have found a mistake in this book, please bring it to our attention. At John Wiley & Sons, we understand how important it is to provide our customers with accurate content, but even with our best efforts an error may occur.

In order to submit your possible errata, please email it to our Customer Service Team at wileysupport@wiley.com with the subject line "Possible Book Errata Submission."

Part I

Day One:
The Hype Cycle

Chapter 1
LEAD AI: A Framework for Building Responsible AI

The path to developing artificial intelligence (AI) responsibly is paved with both opportunities and challenges. As creators in this rapidly evolving field, we have an obligation to build AI that benefits humanity while proactively mitigating risks. This undertaking requires forethought, diligence, and a framework to guide our efforts. The LEAD AI framework provides a roadmap, encompassing key focus areas that are imperative for creating AI that is ethical, unbiased, aligned with human values, and poised to drive positive change.

The LEAD AI Framework

LEAD AI stands for Leadership, Ethical foundations, AI governance and policies, and Designing for inclusivity, AI strategy, and implementation. Each aspect represents a critical pillar that collectively forms the foundation for responsible AI.

Let's break it down even further. Strong leadership entails cultivating a culture rooted in ethical values and a vision focused on stewarding AI for the common good. Robust ethical principles provide a moral compass for AI development, upholding ideals such as fairness, accountability, and transparency. Comprehensive governance policies safeguard against misuse while fostering a climate of responsibility and public trust. Inclusive design broadens perspectives, proactively seeking input from diverse stakeholders to create AI that empowers all communities. An intentional AI strategy aligns business objectives with ethical obligations, guiding technology deployment toward beneficial outcomes. Finally, effective implementation actualizes these ideals through concrete practices, metrics, and continuous oversight throughout an AI system's entire lifecycle.

By internalizing the LEAD AI framework, we can develop the mindset and mechanisms necessary to fulfill the promise of AI while navigating its complexities thoughtfully. The subsequent sections of this chapter delve into each framework component in further detail, providing guidance and illustrative examples to put these responsible AI principles into practice. Building AI that is ethical, unbiased, and aligned with social good requires diligence, collaboration, and unwavering commitment. With the LEAD AI framework as your guide, you can boldly step forward with care, wisdom, and humanity as your lodestars.

L—Leadership

Leadership is like being a lamplighter—it's about igniting the path for others to follow. Imagine a dark, unfamiliar street. The lamplighter walks ahead, lighting each lamp, gradually dispelling the darkness and revealing a way forward. In the same vein, effective leadership illuminates the way for your team, highlighting a path that leads them to success and growth. It's not just about giving orders; it's about guiding, inspiring, and supporting every one of your team members.

Lamplighters are known not only for their ability to light lamps but also for having a deep understanding of the environment in which they operate. They see the nooks and crannies, understand challenges, and consider the needs of those who will benefit from their guidance. They are doers, not just talkers.

Like the lamplighters, it's crucial as a leader in today's dynamic and complex world to have a comprehensive understanding of your team, your industry, and the rapidly evolving landscape of responsible AI. Learning from these lamplighters teaches you to share your light—one lamp at a time—ensuring that your team feels empowered, supported, and driven by a common purpose. You must strive to be the type of leader who doesn't just march ahead but also stands with your team, encouraging them to shine their own light and contribute to the collective illumination.

The journey to becoming this type of leader may have its challenges, but the rewards of viewing the path ahead illuminated with the glow of shared purpose and ambition make every effort worthwhile. You can learn from these luminaries and endeavor to become the lamplighters of your team, nurturing an environment where everyone has the opportunity to thrive and contribute to the greater good.

Some might think leadership is a "soft skill" and ask, "What does this have to do with AI?" Successful AI projects are led with clarity and delivered by a symphony of talented people with diverse lived experiences who provide value to their users by including said users every step of the way. AI projects with strong responsible leadership deliver results early, are completed before their deadlines, and have team members who are eager to do more to serve the organizational values.

Love and Ambition: Starting with Heartfelt Goals

When it comes to building responsible AI, it all starts with heart—the love and ambition that drive you to make a positive impact. Picture this: You're standing at the edge of an unexplored frontier, and possibilities are stretching out before you like a canvas waiting to be painted. At this pivotal moment, what matters most is your heartfelt goals—your deep-rooted desire to create something meaningful and transformative. It's about more than just technology; it's about the human touch—the passion that infuses work with purpose.

Love and ambition are the fuel propelling you forward, igniting the spark of innovation. However, it's not just about personal gain; it's about fostering a collective vision that resonates on a deeper level. When you lead with love and ambition, you set the stage for groundbreaking advancements centering around the betterment of society, making a real difference in people's lives.

So, how do you channel this love and ambition into actionable goals? It begins with introspection—with taking the time to connect with yourself and identify what truly drives you. This introspective journey serves as the compass guiding your actions, leading you toward goals that align with your values and aspirations. Whether it's enhancing accessibility, promoting equity, or optimizing efficiency, each goal is imbued with the genuine intention to contribute positively to the world.

Intertwining love and ambition instills a sense of purpose transcending mere advancement for advancement's sake. It anchors you in a commitment to ethical conduct, steering your efforts toward outcomes that are not only innovative but also responsible. With love as your motivation and ambition as your compass, you cultivate a fertile ground where empathy, creativity, and determination flourish, nurturing AI initiatives that prioritize the well-being of individuals, communities, and Earth.

Starting with heartfelt goals rooted in love and ambition sets your journey's trajectory for one filled with significance and impact. As you embark on this pursuit, remember that the power to create positive change resides within your ability to infuse your endeavors with genuine care and a relentless drive to make a difference. After all, when love and ambition converge, they become the driving force behind AI solutions that elevate humanity and inspire a brighter future.

Mindfulness and Purpose: Staying Centered and Focused

As you navigate the complex landscape of responsible AI, it's essential to address the significance of mindfulness and purpose in your approach. Mindfulness encapsulates the practice of staying present and aware in each moment, fostering a deeper understanding of the core values guiding your actions.

Responsible AI is the intentional development of AI systems to ensure that these systems are helpful, honest, and harmless. This includes ensuring that these systems are transparent, explainable, fair, scalable, and trustworthy.

In the realm of AI leadership, cultivating mindfulness enables you to make conscious decisions, untethered from distractions or impulsive reactions. Mindfulness increases your intentionality by slowing down your reaction times and prioritizing clarity over velocity. By integrating mindfulness into your leadership style, you can effectively manage the challenges and uncertainties inherent in the AI domain.

Purpose also plays a pivotal role in anchoring your endeavors toward building responsible AI. It serves as your North Star, providing clarity and direction as you strive to develop AI solutions that align with ethical standards and societal well-being. Embracing purpose empowers you to remain steadfast amid technology's evolving landscape, ensuring that your initiatives consistently contribute positively to the broader community. As leaders, nurturing mindfulness and purpose within ourselves sets a compelling example for teams and stakeholders. It demonstrates a commitment to making conscientious choices grounded in holistic consideration and long-term impact. Moreover, integrating mindfulness and purpose into organizational culture fosters an environment of trust, authenticity, and integrity. Encouraging your team to embrace mindfulness cultivates resilience and adaptability, enabling them to respond thoughtfully to challenges and complexities.

During my time at Amazon Alexa, I built an Alexa skill for mind-fulness. It guided the user through a 90-second mindfulness exercise. Once it went "live," I asked my teams before every meeting to use this skill. It helped enable people to take a few minutes before each meeting to clear their minds, set their intentions, and create an environment for highly productive meetings.

Instilling a sense of purpose propels collective efforts toward meaningful innovation, reinforcing the importance of ethical considerations in every aspect of AI development. Thus, as you endeavor to build responsible AI, don't overlook the profound influence of mindfulness and purpose. By centering yourself in the present moment and aligning your actions with a clear sense of purpose, you can navigate the intricacies of AI leadership with compassion, wisdom, and ethical resolve.

Leadership and Imagination: Guiding with Vision

Leadership is a journey of imagination and vision. It's about seeing beyond the immediate horizon, envisioning possibilities that others might overlook, and guiding your team toward those aspirations. A strong leader recognizes the power of imagination in shaping the future and uses it to inspire and motivate their team. As you navigate the terrain of AI development, harnessing the force of imagination is essential for steering the course of responsible AI.

Imagination fuels innovation. When you encourage your team to boldly imagine new solutions, you create a breeding ground for creativity and originality. By fostering an environment where imagination flourishes, you empower your team to think "outside the box" and explore uncharted territories in AI development. This can lead to breakthroughs that redefine the boundaries of what's possible, setting your organization apart as a trailblazer in the field.

Vision is the compass that guides your actions. As a leader, your vision provides direction, clarity, and purpose for your team.

It's not just about setting goals; it's about articulating a compelling and inspiring narrative that motivates everyone to work toward a common objective. Your vision should convey a sense of purpose, instilling in your team the belief that their work contributes to something meaningful and transformative. With a clear and compelling vision, you unite your team under a common cause and propel them toward ambitious AI endeavors.

What happens when you don't provide your team with vision? You will often see a lack of direction or focus and confusion about what needs to be done and what tasks to prioritize. The best way to capture a vision and share it with your team is to set targets for where you want to go, whether that is 1 billion views on YouTube or 100 new customers. Setting a target with a specific number helps to crystallize your vision and gets the team excited about meeting their goals.

Leading with vision means navigating uncertainty with poise and confidence. In the ever-evolving AI landscape, change is constant, and the ability to adapt is crucial. Your vision provides stability and guidance in those uncertain times. It enables you to anticipate challenges, identify opportunities, and steer your team toward fruitful outcomes. By anchoring your leadership in a robust and far-reaching vision, you imbue your team with a sense of purpose and resilience, enabling them to weather the storms of innovation with unwavering determination.

Ultimately, leadership and imagination are intertwined forces driving progress and transformation. As a leader at the forefront of responsible AI, you must nurture a culture celebrating imagination and cultivate a vision igniting passion and purpose. Empower your team to embrace bold ideas, rally behind a compelling vision, set aggressive targets, and venture into the uncharted territories of

AI innovation. By harnessing the potent combination of leadership and imagination, you chart a course toward a future where responsible AI thrives and profoundly impacts the world.

Gratitude and Harmony: Building a Positive Culture

Building a positive culture within any organization is crucial for fostering innovation, creativity, and collaboration. It involves nurturing an environment where gratitude and harmony are not only encouraged but also deeply embedded in the organizational ethos. Gratitude serves as a powerful reminder of the value placed on individuals and their contributions. Expressing appreciation for the efforts of colleagues, team members, and partners creates a sense of belonging and motivates everyone to strive for excellence.

Harmony, on the other hand, entails creating a cohesive and supportive atmosphere where diversity is celebrated and differences are viewed as strengths. When individuals feel a sense of harmony within the workplace, they are more likely to engage in open communication, share ideas, and respect varying perspectives. This, in turn, leads to enhanced problem-solving and a heightened collective intelligence.

To cultivate gratitude and harmony, leaders must lead by example, embodying these values in their interactions and decision-making processes. Acts of kindness, achievement recognition, and milestone celebrations all contribute to nurturing a culture of appreciation and interconnectedness. Encouraging mindfulness practices, such as meditation or gratitude exercises, can also help employees develop a heightened awareness of their emotions and the impact of their actions on others.

Although some leaders might mistake these practices as "foo-foo" or "soft skills," the ability to develop emotional intelligence in your team enables them to shift from a mentality of "move fast and break things" to one of "move with intentions and build incrementally." The latter leads to projects with clear direction and audacious goals, which have intentionality that drives increased business value. If you encounter resistance to these practices, do them as a team.

One practice I have implemented is "Thankful Thursdays," a team practice where, as my team was signing off for the day, they would take 15 minutes to write into the team's chat discussion about someone on the team that they were thankful for and why. In the beginning, I started the process and nudged my leaders to follow along. Yet, within a few weeks, the team was excited to add all the people they appreciated during the week in that 15-minute window.

In addition to individual efforts, organizational initiatives play a pivotal role in shaping a positive culture. Establishing regular forums for expressing gratitude, whether through team meetings, newsletters, or dedicated recognition programs, reinforces the importance of acknowledging and valuing each other's contributions. Promoting diversity and inclusion through targeted recruitment, training, and mentorship programs fosters a harmonious work environment where every voice is heard and valued.

The benefits of fostering a positive culture extend beyond mere employee satisfaction. Research has shown that organizations with a strong focus on gratitude and harmony experience higher levels of employee engagement, increased productivity, and greater overall success. Moreover, such organizations are also better equipped to attract top talent and retain their valuable workforce, resulting in a long-term competitive advantage and sustainable growth.

In summary, building a positive culture rooted in gratitude and harmony is not just a fleeting trend but a fundamental requirement for organizations aiming to thrive in an ever-changing landscape. Intentional efforts to instill these values at every organizational level create a ripple effect, influencing behavior, relationships, and outcomes for leaders and their teams. These efforts will travel beyond your business as well. When you cultivate a culture that is positive and empowering, those sentiments also reach your customers and partners. By weaving gratitude and harmony into the fabric of an organization's culture, leaders pave the way for enduring success and fulfillment for all involved.

Trust and Enthusiasm: Inspiring Confidence

Building trust within a team is like constructing a sturdy bridge that connects individuals, allowing them to cross over challenges together. It's about fostering an environment where everyone feels empowered to contribute their best, knowing that their efforts are valued. How do you inspire confidence and cultivate enthusiasm? The essence lies in genuine leadership that embodies integrity, transparency, and empathy. By showcasing these qualities, leaders can instill trust and enthusiasm within their teams.

Transparency is the cornerstone of building trust. When leaders communicate openly and honestly, it creates an atmosphere of transparency and openness, fostering trust among team members. Transparency eliminates uncertainties and allows everyone to align their efforts toward common goals. Leaders must also demonstrate empathy and an understanding of their team members' perspectives and challenges. By showing genuine care and consideration, leaders inspire confidence and foster an enthusiastic work culture. When team members feel understood and supported, they are more likely to invest their energy and talent into achieving collective success.

Moreover, integrity forms the bedrock of trust. Leaders who uphold ethical standards and lead by example establish credibility and earn their team's trust. Their consistent actions and decisions reflect their dedication to ethical conduct, creating a sense of assurance and reliability.

Equally as important is acknowledging and appreciating each team member's contributions. Recognizing their efforts and celebrating their achievements cultivates enthusiasm and fosters a culture of positivity. By expressing gratitude and acknowledging individual strengths, leaders uplift the team's spirit, encouraging collaboration and innovation. Trust and enthusiasm go hand in hand, driving teams to overcome challenges with resilience and determination. When teams trust their leaders and are motivated by genuine enthusiasm, they become more adaptive and resilient in the face of adversity. Challenges are viewed as opportunities for growth and learning, and the collective belief in achieving success strengthens their resolve.

In conclusion, inspiring confidence within a team is a multifaceted endeavor that draws upon the principles of transparency, empathy, integrity, and appreciation. When leaders prioritize these attributes, they pave the way for a culture of trust, enthusiasm, and resilience, enabling their teams to navigate challenges with unwavering confidence and determination.

Recognize your team's efforts by creating a "Wall of Fame." Amazon's lunchroom had a wall celebrating new patents, awards, and press coverage earned by employees. This public recognition motivated teams and gave everyone a reason to celebrate and a desire to make "The Wall."

Resilience and Success: Overcoming Challenges

Resilience is the backbone of any endeavor, especially when it comes to navigating the complexities of AI implementation. In the world of responsible AI, challenges are inevitable. Whether it's technical hiccups, ethical dilemmas, or resistance to change, the journey toward successful AI integration is paved with obstacles. However, it's how you respond to these challenges that truly defines your success. Resilience isn't just about bouncing back; it's also about bouncing forward. It's about embracing those setbacks as opportunities to learn, adapt, and grow.

Successful leaders understand that the path to achieving responsible AI requires grit, determination, and a willingness to face adversity head-on. They know that setbacks aren't roadblocks but rather stepping stones toward progress. To overcome challenges, it's essential that you foster a culture of resilience within your organization. This means encouraging open communication, promoting a growth mindset, and providing support for risk-taking and innovation. You must also lead by example, demonstrating your resilience in the face of adversity. Transparency and vulnerability can inspire and motivate teams to overcome hurdles with optimism and determination. In addition, embracing failure as part of the learn-ing process is crucial for building resilience. Viewing challenges as opportunities for improvement rather than insurmountable barri-ers allows for innovation and continuous refinement.

Celebrating small victories along the way reinforces the belief that overcoming challenges is not just possible but also integral to success. When addressing the unique challenges of responsible AI, you must be prepared to navigate ethical quandaries, ensure transparency, and prioritize the well-being of individuals impacted by AI decisions. This involves staying abreast of evolving ethical standards, seeking diverse perspectives, and upholding a commitment to equity and fairness. It's important because new issues, challenges, and harms are uncovered every day as technology advances. AI often replicates and amplifies existing societal biases and inequities, and you must be proactive to counteract it. Embracing challenges with empathy and understanding cultivates a resilient and empathetic approach to responsible AI lead-ership. Ultimately, resilience is the cornerstone of success in imple-menting responsible AI. It empowers individuals and organizations to weather storms, adapt to change, and emerge stronger on the other side. By fostering such a culture, you can guide your team through the most daunting challenges, reinforcing the shared purpose and propelling your team toward achieving the promise of responsible AI.

E—Ethical Foundations

Ethical considerations form the very foundation on which your approach to AI technology stands. To ensure that your tech is developed and deployed responsibly, it's imperative to establish a solid ethical framework that guides every decision and action. This bedrock will serve as the guide, shaping the trajectory of your AI's development and usage.

At its core, laying ethical foundations for responsible AI involves introspection, empathy, and a steadfast commitment to doing what is right, not just what is expedient. It requires you to scrutinize your intentions, consider the implications of your actions, and prioritize the well-being of individuals and society. By placing ethics at the forefront, you acknowledge the profound impact that AI can have on people's lives and recognize the need to wield this power with prudence and integrity.

One critical aspect of establishing ethical foundations is fostering transparency and accountability within the AI ecosystem. Transparency engenders trust and enables stakeholders to understand how AI systems function, how they make decisions, and how they might affect individuals. Accountability ensures that those responsible for developing and deploying AI are held accountable for their choices and the consequences of their creations. Together, transparency and accountability serve as pillars supporting the AI framework, creating an environment where it is developed and utilized in a manner aligning with societal values and expectations.

The absence of accountability in AI development can create a fertile ground for ethical transgressions. Without repercussions for their actions, developers and organizations might prioritize expediency over ethical considerations, potentially leading them to cut corners and neglect their due diligence. The result will be the deployment of biased, discriminatory, or otherwise harmful AI systems.

This lack of oversight could enable systemic issues to proliferate unchecked, eroding public trust, damaging the organization's brand, and hindering responsible AI advancement.

To ensure ethical AI development and deployment, it's important that you establish clear lines of responsibility and implement mechanisms that hold creators accountable for the consequences of their creations.

In laying ethical foundations for responsible AI, it's essential to address issues of fairness, privacy, and bias. Doing so will enable you to create helpful, honest, and harmless AI systems. Fairness demands that AI systems treat all individuals equitably and without discrimination, whereas privacy necessitates safeguarding personal information and upholding individual confidentiality. Bias mitigation requires a concerted effort to identify and rectify biases within AI algorithms, ensuring that any outcomes are balanced and impartial. By integrating these principles into your AI's ethical framework, you build a sturdy base for AI development and deployment that respects the rights and dignity of all individuals.

Ultimately, the process of laying ethical foundations is both a moral imperative and a pragmatic strategy. It not only reflects your commitment to upholding ethical standards but also mitigates risks, enhances trust, and fosters long-term sustainability in AI innovation. When ethical considerations form the bedrock of responsible AI, you pave the way for technology that serves as a force for good, propelling positive change and contributing to the betterment of your world.

A—AI Governance and Policy

Governance and policy also play a critical role in providing the structure and direction necessary to ensure the responsible development and deployment of AI technology. As you delve more into AI's complexities, it becomes increasingly apparent that a robust governance framework is essential for upholding ethical standards and mitigating potential risks. At its core, governance involves establishing clear guidelines and regulations that govern the use of AI within an organization. By setting up guardrails through well-defined policies, leaders can safeguard against misuse and promote transparency and accountability across all facets of AI implementation. Your comprehensive policy framework should encompass various aspects, including data privacy, algorithmic bias, ethical decision-making, and compliance with legal and regulatory requirements.

Moreover, it must be adaptable to advancements in technology and evolving societal expectations, ensuring that your AI systems remain aligned with ethical principles and societal needs.

Many organizations have created AI governance boards that are responsible for the development of policies, frameworks, and requirements, ensuring that there's a team responsible for the development and upholding of these important processes.

Effective governance also necessitates active participation from diverse stakeholders, incorporating input from experts in AI, ethics, law, and other relevant domains. This collaborative approach fosters a holistic understanding of the implications and consequences associated with AI applications, thereby informing the development of inclusive and ethical policies. Aligning governance with organizational objectives and values is instrumental in embedding ethical considerations into the fabric of AI strategy.

Here are a few examples of effective governance and what could potentially go wrong. For example, a healthcare provider prioritizing patient well-being above all else faces a critical juncture when implementing AI. A misaligned approach might prioritize AI that excels in maximizing diagnoses but, in doing so, overlooks or downplays patient data privacy concerns. This could lead to data breaches, erode patient trust, and ultimately compromise the very well-being the provider aims to uphold. An aligned approach, however, would involve developing AI governance that prioritizes patient data security and transparency alongside diagnostic accuracy. By embedding these values into the framework of its AI strategy, the healthcare provider can build confidence with patients, demonstrating a commitment to care that extends beyond accurate diagnoses to encompass the responsible and ethical handling of sensitive health information.

Another example is a financial institution. Upholding transparency and fairness ensures that these values are deeply embedded in its AI strategy. A misaligned approach might involve deploying AI-driven loan approval systems without a clear understanding of potential biases inherent in the data or algorithms. This could result in discriminatory lending practices that disproportionately impact certain groups, directly contradicting the financial institution's stated commitment to fairness. However, an aligned approach would prioritize governance that mandates rigorous bias audits throughout the AI lifecycle and establishes transparent mechanisms for explaining how AI-driven loan decisions are made. This proactive approach ensures fairness isn't sacrificed for efficiency, aligning the financial institution's AI practices with its core values and fostering trust with customers and the public.

Finally, here's an example of a social media company that champions freedom of expression. Aligning its AI practices with this core value is paramount. A misaligned approach, however, might see the company implementing AI content moderation with a heavy hand, potentially suppressing legitimate discourse due to overly broad definitions of harm or bias within the algorithms. This heavy-handed approach would directly contradict its commitment to free speech, alienating users and potentially stifling valuable conversations. An aligned approach, however, would prioritize AI governance that strives for a nuanced balance. It means developing AI content moderation tools that are effective in mitigating genuine harm but also incorporate robust user appeal processes and clear, readily accessible guidelines that reflect the company's dedication to upholding free speech principles. Its transparency and commitment to due process would foster a platform where its users feel heard and respected, even when navigating complex content moderation decisions.

In essence, alignment builds trust with stakeholders by demonstrating ethical action matches words. It prevents mission drift, ensuring that AI efforts don't contradict the organization's reason for being. It acts as a built-in ethical compass when navigating complex AI decisions, providing guiding principles.

Without this alignment, AI initiatives risk becoming ethically unsound, damaging reputation, and undermining the very values the organization seeks to uphold.

Establishing accountability mechanisms and oversight structures further underscores this commitment, reinforcing a culture of responsibility and integrity. Effective governance goes beyond mere compliance; it represents a commitment to cultivating a culture of responsible innovation and continuous improvement. As such, organizations have the opportunity not only to fulfill their ethical obligations but also to gain a competitive edge by building trust with their customers, employees, and the broader community. In navigating the intricate landscape of AI governance, leaders must prioritize proactive engagement and ongoing evaluation, staying attuned to emerging best practices and industry standards. By doing so, they can navigate the complex interplay between technological advancement and societal impact, ultimately steering their AI development toward a future that embraces diversity, equity, and ethical fortitude.

D—Designing for Inclusivity

In the quest to build responsible AI, designing for inclusivity is paramount. Inclusivity in AI is the active and intentional practice of ensuring that AI systems are designed, developed, and deployed in a way that considers, values, and empowers the full spectrum of human diversity. It's about creating technology that reflects the diverse perspectives and experiences of all individuals. By embracing inclusivity, you foster a sense of togetherness and belonging, ensuring that your AI solutions not only serve everyone but also empower them. When speaking about inclusivity in AI, it's not just about avoiding discrimination or bias; it's about actively seeking out and incorporating voices from various backgrounds and communities. This means engaging with a wide range of stakeholders to understand their unique needs and perspectives.

Designing for inclusivity requires a specific mindset shift. It starts with questioning your assumptions and biases and then actively seeking out diverse viewpoints. It involves building diverse teams that bring together individuals with varied cultural, social, and educational backgrounds. True inclusivity in AI doesn't happen by chance; it requires intentional effort. It involves creating processes and systems that prioritize fairness and equal representation, from data collection and model training to deployment and impact assessment.

Inclusivity also demands a commitment to transparency and accountability. It means openly acknowledging the limitations and potential biases in AI systems while also continuously working to address those challenges. A key aspect of designing for inclusivity is recognizing that AI solutions shouldn't perpetuate existing inequalities or leave certain populations behind. Instead, they must strive to uplift and empower those marginalized communities, which requires a proactive approach to identifying and mitigating potential harms or unintended consequences of AI applications.

Designing for inclusivity, however, also goes beyond technical considerations. It encompasses the entire user experience, ensuring that AI interfaces are accessible and intuitive for people of all abilities and backgrounds. It means fostering an environment where everyone feels heard, valued, and represented, both within your developmental process and in your end products. You must care about fostering an inclusive environment in both the development and deployment of AI because they are interconnected stages that heavily influence each other, and neglecting one undermines the positive impacts of the other.

Development without inclusive deployment is like a tree falling in the forest: You can build the most unbiased, technically sound AI in a vacuum, but if it's deployed without considering the needs and perspectives of diverse users, it risks being ineffective, misused, or even harmful. Inclusivity during deployment ensures that the technology reaches and benefits your intended audience.

Deployment without inclusive development is like putting a bandage on a broken bone: you can try to make an AI system appear inclusive after the fact, but if it wasn't designed with diverse voices and considerations from the start, it's likely built on flawed foundations. It might perpetuate biases, fail to address real needs, and erode trust.

Ultimately, designing for inclusivity in AI is about creating technology that reflects the richness and diversity of human experiences. It's about building bridges rather than barriers, and it's a crucial pillar of responsible AI leadership.

Takeaways

- The LEAD AI framework emphasizes ethical, unbiased AI development aligned with human values.
- Leadership in AI requires guiding teams with vision, empathy, and a commitment to shared goals.
- Mindfulness and purpose are essential for making ethical decisions in AI development.
- Inclusivity in AI design ensures diverse perspectives are integrated for equitable outcomes.
- Robust governance and policy frameworks are crucial for responsible AI deployment.

Reflection Questions

1. How can you incorporate ethical considerations into every stage of AI development?
2. In what ways can inclusive design improve the effectiveness of AI systems?
3. What role does leadership play in fostering a culture of responsible AI?
4. How can mindfulness and purpose be integrated into AI project management?
5. What governance structures can be implemented to ensure that your AI aligns with societal values?

Chapter 2
The Hype of AI:
Capturing the Excitement

Remember the initial excitement and buzz around artificial intelligence (AI)? It's like seeing a cute baby tiger for the first time. You can't help but be drawn in by its potential, its promise, and its allure. It's captivating, thrilling, and full of mystery, much like the first encounter with a captivating new idea or innovation. The possibilities seem endless, and the adrenaline rush is palpable.

Just like encountering a baby tiger, there's an inherent fascination with technology so powerful and yet so untamed. We want to play with it and revel in its charm without fully understanding the dangers lurking beneath the surface. In the same way, the early days of AI captivated our imaginations, enabling us to overlook the complexities and potential risks that lay ahead.

A Wild Ride: The Initial Excitement of AI

The initial excitement of AI was infectious, spreading like wildfire through every industry and niche. It promised to revolutionize how we live, work, and interact with technology. The prospect of intelligent machines that could learn, adapt, and make decisions seemed like something out of science fiction brought to life. The buzz was intoxicating, with everyone eager to witness the arrival of a game-changing force.

Much like the alluring gaze of a baby tiger, the initial phases of AI made us feel invincible and unstoppable. We marveled at the sheer power and potential while underestimating the need for caution and responsibility. Our rush of excitement blinded us to the risks and vulnerabilities lurking within this untamed landscape. However, just as with a baby tiger, the initial euphoria of discovery must be followed by a deeper understanding and respect for the complexities and potential consequences.

As we journey through the wild excitement of AI, it's crucial to acknowledge the allure and captivation that led us into uncharted territory. Much like our encounter with the baby tiger, our initial thrill should serve as a reminder of the need for careful consideration, discernment, and a balanced approach to harnessing the potential of AI without ignoring the dangers that come with it.

Getting to Know That "Baby Tiger" AI

Now that we've hopped onto this wild ride of excitement surrounding AI, it's time to take a closer look at our baby tiger. This metaphorical representation of AI perfectly captures its dual nature—cuddly and cunning. On one hand, AI offers the promise of streamlining processes, improving efficiencies, and enhancing user experiences. That's the cuddly side—the side that makes us marvel at its capabilities and potential. However, just like a real tiger, AI has an equally potent cunning side. Risks and potential dangers lurk beneath its surface. Just as a baby tiger eventually grows into a powerful force, AI can evolve into something beyond our control if not nurtured and managed wisely. Understanding this dichotomy is crucial as we navigate the world of AI. It's not enough to simply be mesmerized by its cuddly qualities; we must also be prepared to handle its cunning instincts. With this understanding, we'll be better equipped to embrace the exciting opportunities while also mitigating the associated risks. As we venture further into the realm of AI, let's keep in mind that our baby tiger might grow into a formidable force, and it's up to us to guide its development responsibly.

Beyond the Fuzz: Seeing the Bigger Picture

You've played with your baby tiger, cooed at its antics, marveled at its cuteness. But now it's time to step back and take in the bigger picture. The world of AI isn't just about its initial excitement or immediate applications; it's about understanding the wider implications and potential consequences of its growth. Just like a real tiger cub that eventually grows into a powerful beast, AI has the potential to evolve into something much larger and more impactful than we can ever imagine. This means considering how AI could potentially integrate into every aspect of our lives, from work to play, and the ethical, social, and economic impacts it could have. We must look beyond the cute facade and start thinking critically about the long-term effects of AI on our society. The following questions must be asked:

- How will AI impact the job market?
- What are potential privacy and security concerns as AI continues to evolve?
- Will AI exacerbate existing societal inequalities or create new ones instead?

It's also essential to acknowledge the power dynamics and control issues that could potentially arise when AI becomes deeply ingrained in our daily lives. By looking at the bigger picture, we can begin to prepare for the inevitable changes and challenges that come with AI's growth. This chapter will delve into these critical considerations and guide you in broadening your perspective beyond the initial appeal of AI, equipping you to navigate the complex landscape of this rapidly evolving technology.

Questions Nobody's Asking: What Happens When AI Grows?

As we marvel at AI's capabilities and the potential it holds, there's an important question that often gets overlooked: what happens when AI grows beyond our initial expectations? Everyone is always excited about the immediate benefits and advantages AI can bring to life, but what about the long-term consequences? Will it evolve in ways we didn't anticipate? Just like a child growing up, AI is constantly learning and adapting. This growth could lead to unforeseen challenges and complexities that we must be prepared to address.

What happens when you don't think about the long-term consequences of AI development? One example of AI gone wrong is an AI system that helped with interviewing candidates. In the short term, it seemed to be an incredible solution, helping recruiters and hiring managers interview more candidates in less time, getting real-time feedback from the AI system on candidates worth moving along and those who had red flags. Over time, the company realized that the model was flagging a lack of eye contact or shiftiness in the seat as negative data points. Other data points were being weighted unevenly. This led the company to shut down the use of the AI system because it was prioritizing candidates who were extroverted and good speakers, and dismissive of those who had more neurodiverse tendencies.

The choices made today in the development and deployment of AI will shape its future trajectory. Considerations around its ethical use, privacy, and security become even more critical as AI matures. The more mature an AI is, the more likely it's taking on more users with more use cases. As I learned at Amazon Alexa, you might start building for one demographic and then realize that your user base expands far beyond what you originally intended. This means that the bounds you start with immediately begin to expand, and your thoughts on ethics, privacy, and security need to expand with them. Additionally, the societal impact of AI's widespread adoption needs careful evaluation. We must ask ourselves the following:

- How will AI's growth affect the job market, economy, and overall human well-being?
- Are we equipped to manage these changes responsibly?

If we want to harness the potential of AI while mitigating the risks, these are the questions that demand our attention. It's not just about *creating AI*; it's about *shaping its growth* in a way that aligns with our values and aspirations. By contemplating the implications of AI's evolution, we can prepare ourselves for the complexities it may introduce while working toward building a future where AI contributes positively to our world.

Teeth, Claws, and All: Potential Risks of AI

As we continue to push the boundaries of AI development, it's crucial to acknowledge potential risks lurking in its shadows. Like a curious new pet, AI comes with its fair share of teeth and claws, and it's essential to understand and address these risks from the outset. It's important to think through the unpopular questions like "How could this go wrong?" "Whom could it hurt?" and "What's the worst thing that could happen?" The earlier you think about these things, the easier it is to mitigate these risks. One significant concern is the ethical implications of AI decision-making. With the power to analyze vast amounts of data and make autonomous decisions, there's a real potential for bias and discrimination to seep into AI systems, potentially perpetuating existing societal inequalities. Remember, AI should be designed with inclusivity in mind.

Additionally, the prospect of job displacement looms large as AI continues to automate tasks traditionally performed by humans.

We've all seen the commercials about how a line worker is eventually replaced by an autonomous computer. Although this automation brings unprecedented efficiency, it also raises concerns about widespread unemployment and the need for retraining the workforce. Some jobs will go away, in the same way that canal boatmen had to rethink their roles when trains became more popular during the Industrial Revolution. For most people, their roles will be augmented with AI. Think about AI more as a task taker as opposed to a job killer. The workforce will need to be retrained to use these systems as a companion, allowing them to delegate mundane tasks to AI so they can take on higher-value work. Every role will be impacted by AI and automation, but remember when you analyze the tasks you do every day, the choice as to where you partner with AI and to what degree is up to you.

Security is another formidable risk in the realm of AI, as increased connectivity and reliance on AI opens the door to cyber threats and vulnerabilities. The potential for malicious use of AI technology, including deepfakes and misinformation campaigns, poses yet another challenge that must be navigated cautiously.

A deepfake is synthesized media that uses AI to synthesize images and video. It has been used successfully by creative designers, marketers, and content creators to help them create more engaging content in multiple languages without having to actually do all the heavy lifting of creating real video. Misinformation campaigns, which often include deepfakes, have the advantage of synthesizing anyone to say anything at any time. Today, there are systems known as *deepfake detectors* used by the media and government to alert consumers when content has been manufactured.

The opacity of some AI models raises questions about transparency and accountability, especially when critical decisions are made without human oversight. We must also consider the environmental impact of AI, as the computational demands of training and running AI models can contribute to significant energy consumption and carbon emissions, creating a burden on our already-stressed local environment. Finally, the reliance on AI has the potential to erode personal privacy, as the collection and analysis of vast amounts of personal data raise concerns about surveillance and its misuse. Acknowledging and confronting these risks head-on is paramount to fostering responsible AI development and deployment. By proactively addressing these challenges, we can work toward harnessing the transformative potential of AI while mitigating its inherent risks.

I was on stage talking to about 3,000 people in Seattle, and most of them had traveled to get to the event. I presented a question to them: "Say I could create a *frictionless* airport experience—one with no waiting or delays—where you get out of the car, walk right in, go right through security, and board your plane. The only catch is that I would need to surveil you to do it. I would need to get to know you—how often you fly; if you fly with or check bags; if you get dropped off or need to park; and if you do get dropped off, who drops you off, a driver or a spouse. If I have all this information, I can create a utopian airport experience for all of us. If I could do this, would you give me all this information?" Ninety percent of the audience said they would gladly trade their data for convenience. In fact, we have been trained to trade data for convenience in many other ways, as we do on Amazon, Netflix, and Spotify.

The Size of Those Paws: Scaling Challenges

As we continue to explore the world of AI, we must confront the daunting aspect of *scaling*, which is the art and science of growing bigger. Scaling can be seen as more and more AI models serving more use cases in more areas of the business. Imagine a small kitten growing into a fully grown tiger; the challenges and adjustments are immense. Similarly, when an AI system is scaled, the implications can be far-reaching. One of the main challenges lies in ensuring that the AI system's performance remains consistent and reliable even as it expands to handle larger datasets and more complex tasks. This requires not just technical scalability but also considerations for ethical and responsible use of AI at a larger scale. The technology needs to keep pace with the increasing demands without sacrificing accuracy or security.

Another critical aspect of scaling AI is the need for adequate resources. From computing power to data storage, scaling up an AI system often requires a significant investment in infrastructure. Organizations must carefully plan for this and ensure that they have the necessary resources to support a scaled AI implementation. Without the correct infrastructure, AI might become bugged or problematic, or not even run at all. Additionally, human resources play a vital role in scaling challenges. As the AI system grows, so does the need for trained professionals to manage and maintain it. The availability of talent who can understand the complexities of scaled AI and ensure its responsible usage becomes increasingly crucial as the infrastructure expands.

Operational challenges also come into play. Integrating a scaled AI system seamlessly into existing workflows and systems requires careful planning and execution. It involves addressing compatibility issues, ensuring smooth interactions with other software and hardware, and managing potential disruptions during the scaling process. These operational challenges can significantly impact the overall efficiency and performance of the AI system if not adequately addressed.

In addition to the internal challenges of scaling AI, external factors such as regulatory compliance and societal impact should also be taken into account. As the scale of AI deployment increases, so do the potential consequences of its actions, making it essential to align with regulatory standards and consider the broader societal implications. A lack of alignment could lead to compliance failures, regulatory fines, and unethical system behaviors. Ensuring that your organization is in alignment involves navigating a complex web of ever-changing regulations and staying attuned to the evolving landscape of AI ethics and policies.

Ultimately, mastering the scaling challenges of AI requires a multidimensional approach that encompasses technological, human, operational, and ethical dimensions. By addressing these challenges proactively, organizations can harness the full potential of AI at scale while safeguarding themselves against associated risks. Embracing the size of those "paws" in scaling AI equips organizations to navigate the vast terrain of possibilities and responsibilities that lie ahead.

Looking Cute Today: Benefits That Blind Us

Have you ever been so enamored with something new and exciting that you completely overlooked any potential downsides? It's almost like when you meet an adorable puppy, and all you can focus on is how cute and cuddly it is, forgetting about the possible challenges of owning a pet. The same phenomenon often occurs in the world of AI. The exhilaration of the limitless possibilities and potential benefits of AI can blind us to the inherent risks and complexities involved. Later, we'll delve deep into the captivating allure of AI and the tendency for its charming qualities to overshadow the cautionary aspects. At first glance, however, AI seems like a miraculous solution to many problems. Its ability to automate tasks, make predictions, and enhance decision-making processes can significantly boost an organization's ability to amplify the productivity and effectiveness of its people, processes, and technologies. Additionally, the technological advancements driven by AI hold the promise of solving complex issues across various industries, from healthcare to finance and beyond. This dazzling allure often mesmerizes individuals and organizations, fueling an insatiable appetite for integrating AI into every facet of their operations. However, as with any captivating charm, it's essential to recognize that the enchantment with

AI's potential benefits can obscure the imperative need for thorough risk assessment and ethical considerations. Embracing the art of asking unpopular questions and being willing to "Say something when you see something" will empower teams to think differently about the early stages of AI and implement strategies that can minimize challenges in the long term.

Taming the Beast: Partnering with AI Experts

In the wild world of AI, partnering with experts is like enlisting the help of seasoned animal trainers to handle a magnificent yet unpredictable creature. Just as tigers require skilled handlers to ensure their safety and the safety of those around them, AI technologies demand the wisdom and experience of professionals who understand their intricate behaviors and potential dangers. Partnering with experts allows organizations to tap into a wealth of knowledge and best practices, gaining insights that can guide them through the often-bewildering jungle of AI development and deployment. These experts bring a critical perspective with them, helping businesses navigate the complexities of building responsible, effective AI solutions while also mitigating risks. By seeking out and collaborating with individuals and teams who've already forged paths through the dense underbrush of AI, organizations can benefit from their hard-won wisdom and avoid potential traps and pitfalls.

Whether consulting with ethical AI specialists, data scientists, or industry leaders, partnering with such experts provides invaluable mentorship and guidance. Through collaborative efforts, organizations can harness the power of AI while also ensuring that it remains in check. The process of taming the AI beast doesn't happen overnight, but by forming strong relationships with seasoned professionals, businesses can build a solid foundation for their AI initiatives. These partnerships not only assist in managing the inherent risks of AI but also foster a culture of transparency, responsibility, and continual learning for all involved. Ultimately, as organizations combine their own domain expertise with the insights and guidance of AI specialists, they become better equipped to comprehend AI's uses and harness its potential for positive transformation. Such collaboration between businesses and AI experts paves the way for awe-inspiring innovation and responsible, sustainable progress.

Eyes Wide Open: Realistic Expectations

Setting realistic expectations when it comes to AI is critical. It's important to approach the potential of AI with a clear understanding of what it can and cannot achieve. With all the hype surrounding AI, it's easy to get carried away with inflated expectations and grand visions of what AI can do. However, the reality is that AI is still in its infancy in many ways. It's a powerful tool, but it's not a magic wand that can instantly solve all problems. So, let's take a step back and examine what realistic expectations look like when it comes to AI.

First and foremost, it's crucial to understand that AI isn't perfect. It has limitations and constraints, just like any other technology. Although it can process vast amounts of data and perform complex tasks at incredible speeds, it's not immune to errors or biases. Organizations need to be aware of these limitations and approach AI with caution and skepticism. Another aspect of realistic expectations is the timeline for AI implementation. Building and deploying AI solutions takes time and resources. It's not something that happens overnight and requires careful planning and consideration. Rushing into AI without a clear strategy is a recipe for disappointment. Additionally, we need to be realistic about the impact AI has on the workforce. AI can automate certain tasks and improve efficiency, but it's unlikely to replace human workers entirely. Instead, it's more likely to augment human capabilities and create new opportunities. For example, digital marketers and social media managers will now be able to create better first-draft content of ad copy and imagery, rather than having to battle with a blank page. IT administrators will be able to automate the graceful handling of password resets and common questions being asked 24/7 and provide immediate responses, even if the team isn't online when the questions come in. My favorite example is the audio/visual teams that run the events at which I speak. Although AI is helping with audio levels, predictive maintenance, and team communication, these teams are in no danger of losing their jobs. In fact, in a world that is now looking to meet more often at conferences and live events, these teams can scale the number of events they support, creating new employment opportunities for everyone.

Understanding these nuances is essential for setting realistic expectations. We must consider the ethical and societal implications of AI. Realistic expectations account for the potential drawbacks and consequences of AI adoption. It's important to have open discussions about the ethical considerations and ensure that AI is deployed responsibly. By keeping our eyes wide open and approaching AI with realism and caution, we can harness its potential while avoiding unrealistic hype and disappointment.

Preparing for Tomorrow: Responsible Enthusiasm

We've come a long way in understanding the potential of AI, but with great power comes great responsibility. As we prepare for tomorrow, it's essential to balance our enthusiasm with a healthy dose of responsibility. Instead of getting carried away by the hype, let's focus on harnessing the transformative power of AI while mitigating the associated risks. Responsible enthusiasm involves aligning our visions for AI with ethical considerations and long-term sustainability. It requires us to think beyond immediate gains and consider the broader impact that AI has on society, the environment, and future generations.

We must cultivate a culture of continuous learning, adapting, and innovating to ensure that our enthusiasm for AI drives meaningful progress. This means staying curious, open-minded, and receptive to feedback and diverse perspectives. Embracing responsible enthusiasm also entails collaborating with diverse stakeholders—experts, policymakers, communities, and end users—to co-create AI solutions that are inclusive, fair, and beneficial for all. It's about ensuring that everyone has a seat at the table and that no one is left behind in this journey toward an AI-powered future.

Responsible enthusiasm invites us to examine our assumptions, biases, and blind spots when it comes to AI. By critically assessing the implications of our excitement, we can better anticipate and address potential pitfalls before they escalate. This proactive approach fosters a culture of accountability, transparency, and trust, which are vital for sustaining positive momentum in the AI space.

Finally, preparing for tomorrow involves equipping ourselves with the necessary tools and frameworks to navigate the evolving landscape of AI. This includes investing in ongoing education, upskilling, and reskilling to adapt to the changing demands of the AI era. By embracing responsible enthusiasm, we can channel our collective energy and passion for AI into building a future that isn't only technologically advanced but also ethical, equitable, and sustainable. So, gear up, stay grounded, and embark on this journey with a sense of purpose and responsible enthusiasm.

Takeaways

- Leaders must prioritize ethical decision-making so they can understand the far-reaching impacts of AI on society and individuals.
- Building and maintaining trust through transparency and accountability is crucial for effective leadership in AI projects.
- Businesses should embrace and advocate for diverse perspectives in AI development to create more equitable and innovative solutions.
- Organizations can stay informed and adaptable by continuously expanding your knowledge of emerging AI technologies and challenges.

Reflection Questions

- How can you apply the principles of ethical leadership to ensure responsible AI implementation within your team?
- What strategies can you adopt to build and sustain trust, particularly when making critical decisions involving AI?
- How will you incorporate diverse perspectives and promote inclusivity in your AI projects to drive better outcomes?

Chapter 3
Building the AI Sandbox: Safe, Responsible Spaces for Innovation

Experimentation is the heart of innovation, but when it comes to artificial intelligence (AI), the stakes are higher. To truly understand the potential and risks associated with AI applications, we need a safe, controlled environment for ideation, testing, and development—this is where the concept of an AI sandbox becomes indispensable.

The Basics: What Exactly Is an AI Sandbox?

An *AI sandbox* is a safe and controlled environment where organizations can experiment and innovate with AI technologies without risking their operational systems. Think of it as a virtual playground for AI where data scientists and engineers can freely test new algorithms, models, and applications without the fear of unintended consequences. It provides a space for exploration and trial and error, fostering creativity and learning within a secure framework. It's like an AI laboratory equipped with safeguards and guidelines to ensure that the experiments remain contained and ethical.

In practical terms, an AI sandbox typically involves a separate infrastructure or cloud environment isolated from an organization's production systems. This separation helps mitigate the potential impact of any issues or errors that may arise during the experimentation process. Additionally, the sandbox environment enables teams to work with *synthetic* or *de-identified data*, reducing privacy and security concerns while still enabling meaningful research and development. By mimicking real-world conditions in a controlled setting, organizations can validate AI concepts, train algorithms, and assess performance without disrupting their everyday operations.

Synthetic data is data that has been created by a machine. Generative AI can be used to take information that is known about a specific data point or set of data points and synthesize datasets that can be used for training models. For example, in healthcare, patient care information is needed to help train models, but it is often unavailable or resource-intensive to acquire. One option is to interview patients or find smaller datasets and use them to generate larger datasets that can be used for training.

De-identified data is data that has been anonymized to remove any personal, identifying information, sometimes referred to as personal identifiable information (PII). Examples include call center log files that record call transcripts. If you want to acquire these call transcripts, you must have all the personal identifying information redacted from the transcript to avoid any violation of privacy.

Another key aspect of the AI sandbox is its role in facilitating collaboration and knowledge sharing. Within this designated space, cross-functional teams can come together to explore AI solutions, leveraging their diverse expertise to drive innovation. It becomes a hub for exchanging ideas, refining approaches, and consolidating best practices in responsible AI development. With clear boundaries and protocols set in place, participants are encouraged to push the boundaries of what's possible while adhering to principles of transparency, fairness, and accountability.

Overall, the AI sandbox serves as a critical enabler for responsible AI deployment, offering a structured playground for creativity, experimentation, and learning. It represents a commitment to unlocking the potential of AI while safeguarding against potential risks and ensuring alignment with ethical standards. By understanding the basics of what an AI sandbox entails, organizations can lay a strong foundation for building safe and responsible spaces for innovation in the AI realm.

Why an AI Sandbox Matters

Having and using an AI sandbox instills confidence in decision-makers, enabling them to make informed choices about scaling AI initiatives. Without this crucial foundation, the journey toward responsible and effective AI implementation would be unnecessarily risky and marked by uncertainty. In essence, the presence of an AI sandbox underscores the commitment to safe and responsible AI innovation, ensuring that every stride toward progress is rooted in careful consideration of potential implications and outcomes.

Establishing Policies for Safe AI Usage

When it comes to integrating AI into your organization, establishing clear policies for safe and responsible usage is paramount. Policy establishment ensures that everyone in the organization understands the rules of engagement and can contribute to a culture of ethical AI practices. Start by clearly outlining the purpose of these policies— they aren't meant to stifle innovation but rather to provide guardrails that enable exploration while safeguarding against potential risks.

One key aspect of establishing policies is defining the scope of AI usage within your organization. Determine which areas can benefit from AI technologies, and then identify the specific use cases where AI will be employed. By doing so, you can tailor your policies to address the unique considerations and challenges presented by these applications. Also, be sure to involve stakeholders from different departments and levels of the organization in this process to gain diverse perspectives and ensure broad buy-in.

Another critical element is setting guidelines for data privacy and security. Clearly define how data will be collected, stored, processed, and accessed to uphold the highest standards of privacy and protection. This might involve encryption protocols, access controls, and regular audits to monitor compliance with established policies. Additionally, consider any legal or regulatory requirements that must be adhered to, ensuring that your AI initiatives align with industry best practices and legal standards.

In parallel, it's important to establish governance structures to oversee AI implementation. Assign roles and responsibilities for managing AI projects and ensuring adherence to policies. This includes designating individuals or teams responsible for ethical considerations, risk assessment, and compliance monitoring. It's also beneficial to create channels for feedback and reporting to enable continuous improvement and refinement of these policies as new challenges and opportunities emerge. It is important to establish these feedback processes because they will help you to identify concerns before they become a production challenge. When building AI systems, failures may be difficult to detect with routine testing: you will need a dedicated, inclusive team of testers to ensure these policies and guardrails are meeting the needs of the business. This is also known as *AI Red Teaming*, which is covered more in later chapters.

Finally, training and educational programs should be leveraged to communicate the established policies effectively across the organization. Equip employees with the knowledge and skills necessary to navigate the AI landscape responsibly. This should encompass not only technical aspects but also ethical decision-making frameworks and case studies that illustrate the real-world implications of AI usage. By communicating these policies, every team member has all the tools needed to succeed responsibly.

By taking these foundational steps to establish policies for safe AI usage, organizations can create an environment where innovation flourishes within clearly defined boundaries, promoting trust, transparency, and accountability.

Inside the Firewall: Building Your Walled Garden

In building your AI sandbox, one of the critical aspects is creating a secure environment, often referred to as the *walled garden*. Think of it as the protective barrier that shields your AI initiatives from external threats and unauthorized access while fostering a climate of trust and innovation within it. The walled garden entails strict access controls, robust authentication mechanisms, and detailed monitoring to ensure that only authorized personnel can modify, access, or interact with the AI applications and housed data. Consider it the digital fortress where your AI projects can flourish without being compromised by potential vulnerabilities. As you construct this digital citadel, it's essential to integrate multilayered security measures, ranging from encryption protocols to advanced intrusion detection systems. This way, you're not only safeguarding your AI assets against cyber attacks but also instilling confidence in stakeholders regarding the protection of sensitive data and intellectual property (IP).

The walled garden should be designed with flexibility in mind, allowing for controlled collaboration and information sharing both within and outside the confines of your organization. This ensures that while security remains paramount, it doesn't impede the collaborative nature of AI development. Additionally, partnerships and integrations with trusted third-party providers can enhance the capabilities of your walled garden, bringing in specialized tools and expertise without compromising the security perimeter. The concept of the walled garden is not about isolation but rather is about creating a haven where innovation can thrive unimpeded. It's a space where the boundaries are carefully crafted to nurture creativity and experimentation yet fortified enough to shield against potential threats. Remember, the strength of these walls lies in their adaptability and resilience, reflecting an ongoing commitment to fortifying your AI sandbox amid the evolving landscape of technological and regulatory challenges. By establishing and reinforcing the walled garden within your AI sandbox, you lay the groundwork for a culture of innovation that flourishes under the protective embrace of responsible and secure practices.

Safe Innovation: Identifying Low-Risk Use Cases

Innovation is at the heart of AI exploration, and identifying low-risk use cases enables organizations to push boundaries while maintaining a safety net. These use cases act as stepping stones in the AI journey, fostering learning and growth without excessive risk. When venturing into uncharted AI territory, starting with low-risk use cases provides an opportunity to test the waters and build confidence. By selecting use cases with minimal impact on critical business operations, teams can innovate safely, free from the constraints of high-stakes repercussions.

So, what exactly constitutes a *low-risk use case*? It typically revolves around processes or areas where the consequences of failure are manageable. For instance, automating routine data-entry tasks and implementing chatbots as customer support interfaces are considered low-risk use cases due to their limited impact on core business functions. By identifying these scenarios, organizations can carve out safe spaces for AI experimentation, laying the foundation for future success.

Additionally, low-risk use cases often allow for relatively simple implementation compared to mission-critical applications. This accessibility gives teams the freedom to experiment, iterate, and refine their

AI solutions without being paralyzed by fear of failure. In doing so, they can gradually build expertise and trust in their AI technologies, paving the way for more ambitious projects further down the line.

Nevertheless, the identification of low-risk use cases demands a thoughtful approach involving a thorough analysis of potential ripple effects and a realistic assessment of the risks entailed. Organizations must consider factors such as data quality and availability, regulatory compliance, and potential ethical considerations when evaluating a use case's risk profile.

By adopting a proactive mindset and conducting careful due diligence, organizations can safeguard against unforeseen pitfalls and unintended consequences. Once potential use cases have been vetted, it's essential to involve stakeholders from across the organization to gain diverse perspectives and ensure buy-in. Bringing together multidisciplinary teams can help identify and mitigate risks early on, setting the stage for successful innovation in a safe environment.

Vetting Use Cases

I have developed a specific framework for ensuring that the use cases brought to market are the right ones at the right time for businesses. I narrow down use cases with the following rubric:

First, ensure that the organization has clarity on the core values of the company. Only choose use cases that directly influence or impact one of these core values. Only the highest-value use cases should be considered.

Second, understand what is risky for your organization. This is different for every company. What would you consider to be a risk with AI? Is it your brand? Customer loyalty? Personal connection? Whatever you are worried about, don't go after those use cases first. This will leave you with only the highest-value, lowest-risk use cases to go after. But we aren't done.

Third, evaluate complexity. Go after the minimum remarkable product (MRP). When it comes to AI, don't try to boil
the ocean. Find a use case that is high value, low risk, and
easy to implement. Find a use case that will delight the
user—that will be remarkable to the user—and the smaller,
the better.
Following this rubric will help ensure that you gain
momentum with your AI projects and have an opportunity
to deliver more features and value over the long term.

Ultimately, the process of identifying low-risk use cases embodies a strategic balance between innovation and prudence. It empowers organizations to embrace new AI possibilities without exposing
themselves to unnecessary vulnerabilities. As we embark on this
journey, keep in mind that innovating safely matters. It serves as the
catalyst for sustainable, responsible AI innovation that adds true
value to the business and society.

Aligning with Values: Ensuring Ethical AI Practices

As businesses dive deeper into the realm of AI, it becomes increasingly crucial to align technological advancements with ethical
principles and societal values. AI's use brings forth a myriad of
opportunities but also necessitates a strong commitment to upholding ethical standards. To ensure that AI technologies are developed
and deployed ethically, it is imperative for organizations to place
a significant emphasis on aligning their AI initiatives with core
values and ethical practices.

One fundamental aspect of aligning with values involves establishing clear guidelines and principles for the ethical use of AI. This
includes defining what constitutes ethical behavior in the context
of AI applications, empowering employees to make conscientious
decisions, and outlining consequences for unethical actions. By

establishing transparent and comprehensive ethical guidelines, organizations lay the foundation for responsible AI implementation.

Ensuring ethical AI practices requires a close examination of potential biases within AI systems. Bias can permeate every stage of the AI lifecycle, from data collection and preprocessing to model training and deployment. It's essential for organizations to actively identify, mitigate, and monitor biases to refrain from perpetuating or exacerbating societal inequities through AI technologies. Implementing fairness and bias-mitigation techniques, such as thorough dataset evaluation and diverse model testing, is central to achieving ethical AI outcomes. The best way for organizations to be able to identify, mitigate, and monitor biases is by having a diverse and inclusive team who are testing the models early and often. This team is often referred to as an *AI Red Team*.

Building upon this, promoting transparency and accountability in AI operations is integral in aligning with ethical values. Organizations must endeavor to provide explanations for AI-generated decisions, especially if they have substantial impacts on individuals or communities. Additionally, maintaining accountability mechanisms, such as audit trails and oversight processes, fosters trust and demonstrates a commitment to ethical conduct. Transparency not only enhances ethical practices but also serves to establish credibility and foster public trust in the organization's AI endeavors.

Ensuring ethical AI practices goes beyond regulatory compliance. It involves an ongoing commitment to actively engage with stakeholders and the broader community to understand their concerns and address any ethical implications of AI implementations. Seeking feedback from diverse perspectives and integrating ethical considerations into the development and deployment of AI technologies can lead to more inclusive and responsible outcomes. Organizations that prioritize constructive dialogue and continuously adapt their AI strategies based on ethical insights are better positioned to align with evolving societal values and expectations.

In conclusion, aligning with values and ensuring ethical AI practices demands diligent efforts across all facets of AI development and deployment. By setting clear ethical guidelines, mitigating biases, promoting transparency and accountability, and engaging with stakeholders, organizations can navigate AI's complexities while upholding ethical standards and contributing positively to society.

From Prototypes to Policies: Practical Implementation Steps

Once you've successfully aligned your AI initiatives with ethical practices, it's time to move from the testing phase to full-fledged implementation. This transition can be a critical juncture, as it involves translating your prototypes into practical policies that govern the use of AI across your organization. In this section, we'll delve into the nitty-gritty of this process, offering a comprehensive guide to help you navigate this crucial stage effectively.

The first step in transitioning from prototypes to policies is to conduct a thorough evaluation of your AI prototypes. This involves rigorously assessing their performance, ethical implications, and alignment with your organizational goals. Once you've gained a clear understanding of the strengths and limitations of your prototypes, you can begin formulating policies that encapsulate the best practices derived from these insights.

Next, it's essential to engage key stakeholders from various departments within your organization. By involving individuals from legal, compliance, information technology (IT), and other relevant departments, you can ensure that your policies are well-informed, comprehensive, and reflective of the diverse perspectives within your organization. This collaborative approach not only enhances the quality of your policies but also fosters a culture of shared responsibility across departments when it comes to AI governance.

Simultaneously, as you devise your organization's policies, it's vital to develop robust frameworks for monitoring and enforcement. These frameworks include establishing clear guidelines for data privacy, security measures, and ongoing AI application oversight. Additionally, it's essential to equip your teams with the necessary training and resources to adhere to these policies effectively.

By investing in continuous education and support, you can cultivate a culture of responsible AI usage throughout your organization.

Fostering transparency and accountability should be central tenets of your policy development. It's crucial to communicate the rationale behind these policies to all stakeholders and ensure that there are mechanisms in place for reporting, feedback, and continuous improvement. By promoting openness and responsiveness, you can instill trust and confidence in the deployment of AI solutions while encouraging innovation and experimentation within the established ethical boundaries.

Finally, as you progress through the practical implementation steps, it's essential to iterate and refine your policies based on real-world experiences and evolving regulatory landscapes. Embracing a flexible, adaptive approach will enable you to adapt to emerging challenges and seize new opportunities while upholding the ethical standards underpinning your AI initiatives.

An insurance company was self-disclosed to have consistently been a laggard when it comes to innovation, especially AI. But something about the world of generative AI felt different to the leadership. They decided to have an AI Leadership Essentials workshop to uncover the art of the possible for AI in their company and see what was practical to start immediately.

In gathering the meeting's attendees, they collected representation across five different lines of business and three functional areas. They admitted at the time that these people had very rarely been in the same room at the same time before. We then spent two days working through the rubric for AI Project Success. At the end of the two days, we had three use cases, or MRPs, in which the business was going to invest. We developed an AI strategy and set of policies to govern the projects and got a commitment from the team to invest in the effort. Then everyone got

(continued)

(continued)

to work. Three weeks into the project, guidance from the United States Federal Government was released in the form of an Executive Order on Artificial Intelligence.

The governance board immediately met and integrated the new guidance that was revealed in that order. They remained agile and fluid in adoption strategies and, most importantly, kept the leadership group meeting consistently so there was no delay in adoption. The project was able to pivot with the new guidance and deliver value to the company's customers faster than its competitors. The biggest lesson learned is the importance of identifying a leadership team on AI and having that team meet regularly to evaluate the metrics of success for all ongoing projects and evaluate new available information.

It's important that this team in your company is comprised of leadership from across the organization. Leaders to consider include those from legal, security, compliance, engineering, and customer success departments, as well as representatives from every line of business. This team will serve as the AI governance board and ethics review board for new projects.

Boosting Productivity: Internal Generative Applications

When it comes to leveraging the power of AI within an organization, one of the most compelling strategies is to explore the potential of internal generative applications. These applications have the capacity to revolutionize workflow processes, unlock new levels of efficiency, and drive innovation from within. By harnessing the capabilities of AI to generate solutions, optimize tasks, and automate repetitive processes, internal generative applications hold the key to unlocking unprecedented productivity gains.

Imagine a scenario where routine administrative tasks are seamlessly streamlined through intelligent automation, freeing up valuable time for employees to focus on higher-value, strategic initiatives. With internal generative applications, organizations can empower their workforce to innovate, experiment, and create without being bogged down by mundane, time-consuming tasks. Moreover, these applications can also take data analysis to the next level, uncovering actionable insights, trends, and patterns that might have otherwise remained hidden.

Incorporating AI-driven generative applications into the fabric of an organization requires a thoughtful approach. It demands a thorough understanding of existing workflows, identification of pain points, and a clear vision of how AI can augment and enhance these processes. Additionally, it necessitates building a culture that embraces continuous learning and adaptation, where employees are encouraged to engage with AI technologies to foster innovative solutions.

These applications have the potential to create a domino effect, catalyzing a ripple of positive change throughout the organization. They can enable teams to pursue ambitious projects, test new ideas, and bring concepts to life with greater speed and precision. By integrating generative applications into various departments and functions, organizations can develop a comprehensive ecosystem of AI-driven tools that work in harmony to bolster overall productivity and drive sustained success.

As we venture further into the era of responsible AI, internal generative applications offer a unique opportunity to reshape the future of work. They represent a testament to the transformative capabilities of AI, demonstrating its capacity to empower individuals, elevate collaboration, and fuel meaningful progress. Embracing and harnessing the potential of internal generative applications isn't just about implementing technology; it's about fostering a culture of creativity, ingenuity, and adaptability. When utilized thoughtfully, these applications have the power to propel organizations toward a future where productivity knows no bounds.

Success Stories from the AI Sandbox

In the AI realm, success stories aren't just about achieving milestones; they're about transforming the way organizations operate. The following real-world examples detail how companies have leveraged their AI sandboxes to drive innovation and impact.

One notable story comes from a leading healthcare provider that used its AI sandbox to develop predictive analytics models for patient outcomes. By testing and refining these models within the sandbox, the organization was able to significantly enhance its ability to anticipate and address critical health issues, ultimately improving patient care and outcomes.

Another inspiring example comes from the finance sector, where a major bank utilized its AI sandbox to experiment with natural language processing algorithms for fraud detection. Through rigorous testing and iteration, the bank successfully deployed these models into production, leading to a substantial decrease in fraudulent activities and safeguarding the financial well-being of its customers.

An e-commerce giant harnessed its AI sandbox to explore personalized recommendation engines, resulting in a remarkable increase in customer engagement and sales.

These success stories demonstrate the profound impact that AI sandboxes can have when embraced as platforms for responsible experimentation and innovation. They underscore the value of creating safe spaces for teams to push boundaries, learn from failures, and ultimately deliver game-changing solutions. As you consider the potential of your own AI sandbox, these stories serve as beacons of inspiration, illuminating the transformative power of responsible AI. They remind us that beyond the hype and buzzwords, AI has the capacity to create tangible, positive change when approached with intention, empathy, and a commitment to ethical practice.

Looking Forward: Scaling Up from Your Sandbox

Every success story in the AI world stems from a humble beginning—a point of inception where an idea or prototype takes shape within the confines of an AI sandbox. As these ideas flourish and demonstrate their potential, the need to scale up becomes inevitable. We'll now explore the pivotal phase of transitioning from the safe cocoon of the AI sandbox into the expansive realm of real-world impact.

Scaling up from an AI sandbox is like nurturing a seedling into a towering tree. It requires careful planning, nourishment, and a supportive environment. The first step is to evaluate the success stories from your sandbox, identifying the solutions that have shown promise and align with strategic business objectives.

Once you've pinpointed the frontrunners, it's time to lay the groundwork for their integration into the broader organizational framework. This demands close collaboration between the teams operating within the sandbox and those responsible for enterprise-wide implementation. It's crucial to ensure that the ethics and values upheld within the sandbox are seamlessly translated as these solutions scale up.

Naturally, scaling up also means stepping beyond the safe boundaries of controlled experimentation. Real-world challenges, such as regulatory compliance, privacy concerns, and security protocols, come into play. Addressing them demands a shift from hypothetical scenarios to actual practical problem-solving. One cannot overestimate the importance of maintaining ethical and legal standards as innovative solutions expand their reach.

Scaling up from the sandbox also necessitates revisiting architectural considerations. What worked perfectly within a contained environment might encounter bottlenecks when introduced at enterprise scale. Hence, a reassessment of infrastructure, data pipelines, and computing resources is integral to smooth, seamless expansion. You must mitigate these issues to be able to expand your AI.

The human element must not be overlooked, either. As AI solutions make their way out of the sandbox into the real world, there's a subsequent need for upskilling, change management, and a fortification of the cultural fabric that embraces these transformative technologies. Communicating the value proposition of these solutions and fostering a mindset of adaptability among the workforce becomes non-negotiable. The greatest advantage you have as a leader is the people who work in your organization. Your workforce can unlock the most important use cases that will shift the needle for your business in terms of time saved and revenue growth. Once your workforce understands that they not only play a role in the new world of AI but are critical to reinventing how the organization will function, they will become more engaged and begin to embody leadership. During my time at Amazon, I learned to invent and simplify. Every employee will become an engine of innovation in the work they do every day, finding small inventions through AI that will revolutionize the entire company.

In conclusion, scaling up from the AI sandbox marks a critical juncture in the journey of responsible AI deployment. It represents the transition from experimental endeavors to tangible, real-world impact. Although it presents its set of challenges, the prospect of extending the reach of successful sandbox initiatives holds the promise of meaningful transformation and sustainable innovation.

Takeaways

- The AI sandbox provides a safe space for experimentation and innovation without putting operational systems at risk. It enables the testing of models, algorithms, and applications while mitigating unintended consequences.
- Policies and governance structures are critical for overseeing AI implementation responsibly. This includes guidelines for data

privacy, security, ethical practices, risk assessments, and compliance monitoring.
- Identifying low-risk use cases can help build confidence and expertise gradually. Choose projects with minimal disruption to core operations first.
- Aligning AI with ethical values and societal principles is crucial. Mitigate biases, ensure transparency, promote accountability, and engage stakeholders throughout the process.
- Moving from prototypes to full implementation requires thorough testing, stakeholder input, robust monitoring frameworks, and communication of rationale behind policies.
- Generative AI applications can boost productivity by automating repetitive tasks and providing data-driven insights to employees. But they require strategic integration.

Reflection Questions

- Do you have clear policies and governance structures in place to guide ethical and responsible AI development?
- How can you identify low-risk, high-value AI use cases to pursue as starting points?
- What potential biases exist in your data or proposed models? How can you proactively mitigate them?
- Are you communicating the rationale and ethical principles behind your AI policies effectively?
- How can you scale up AI solutions responsibly while managing real-world challenges?
- What cultural changes do you need to embrace generative AI and prepare your workforce?

Chapter 4

From Ideation to Action: Setting Up for Successful Business Outcomes

In the ever-evolving landscape of business technology, the journey from ideation to actionable outcomes forms the backbone of successful innovation. This chapter delves into the fundamental steps and strategies necessary to translate visionary concepts into tangible results within the business context. By setting up robust frameworks and aligning initiatives with core values, businesses can navigate the complexities of modern technological advancements, especially in the realm of artificial intelligence (AI). Understanding how to effectively bridge the gap between ideas and implementation is crucial for achieving sustainable growth and maintaining a competitive edge in today's dynamic market.

Aligning AI with Business Vision and Core Values

When it comes to leveraging the power of artificial intelligence (AI) within a business, one of the fundamental considerations is ensuring that the AI projects align with the company's overall business vision and core values. This alignment is crucial for multiple reasons. First and foremost, it ensures that the efforts put into AI development are aimed at advancing the strategic goals and long-term vision of the organization. Additionally, aligning with core values helps in maintaining consistency in the brand image and the ethical standards upheld by the company. It also aids in building trust among stakeholders, including customers, partners, and employees. Embracing AI without considering its alignment with the company's vision and values can lead to misguided pursuits and potential conflicts with the organizational ethos. Consequently, this often necessitates a reevaluation of what those core values represent in the context of AI integration. For some companies, this might involve amplifying the significance of transparency, privacy, or fairness, whereas for others, innovation, customer-centricity, or sustainability may take precedence. The process of refining core values usually involves engaging with various layers of the organization, from the leadership team to the front-line employees. It demands candid conversations and deep reflection on how AI initiatives can best serve the company's overarching mission while staying true to its principles. Ultimately, the goal is not just to apply AI for the sake of adopting the latest technology trend but rather to utilize it wisely and responsibly, comprehensively integrating it into the fabric of the organization. In doing so, the company can propel itself toward a future where AI is not just a tool but a catalyst for positive change.

Here is an exercise that we do in our AI Leadership Essentials workshop at the AI Leadership Institute. It helps organizations refine their core values, understand risk, and evaluate complexity to ensure the right use case is selected to ensure the highest level of return on investment (ROI) possible. The first step is to dive deeper into what the organization values.

Defining Organizational Core Values

To define your organization's core values, begin by answering the following questions about your organization. I have provided prompts to help you define these values:

- *What are the core principles that your organization stands for?*
  Identify the fundamental beliefs and values that guide your organization's actions and decisions.

- *How do your core values align with your mission and vision?*
  Ensure that the values are consistent with the long-term goals and purpose of the organization.

- *Which ethical principles are non-negotiable for your organization?*
  Determine the ethical standards that must be upheld in all circumstances, particularly in the context of AI development and deployment.

- *What societal impact do you aim to achieve with your AI initiatives?*
  Consider how your AI technologies can positively contribute to society and align with your ethical commitments.

- *Who are the key stakeholders affected by your AI technologies, and what are their values?*
  Identify and understand the values of those who will be impacted by your AI solutions, including customers, employees, and the broader community.

- *How can you ensure transparency and accountability in your AI operations?*
  Develop strategies to provide clear explanations for AI decisions and maintain mechanisms for oversight and accountability.

- *What measures are in place to identify and mitigate biases in your AI systems?*
  Establish procedures for detecting, reducing, and monitoring biases to uphold fairness and ethical standards.

- *How do you promote diversity and inclusivity within your AI development teams?*
  Ensure that a diverse range of perspectives is represented in your AI teams to enhance ethical decision-making and reduce biases.

- *What feedback mechanisms do you have to engage with stakeholders about your AI initiatives?*
  Create channels for continuous dialogue with stakeholders to address ethical concerns and incorporate their insights into AI development.

- *Are your organization's core values reflected in your AI policies and guidelines?*
  Verify that your AI policies and guidelines are consistent with and reinforce your organization's core values.

- *How do you measure success in upholding your core values through your AI projects?*
  Establish metrics and benchmarks to evaluate the effectiveness of your AI initiatives in adhering to your defined core values.

Embedding Core Values in AI Practices

To define how to embed your organization's core values in its AI practices, begin by answering the following questions about your organization. I have provided answers to help you define these values:

- *How frequently do you revisit and update your organization's core values to ensure that they remain relevant?*
  Schedule regular reviews of your core values to ensure that they evolve with changes in societal expectations and organizational goals.

- *In what ways do your core values influence your organization's decision-making processes in AI projects?*
  Analyze how your core values shape decisions at every stage of your organization's AI development, from conception to deployment.

- *What training and resources can you provide to your employees to uphold your core values in AI development?*
  Offer ongoing education and tools to empower your employees to make decisions that reflect the organization's core values.

Second, understand what is risky for your organization. This is different for every company. The following section contains some vital questions to consider.

Evaluating AI Use Case Risks: Key Questions

Ask these questions to evaluate your organization's reputation risks in AI use:

- How might the AI application's outcomes impact your brand's image and public perception?
- Are there potential ethical concerns that could arise from the use of this AI technology?
- Could the deployment of this AI system lead to public backlash or negative media coverage?
- What steps are in place to ensure transparency and accountability in your AI processes?
- How do you plan to address any potential biases in AI decisions that could harm your organization's reputation?

Ask these questions to assess your employee risks in AI use:

- How will the introduction of AI affect your employees' roles and job security?
- What training and resources are available to help your employees adapt to AI-driven changes?
- Are there any potential health and safety risks associated with your AI systems in your workplace?
- How do you ensure that AI tools do not inadvertently introduce biases in your organization's recruitment or performance evaluations?
- What mechanisms are in place to address any employee concerns related to your organization's AI use?

Ask these questions to assess your customer risks in AI use:

- How might AI applications affect your organization's customer experience and satisfaction?

- What data privacy and security measures are implemented to protect your customer information?
- Could AI decisions negatively impact your customers' trust and loyalty?
- How do you ensure that AI-driven interactions are fair and unbiased toward all of your customers' demographics?
- What protocols are established for addressing any customer grievances related to their AI usage?

Ask these questions to assess your partner risks in AI use:

- How might your organization's AI initiatives influence your relationships with business partners?
- Are there risks of data sharing or collaboration that could compromise your organization's partner confidentiality?
- What steps are taken to align your AI practices with the ethical standards of your organization's partners?
- How do you ensure that your AI applications do not create competitive disadvantages for your organization's partners?
- What communication strategies are in place to keep partners informed about your organization's AI developments and associated risks?

Whatever you are worried about, don't go after those use cases first. Doing so will leave you with only the highest-value, lowest-risk use cases to pursue. AI is complex; it's time to think about its complexity.

Evaluate that complexity. Go after the minimum remarkable product (MRP). When it comes to AI, don't try to boil the ocean. Find a use case that is high value, low risk, and easy to implement. Find a use case that will delight the user and be remarkable to the user. Finally, the smaller, the better.

Guiding Toward a Minimum Remarkable Product (MRP)

Use the following questions to help guide your organization in selecting its MRP.

Understanding Scope and Feasibility

For your organization to define your MRP's scope and feasibility, ask the following:

- What is the primary objective of this AI solution?
- How well-defined are the requirements and desired outcomes?
- What specific problem does your AI solution aim to solve?
- Is the use case clearly articulated and understood by your organization's stakeholders?

Assessing Technical Complexity

For your organization to frame your MRP's technical complexity, ask the following:

- What data is required for this AI solution, and how accessible is it?
- Are there any existing models or algorithms that can be leveraged, or do you need to develop new ones?
- What are the computational requirements for developing and deploying this solution?
- How complex are the integration points with your existing systems and workflows?

Evaluating Implementation Challenges

For your organization to outline your MRP's implementation challenges, ask the following:

- What are the potential risks and barriers to implementing this solution?
- How much time and resources will it take to develop and deploy this solution?
- Are there any dependencies or prerequisites that need to be addressed before implementation?
- What is the level of expertise required to successfully implement and maintain this solution?

Determining User Impact and Value

For your organization to determine your MRP's user impact and value, ask the following:

- How will this solution impact the end users and their workflows?
- What metrics will be used to measure the success and value of this AI solution?
- How can the solution be designed to be intuitive and user-friendly?
- What feedback mechanisms will be in place to capture user experiences and make iterative improvements?

Ensuring Ethical and Responsible Use

For your organization to ensure your MRP's ethical and responsible use, ask the following:

- What ethical considerations need to be addressed in the development and deployment of this solution?
- How can you ensure transparency and accountability in AI-driven decisions?
- What measures will be taken to mitigate biases and ensure fairness?
- How will you engage with stakeholders to address ethical implications and gather diverse perspectives?

Balancing Innovation and Prudence

Finally, for your organization to balance your MRP's innovation and prudence, ask the following:

- Does this AI solution align with your company's strategic goals and ethical standards?
- What is the minimum viable product (MVP) that can be developed to test the concept?
- How can you scale the solution incrementally to manage risks and optimize resource use?

- What are the potential long-term benefits and challenges associated with this AI solution?

The Art of Possible: Pushing Boundaries Responsibly

When it comes to harnessing the potential of AI for business growth, it's crucial to recognize the art of possible and responsibly push boundaries. In today's dynamic landscape, businesses are constantly seeking new and innovative ways to leverage AI to gain a competitive edge. This requires a mindset embracing exploration and creativity while also remaining steadfast in ethical considerations and societal impact. Pushing boundaries responsibly involves balancing ambition with prudence to ensure that the outcomes of AI initiatives align with the organization's values and contribute positively to the broader community. As organizations immerse themselves in the possibilities that AI presents, they must also acknowledge the importance of ethical guidelines, regulatory compliance, and a deep understanding of the potential impact on various stakeholders.

Additionally, responsibly pushing boundaries demands a commitment to continuous learning and improvement, as well as a willingness to adapt and refine strategies in response to emerging challenges and opportunities. Embracing the art of possible requires an open-minded approach that fosters collaboration and diverse perspectives, enabling teams to explore new horizons while maintaining a strong ethical compass. It means embracing a culture of innovation grounded in empathy and consideration for the wider implications of AI advancements. When companies pursue the art of possible through responsible boundary-pushing, they position themselves as industry leaders who not only drive transformative change within their own operations but also contribute meaningfully to the greater good.

The journey of exploring the art of possible involves a delicate balance between audacity and restraint, in addition to courage and prudence. By fostering an environment that encourages bold thinking within the boundaries of ethical responsibility, businesses can unlock the full potential of AI while safeguarding against unintended consequences. This approach sets the stage for groundbreaking developments that elevate businesses and society, demonstrating a commitment to harnessing AI's transformative power for the betterment of all.

Core Value Selection: The Key to Long-Term Success

Selecting the right core values for your AI initiatives is crucial for ensuring long-term success. *Core values* serve as guiding principles that drive decision-making, behavior, and culture within an organization. When it comes to AI, having the *right* core values can shape the ethical and responsible use of technology, as well as align the business with broader societal needs and expectations. As you embark on integrating AI into your business strategy, here are some key considerations for selecting core values that will underpin your AI initiatives.

First, it's important to consider AI's impact on society and the environment. Choosing core values that prioritize sustainability, equity, and social responsibility can help steer AI initiatives toward positive contributions to society while minimizing negative externalities. Additionally, core values centered around transparency and accountability can foster trust among stakeholders, including customers, employees, and regulators. By prioritizing transparency, organizations can demonstrate a commitment to open communication and earn the confidence of those affected by AI-driven decisions.

The selection of core values should reflect a commitment to diversity, equity, and inclusion. Embracing diversity in both teams and perspectives can lead to more comprehensive and empathetic AI solutions that cater to the needs of diverse user groups. It's essential to integrate these principles into the fabric of your organization to ensure that AI systems are designed with inclusivity in mind. Moreover, core values related to continuous learning and improvement can position your AI initiatives for long-term adaptability and relevance.

Given the rapid evolution of AI technologies, embracing a culture of learning and iteration can enable organizations to stay ahead in a fast-changing landscape. Finally, core values centered around ethical decision-making and human-centric design can guide the development and deployment of AI solutions that prioritize human well-being and ethical considerations. Ultimately, the selection of core values to underpin your AI initiatives should reinforce your organization's commitment to ethical, responsible, and impactful AI. By consciously choosing core values that align with these principles, you can set the foundation for sustainable success in the era of AI.

Understanding Organizational Risk

Operationalizing AI within an organization involves a multitude of risks that must be carefully understood and managed to ensure the successful deployment of responsible and ethical AI solutions. As organizations embrace AI, it becomes imperative to recognize the diverse spectrum of risks stemming from various sources, including technical, operational, legal, and ethical factors.

Recognizing the diverse spectrum of risks is imperative because it ensures a holistic approach to AI deployment, enabling organizations to anticipate and address potential challenges comprehensively. Technical risks, such as algorithmic biases and system failures, can undermine the reliability and fairness of AI applications. Operational risks, including workflow disruptions and integration issues, can hinder the seamless adoption of AI technologies. Legal risks stemming from non-compliance with evolving regulations and standards can result in significant penalties and damage to the organization's reputation. Ethical risks involving the misuse of AI or unintended societal impacts can erode public trust and lead to adverse social consequences.

By understanding and managing these risks, organizations can develop robust strategies that not only mitigate potential downsides but also enhance the positive impact of AI. This proactive approach fosters a culture of responsibility and accountability, ensuring that AI initiatives align with the organization's values and societal expectations. Moreover, addressing these risks early in the deployment process can lead to more resilient and adaptive AI systems capable of evolving with the changing technological and regulatory landscape.

One of the fundamental aspects of comprehending organizational risk is identifying the specific areas within the organization that can be susceptible to disruptions or adverse outcomes due to AI integration.

Areas in an organization susceptible to disruptions or adverse outcomes due to AI include:

Operational processes: AI deployment can affect existing workflows and dependencies, potentially revealing points of failure or vulnerability.

Human resources: AI might lead to workforce displacement, skill gaps, and changes in job roles, impacting employee well-being, job satisfaction, and career development.

Regulatory compliance: Ensuring adherence to evolving AI governance, legislation, and industry standards is crucial to avoid legal repercussions.

Data privacy and security: AI applications must safeguard consumer privacy and data protection to maintain trust and integrity.

Technological infrastructure: The existing infrastructure must be assessed to identify potential integration issues and system failures.

It is important to evaluate how AI deployment may affect existing processes, workflows, and dependencies within the organizational ecosystem. Also, understanding the interplay between AI technologies and the existing infrastructure can facilitate the identification of potential points of failure or vulnerability, enabling proactive risk-mitigation strategies.

Organizational risk encompasses the potential impact on human resources, including workforce displacement, skill gaps, and changes in job roles. The introduction of AI might lead to significant shifts in how we work, necessitating an assessment of the implications on employee well-being, job satisfaction, and career development. Understanding these dimensions of risk is crucial for fostering a culture of transparency, empathy, and inclusivity within the organization, thereby mitigating any potential negative socio-economic consequences.

In addition to internal considerations, organizations must also grapple with external factors that contribute to risk, such as regulatory compliance, data privacy, and security concerns. The evolving landscape of AI governance and legislation necessitates a robust understanding of the legal and ethical ramifications of AI application within specific industries and jurisdictions. This entails staying abreast of regulatory frameworks, industry standards, and best practices to ensure adherence to legal requirements and ethical guidelines. Furthermore, organizations must proactively assess the potential impact of AI on consumer privacy, data protection, and cybersecurity to uphold trust and integrity amidst increasing public scrutiny and awareness.

Ultimately, understanding organizational risk demands a holistic approach that integrates technological awareness, human-centric perspectives, and legal–ethical diligence. By perceiving risk as a multidimensional facet of AI adoption, organizations can proactively identify, evaluate, and address potential vulnerabilities, thereby laying the groundwork for responsible, sustainable, and impactful AI deployment.

Evaluating Risks Systematically

Every significant business endeavor involves risk, and the integration of AI into operations and decision-making processes is no exception. Systematically evaluating risks is a critical step in ensuring the successful implementation of AI solutions. To begin with, it's important to comprehensively assess the potential risks associated with AI initiatives, including technological, ethical, legal, and organizational risks. Technological risks may involve technical complexities, system failures, or algorithmic biases, whereas ethical risks pertain to considerations such as privacy violations or unfair discrimination. Legal risks could encompass regulatory compliance and intellectual property issues, and organizational risks might relate to cultural resistance or operational disruptions.

Once these risks are identified, it's essential to prioritize them based on the likelihood of occurrence and the potential impact. This prioritization helps allocate resources effectively and address the most pertinent risks proactively. An effective method for evaluating risks systematically is to utilize frameworks and tools specifically designed for risk assessment in AI projects, such as AI Impact Assessments or Ethical Risk Frameworks. These frameworks provide structured approaches for identifying, analyzing, and mitigating risks throughout the AI lifecycle. Besides, engaging diverse stakeholders across the organization, including legal, compliance, technology, and business teams, can bring valuable perspectives to the risk assessment process. In doing so, it's crucial to ensure open communication and collaboration to gain a holistic understanding of the risks involved.

Continuous monitoring and reassessment of risks should also be embedded into project management processes to adapt to evolving circumstances and new insights. Through this systematic approach to evaluating risks, organizations can not only mitigate potential negative impacts but also harness the opportunities presented by AI technology. Additionally, cultivating a culture that values transparency, accountability, and continuous improvement in risk management will foster an environment where potential risks are transparently acknowledged and responsibly managed. By embracing a rigorous and systematic approach to evaluating risks, businesses can pave the way for the successful deployment of AI solutions, leading to sustainable business growth and competitive advantage.

Level of Complexity: Avoiding Overcommitment

When venturing into the realm of AI implementation, it's crucial to strike a delicate balance in the level of complexity. The key is to avoid overcommitment, which can lead to delays, cost overruns, and, ultimately, frustration. It's tempting to aim for the most advanced and intricate AI solutions, but it's equally important to consider the organization's current capabilities and the resources available. Choosing an AI solution that is overly complex for the current state of the organization might lead to unnecessary complications and hinder progress. As such, it's advisable to assess the readiness of the organization to embrace and sustain complex AI solutions. This assessment should consider factors such as the existing technological infrastructure, the workforce's skill set, and the organizational culture. By aligning the complexity of the AI solution with the organization's readiness, businesses can avoid overcommitment and set realistic expectations.

It's also essential to consider the impact of complexity on the end user. Implementing overly complex AI solutions can result in user frustration, reduced adoption rates, and even resistance toward AI-driven initiatives. Therefore, it's vital to prioritize user experience and ensure that the level of complexity does not compromise usability. One approach to managing complexity is to break down the AI implementation into manageable phases or iterations. This iterative approach allows organizations to gradually build complexity as they gain experience and confidence in leveraging AI. By starting with simpler AI solutions and progressively increasing the complexity, organizations can mitigate the risks associated with overcommitment. Additionally, engaging in continuous communication and feedback loops with stakeholders can provide valuable insights into the optimal level of complexity. This collaborative approach enables organizations to adapt AI solutions in response to real-world feedback, ensuring that the level of complexity remains aligned with the evolving needs and capabilities of the organization. Ultimately, by carefully navigating the level of complexity and avoiding over-commitment, organizations can set themselves up for successful AI implementation, driving innovation and achieving tangible business outcomes.

Identifying Minimum Remarkable Products

When it comes to developing AI solutions, identifying *minimum remarkable products* (MRPs) is a critical step in achieving success-ful business outcomes. An MRP is essentially the smallest set of features that can be delivered to the market and still provide signifi-cant value to users. In the context of AI, this means identifying the core functionalities or capabilities that will make the solution truly remarkable to users and stakeholders. It's about finding the balance between delivering enough value to make an impact while avoid-ing unnecessary complexity and scope creep. The goal is to create a product that addresses a specific need or pain point in a way that delights users. So, how do you go about identifying an MRP for your AI solution?

Start identifying an MRP by understanding the user's jour-ney and pain points. What are the critical tasks or challenges that users face, and how can AI help address those? This requires deep empathy and understanding of the user's needs, behaviors, and motivations. After all, the primary goal of AI is to enhance human experiences and make everyday tasks easier.

Next, prioritize the features that will have the most signifi-cant impact on the user experience. This involves distinguishing between must-have features and nice-to-have ones. By focusing on these essentials, you can deliver a product that resonates with users and provides immediate value. Moreover, it ensures that your development efforts are efficiently directed toward the elements that matter most.

Another key aspect of identifying an MRP is considering the scalability and sustainability of the solution. Although starting small is essential, it's also crucial to envision how the product can evolve and grow over time. This requires a careful balancing act, ensuring that the MRP meets your organization's immediate needs while laying the foundation for future enhancements.

Additionally, gathering feedback from users and stakeholders throughout the process is invaluable. This iterative approach allows you to finetune the MRP based on real-world insights and validate its impact on user engagement and usability. Ultimately, the goal of identifying an MRP is to create a lean yet impactful AI solution that addresses a genuine need and delivers an exceptional user experience. By focusing on the core value proposition and continuously refining the product based on user feedback, you can set the stage for successful adoption and long-term satisfaction. In the next section, we'll delve deeper into the principles of delighting the user and ensuring sustained engagement and usability in AI solutions.

Delighting the User: Ensuring Engagement and Usability

When it comes to AI solutions, it's crucial to ensure that the end-user experience is engaging and usable. After all, what good is a powerful AI system if it's not accessible or enjoyable for the people who interact with it? *Creating delight for users* means going beyond simple functionality and focusing on how the solution fits into their lives. It involves understanding their needs, pain points, and desires. In the context of AI, this means providing meaningful insights and recommendations while respecting the user's privacy and data. It's about creating experiences that are intuitive, seamless, and valuable. Research and user feedback play a crucial role in achieving this. By gaining insight into how users interact with the AI solution, we can refine its usability and enhance their overall experience. This might involve conducting usability tests, gathering feedback through surveys or interviews, and closely monitoring how users engage with the system. Additionally, it's important to consider accessibility for diverse user groups. AI solutions must be designed to accommodate different abilities, languages, and cultural norms. This inclusivity ensures that everyone can benefit from AI technology and that no one is left behind. Leveraging design-thinking approaches can help ensure that the AI solutions resonate with a wide user range.

Establishing a multidisciplinary team is essential for creating AI solutions that truly delight users. Collaborating with experts on user experience, human-computer interaction, psychology, and other relevant fields allows for a holistic approach to designing AI systems. By integrating diverse perspectives, we can develop user-centric solutions that not only meet functional requirements but also elevate the user experience. A well-designed AI solution should feel natural and unobtrusive to the user. It should seamlessly fit into their workflow, anticipate their needs, and adapt to their preferences. Achieving this level of user delight requires a deep understanding of the user's context and the ability to translate it into an AI system that feels almost intuitive to use. Ultimately, delighting the user with AI solutions is about fostering trust and building a positive relationship. By prioritizing the user's experience and

---

Microsoft established a Responsible AI Standard that showcases the value of interdisciplinary teams. Microsoft created the following teams to ensure a broad understanding of how AI could impact different products and communities:

- **AI Red Team:** A group of experts who think like potential threats to probe AI systems for vulnerabilities. They take on different personas, such as a teenager or an adversary, to identify potential hazards.
- **Aether Committee:** A group that provides expertise on the latest trends in responsible AI, using scientific and engineering talent.
- **Office of Responsible AI:** A team that sets the company's policies and governance processes.
- **Responsible AI Strategy in Engineering (RAISE):** A group that helps engineering teams implement responsible AI processes through tools and systems.

- **Responsible AI Champs:** A community of appointed employees who raise awareness about responsible AI and help teams assess ethical and societal considerations.
- **ACM Conference on Fairness, Accountability, and Transparency (ACM FAccT):** A Microsoft-sponsored event that supports research on responsible AI.

These teams and groups offer good examples of the types of groups that companies should be thinking about to ensure that the model is being used and tested as broadly as possible. At the AI Leadership Institute, AI Red Team workshops are offered to help organizations mirror the success of companies like Microsoft to reduce the time and effort it takes to get positive results with AI.

striving for excellence in engagement and usability, we can create AI solutions that make a meaningful impact in people's lives.

Building Inclusive Teams for Better AI Solutions

In the rapidly advancing world of AI, the success of any project relies heavily on the diversity and inclusivity of its team. Building inclusive teams is not just about meeting diversity quotas but also about creating an environment where a variety of perspectives and experiences come together to drive innovation and better decision-making. When it comes to developing AI solutions, this becomes even more crucial. A diverse team not only brings unique insights to the table but also helps address biases and ensure that the AI model reflects the needs of a wide range of users.

Creating an inclusive culture starts from the top. Leadership must foster an environment where all voices are valued and heard and where individuals feel empowered to contribute authentically. This means embracing different backgrounds, cultures, and ways of thinking. It involves actively seeking out talent from underrepresented groups and then providing them with opportunities to thrive and grow within the organization. In addition, creating an inclusive team also means investing in education and awareness around issues of bias, fairness, and inclusivity. Team members should be equipped to recognize and address bias in AI algorithms, data, and decision-making processes. It's important to implement policies and practices that promote equal opportunities, fair treatment, and representation at all levels. This could involve establishing mentorship programs, offering unconscious bias training, and consciously designing inclusive recruitment and promotion processes.

Beyond fostering an inclusive internal team, organizations should also prioritize building diverse external collaborations. Partnering with a wide range of stakeholders, including community groups, academic institutions, and industry peers, can lead to richer insights and more robust AI solutions. By intentionally seeking out diverse perspectives and engaging with a broader ecosystem, teams can ensure that their AI solutions are relevant, ethical, and beneficial to a wider audience. Ultimately, building inclusive teams for better AI solutions isn't just the right thing to do—it's also a strategic imperative in today's complex, interconnected world. Organizations that prioritize diversity and inclusivity in their AI initiatives stand to gain a competitive edge as they harness the power of varied perspectives to create more effective, impactful, and responsible AI solutions.

Monitoring and Measuring Systems at Scale for Success and ROI

When it comes to implementing AI solutions, monitoring and measuring systems at scale play a crucial role in determining success and ROI. Once an AI system is deployed, it's important to have mechanisms in place to continuously monitor its performance. This involves tracking key metrics and key performance indicators (KPIs) to ensure that the system is delivering the expected outcomes.

To achieve this, organizations need to develop robust monitoring frameworks that can handle the complexities of AI systems operating at scale.

One of the fundamental aspects of monitoring AI systems is real-time data collection. Real-time monitoring allows for immediate detection of any anomalies or issues, enabling quick remediation and preventing potential negative impacts on business operations. An effective monitoring system should be capable of capturing various types of data, including user interactions, system performance, and other relevant operational parameters. During my time at Amazon, the organization understood the importance of this type of monitoring. It established multiple teams to measure the most important indicators of success. One team was focused on accuracy, ensuring that the model was telling the truth and providing accurate outcomes for users. Another team was focused on scale, ensuring the elasticity of the architecture so that the system would maintain its robustness as the user base grew. These teams met daily to review metrics and anomalies, detecting unexpected behavior very quickly.

In addition to real-time monitoring, organizations must also focus on establishing comprehensive measurement criteria for evaluating the overall success and ROI of their AI initiatives. This is important because if you fail to set clear, measurable objectives, it will be very difficult to tell if the project has been successful. Having clarity on the outcome of an AI system will ensure that you do not overengineer and that you consistently get the ROI you envisioned. This involves setting clear benchmarks and performance targets aligned with the business objectives. By defining these benchmarks, organizations can track the progress of their AI systems and assess whether they are delivering the anticipated value.

The ability to measure the impact of AI solutions on business outcomes is essential for demonstrating the value they bring to the organization. This requires the implementation of robust analytics and reporting mechanisms that can provide actionable insights into the performance of AI systems. Organizations should leverage advanced analytics tools to gain a deeper understanding of how AI is contributing to key business metrics such as revenue generation, cost savings, customer satisfaction, and operational efficiency.

To optimize the monitoring and measurement process, it's crucial to integrate feedback loops that enable continuous refinement and improvement of AI systems. This iterative approach enables organizations to adapt to changing business dynamics and evolving customer needs. This happens by not just capturing the data in feedback loops but also having a team review that data and select how to evolve the solution to meet the evolving needs of the business. This is done in small and frequent iterations. By leveraging feedback from users, stakeholders, and domain experts, organizations can identify areas for enhancement and make informed decisions to optimize the performance of their AI systems.

Ultimately, effective monitoring and measurement of AI systems at scale not only ensures their continued performance but also enables organizations to maximize their ROI. By proactively identifying and addressing issues, organizations can maintain the reliability and effectiveness of their AI solutions. Additionally, the ability to demonstrate AI's tangible impacts on key business outcomes strengthens the case for further investment in AI capabilities and encourages a culture of continuous improvement and innovation. As your organization consistently delivers on the promise of AI by building AI systems that meet the expectations set at the beginning, trust begins to build.

When organizations can clearly demonstrate the tangible benefits of their AI systems—such as improved revenue, cost savings, enhanced customer satisfaction, and greater operational efficiency—they build a compelling business case for further investment. Stakeholders are more likely to support additional funding and resources when they see concrete evidence of AI's positive impact on key business metrics. This financial backing provides the means to explore new AI capabilities, experiment with innovative technologies, and scale successful solutions across the organization.

Furthermore, a culture of continuous improvement and innovation is fostered when organizations commit to regular monitoring and evaluation of their AI systems. By systematically collecting and analyzing data, teams can identify areas for enhancement, uncover new opportunities, and swiftly address any issues.

This iterative process not only improves the performance and reliability of AI solutions but also cultivates a mindset of ongoing learning and development among employees. As team members witness the successful outcomes of their efforts, they are motivated to maintain high standards and drive further advancements, thereby creating a virtuous cycle of innovation and excellence.

Takeaways

- Aligning AI initiatives with the company's overall business vision and core values is critical for ensuring ethical and responsible technology development. This provides direction and helps maintain brand integrity.
- Responsibly pushing boundaries involves balancing ambition and ethical considerations. Companies should foster a culture of bold thinking within the framework of inclusivity, transparency, and social responsibility.
- Choosing the right core values to underpin AI projects sets the stage for long-term success. Values like accountability, sustainability, and human-centric design guide development.
- Understanding all dimensions of risk—technological, ethical, legal, and organizational—enables proactive mitigation strategies when adopting AI. A multifaceted view of risk is key.
- The complexity of AI solutions should align with the company's capabilities and resources. Overly advanced systems can lead to frustration, delays, and resistance. A phased and iterative approach is advisable.

- Identifying the minimum set of features that provide remarkable value (i.e., minimum remarkable product) creates focused, impactful AI solutions that meet user needs.
- Delighting users involves intuitive design, inclusive functionality, and seamless workflow integration. Multidisciplinary collaboration and iterative refinement based on user feedback is key.

Reflection Questions

- How can you ensure that your AI initiatives align with and advance the company's core mission and values? What values are most important?
- In what ways can you push boundaries and innovate responsibly? How do you balance ambition and ethical considerations?
- What are the greatest risks associated with AI adoption in your company? How can you proactively address them?
- What is the right level of complexity for your current AI solutions? Do you need to scale back or move forward gradually?
- How might you identify the minimum set of features that will delight users and provide remarkable value?
- How can you best gather user feedback to refine the usability and experience of your AI systems?

Part II

Day Two: The Road to Reality

Chapter 5

From Playground to Production: Embracing the Challenges

Making the leap from concept to practical implementation in the world of artificial intelligence (AI) involves navigating a landscape often riddled with unexpected challenges. Once the initial excitement and fanfare surrounding an AI project starts to fade, reality sets in, and the daily grind begins. It's important to acknowledge that this transition is natural and expected, and it's where the true mettle of a project is tested. To truly embrace these challenges means recognizing that they are not obstacles but rather opportunities for growth and innovation.

Bridging the Gap: Transitioning from Proof to Production

Real-world examples abound of AI projects that faced significant hurdles during their journey from *proof of concept* to full-fledged production. Take the case of a leading technology company that

invested heavily in an ambitious AI-driven customer service platform. After an initial successful pilot phase, the team encountered
unexpected roadblocks during the scaling process, leading to delays
and performance issues. Instead of being deterred, the team ral-
lied together, reassessed their approach, and leveraged the setbacks
as valuable learning experiences. By embracing their challenges
head-on, they restructured their deployment strategy, refined their
model-training processes, and ultimately achieved a successful
production rollout.

A proof of concept is a tightly scoped demonstration of how
the AI system will solve a specific business problem. This
requires clarity on the business problem to be solved, a metric that will be used to measure the project's success, and a
timeline for delivery, which is typically less than 6 weeks.

Similarly, a healthcare organization embarked on an AI initiative to optimize patient care through predictive analytics, which
enables the organization to use data from past patient interactions
to help predict how to take care of future patient problems. With
the use of this data, the organization could tell what patients might
have problems with certain medications, or what the best cadence
was for checking in with patients after a procedure. However, it
encountered resistance from frontline healthcare professionals
who were skeptical about integrating AI into their daily workflows.
Rather than shying away from the resistance, the project leaders
engaged in open dialogue with their staff, provided extensive training (including teaching everyone how to build an AI bot) and support to them, and gradually won over their support by showcasing
the tangible benefits of the AI-driven insights in improving patient
outcomes. By acknowledging the initial skepticism and leveraging
it as an opportunity to communicate effectively and build trust,
the project leaders successfully bridged the gap from the project's

proof of concept to adding it as an integral part of their team's daily operations.

These examples underscore the significance of embracing the daily challenges that arise when transitioning from AI dreams to the everyday reality of implementation. They emphasize the value of persistence, adaptability, and a willingness to learn from setbacks. By sharing these stories and dissecting the strategies employed to overcome obstacles, we can gain valuable insights into the resilience required to navigate the intricate path from vision to productivity in the realm of AI.

Transitioning from proof of concept to a full-scale production environment can be both thrilling and daunting. It's the critical phase where your innovative ideas begin to take concrete shape, and the pressure is on to deliver real product value. Bridging the gap requires careful planning, execution, and an unwavering commitment to your vision.

As you transition toward a production setting, it's essential to assess the scalability of your AI solution. What worked in a controlled testing environment, your AI sandbox, might not necessarily seamlessly function when deployed at scale. Consider all potential bottlenecks, resource requirements, and performance benchmarks to ensure a smooth transition.

Infrastructure Matters: Building the Right Foundation

Infrastructure, which is the framework upon which you build your AI platform, plays a pivotal role in this transition. Building the right foundation involves evaluating the existing systems, acquiring or upgrading hardware if necessary, and optimizing your network's architecture to support the demands of your AI solution. You'll need to strike a balance between computational power, storage capacity, and networking capabilities to create an environment that can accommodate the evolving needs of your AI applications.

This is needed because as your AI system scales and becomes more heavily used, you will want the system to scale elastically. Having an elastic system means the infrastructure will grow as the demand grows and will shrink when the demand for the application slows. This enables you to ensure that you don't overprovision resources that the application doesn't need but also can grow to meet the users' needs in real time. If you fail to consider scale, you may build a system that crumbles under the pressure of growth. As an example, an airline built AI into its customer service support channels. The AI system enabled asynchronous communication with passengers, pilots, and staff during irregular operations like flight delays and staff availability. However, the airline didn't plan for scale and neglected to create an elastically scalable architecture. So when bad weather hit and these systems came under heavy load by users, the system became slow and eventually unresponsive. When we build responsible AI systems, robustness needs to be a key consideration.

Moreover, transitioning to production involves aligning with organizational objectives and policies. Understanding the compliance and security standards governing your industry is paramount. For regulated industries like healthcare and finance, this is business as usual. But with AI, every industry will need to keep an eye on upcoming regulations and policies that will impact operations. It is important to look at this information through three lenses. The first is academia, where you should create an alliance with an academic organization that can help you keep in touch with the research happening in your industry. Second, align with someone in the policy and regulatory arena to help ensure that you understand the global regulatory scene and can take action as early as possible. The General Data Protection Regulation (GDPR) is a good example. When the GDPR was announced, it required all global, national organizations to change how they managed their data. For those companies who knew this was coming, the impact was far less than it was for companies that weren't prepared. Finally, integrating your AI solution into the existing IT landscape while adhering to regulatory requirements demands meticulous attention to detail, from data protection protocols to access controls.

Team Dynamics

But it's not just about the tech—team dynamics, which is how the organization works across functional areas, play a vital role in this process. Effective collaboration among cross-functional teams, including data scientists, software engineers, and business stakeholders, is crucial for your project's success. The ability to effectively communicate and bridge the gap between technical and business perspectives is essential to ensure that the AI solution meets both your organization's functional and strategic objectives.

As you leap from the controlled environment of a proof of concept to the complex realities of your product's production setup, you must remain agile and adaptable. AI systems require consistent and constant supervision and monitoring. It isn't enough to get the data; a team must monitor the data and be empowered to use that data to adjust how the system is performing. The nimbler and more empowered a team is, the better they will be able to react and respond to business needs in a timely fashion. Embrace an iterative approach to problem-solving, and be open to refining your strategies based on real-world feedback. This phase is as much about learning and adapting as it is about execution.

Ultimately, moving from proof to production is about more than just deploying technology; it's about transforming your organization's capabilities and shaping its future. This transition is an opportunity to innovate, collaborate, and make a tangible impact on the world around you.

As you transition from the proof-of-concept phase to full-fledged production, the backbone of your AI operations becomes increasingly crucial. The infrastructure that supports your AI initiatives lays the groundwork for success and forms the bedrock upon which you can build robust and scalable solutions. We will now delve into the pivotal aspects of infrastructure management and highlight the key considerations that can make or break your AI journey.

Technology

First and foremost, addressing your organization's underlying infrastructure involves a holistic evaluation of your technology stack. Are your hardware and software resources equipped to handle the demands of AI at scale? Assessing your computational capabilities, storage systems, and network infrastructure is essential to ensure seamless integration and efficient data processing. You need to ensure that your organization's tech foundation can support all it needs to do and more. Additionally, your choice of cloud services, on-premises solutions, or hybrid models necessitates careful deliberation to align with your business objectives and regulatory requirements.

The security and compliance implications of your infrastructure cannot be overstated. As AI deployments often deal with sensitive data and critical business processes, fortifying your infrastructure against cyber threats and ensuring adherence to relevant regulations are paramount. Implementing robust access controls, encryption mechanisms, and audit trails not only safeguards your AI assets but also fosters trust among stakeholders. Additionally, incorporating ethical considerations into the fabric of your infrastructure fosters responsible AI practices, thereby enhancing organizational reputation and mitigating potential risks.

Scalability and flexibility form the cornerstone of a future-ready infrastructure. Anticipating the dynamic nature of AI workloads and the evolving nature of technological advancements, the architecture should accommodate seamless scalability and agility. Embracing containerization, microservices, and interoperable frameworks empowers your infrastructure to adapt to changing demands without incurring extensive reengineering efforts. Moreover, tapping into automation and orchestration tools streamlines the management of infrastructure components, allowing your teams to focus more on innovation and value creation.

Finally, the human element must not be overlooked in the infrastructure equation. Empowering your teams with the necessary skill sets, training programs, and collaborative environments is imperative to harness the full potential of your infrastructure. Cultivating a culture of continuous learning and knowledge sharing fosters cross-functional synergy and propels your AI endeavors toward success. Recognizing and addressing inherent biases and diversity within the AI talent pool augments the creativity and inclusivity of your infrastructure team, paving the way for groundbreaking innovations.

In essence, the foundation of your AI journey rests upon the strength of your overall infrastructure. By embracing a comprehensive approach encompassing technological robustness, security, scalability, and human capital, you can fortify your organization for the challenges and opportunities that lie ahead in the realm of AI.

Assembling Your AI Avengers

When it comes to building and deploying responsible AI, assembling the right team is essential for success. Just like in superhero movies, you need your own team of AI avengers who bring diverse skills, experiences, and perspectives to the table. But unlike the movies, this team isn't about fighting villains; it's about solving complex problems and delivering real value. So, who are your key players?

First, you need a data scientist, the master of algorithms and model building, who can wrangle the data and uncover insights that drive AI innovation. Then there's the domain expert, someone who understands the specific industry or business context in which the AI will be applied. This person brings invaluable knowledge that ensures the AI solutions are not only technically sound but also practical and impactful. Next, you'll want a software engineer who is adept at turning machine-learning models into production-ready applications. Their expertise in coding and deployment is crucial for bringing AI from the lab into the real world. Alongside them, you'll require an ethical AI specialist who plays a critical role in ensuring that the AI systems being developed consider fairness, accountability, and transparency. They'll help mitigate the risks of unintended biases or negative impacts. Last but not least, you'll need a project manager to orchestrate the entire process, coordinate efforts, manage timelines, and align the team with broader organizational goals.

The team's dynamics go beyond just individual roles, however. Collaboration, communication, and a shared sense of purpose are vital for harnessing their collective potential. Building a culture that values diverse perspectives, encourages open dialogue, and fosters continuous learning is key to unleashing the full power of your team. Embracing collaboration tools, agile methodologies, and cross-functional interactions can help amplify the strengths of each team member while addressing any weaknesses found. After all, true success in the AI realm isn't just about the technology itself; it's about the people behind it all. By assembling your AI Avengers thoughtfully, nurturing a culture of teamwork and growth, and empowering them with the right resources, you set the stage for transformative AI innovations that truly make a difference.

Data, Data Everywhere: Managing and Maintaining Quality

You've probably heard the phrase "Garbage in, garbage out." That's especially true when it comes to AI and machine learning. Your data is the lifeblood of your AI systems, and ensuring its quality is paramount. In today's world, data is everywhere—streaming in from multiple sources, constantly evolving, and sometimes being unpredictable. Managing this influx of data and ensuring its quality can be a challenging task, but it's a critical one for the success of your AI initiatives. The importance of balancing fast iteration with steady progress in AI development stems from the necessity to adapt quickly to new information while maintaining a solid, scalable foundation. Rapid iteration enables teams to respond to emerging challenges and integrate new insights, keeping pace with the fast-evolving AI landscape. However, without a methodical approach, this can result in technical debt and inefficiencies that undermine long-term success. To navigate this balance, teams must employ clear guidelines, continuous evaluation, and risk management strategies, ensuring that each step forward is both innovative and sustainable.

Managing and maintaining data quality involves several key steps. First, you need to establish clear data governance policies and procedures. This means defining standards for data collection, storage, and usage, as well as assigning responsibility to a team member for maintaining data quality. It's crucial to have a solid understanding of your data sources and how they impact the quality of your AI models. Additionally, implementing data quality checks and validation processes will help identify and correct any issues early on.

Data profiling and cleaning tools can also be invaluable in maintaining data integrity. One of the biggest challenges in managing and maintaining data quality is dealing with the sheer volume and velocity of data. With the rapid pace of data accumulation, it can be easy for inconsistencies and errors to slip through the cracks and cause havoc. This is where automation tools and processes come into play. By automating data quality checks and monitoring, your team can stay on top of data integrity without being overwhelmed by its sheer volume.

Data quality is an ongoing process. As your AI systems evolve and grow, so, too, must your data management practices. Regular audits, reviews, and updates to your data governance policies ensure that your data remains an asset rather than a liability. Ultimately, managing and maintaining data quality is not just a technical concern—it's a strategic imperative. High-quality data fuels accurate insights and decisions, whereas poor-quality data can lead to costly errors and missteps. By prioritizing data quality and putting in place robust processes to manage and maintain it, you'll be setting your AI initiatives up for success in the long run.

A Balancing Act: Fast Iteration vs. Steady Progress

Finding the right balance between achieving fast iteration or working in 2- to 4-week sprints/cycles and ensuring steady progress is crucial in the world of AI development. On the one hand, the need for rapid iteration allows teams to test and refine their AI models quickly, incorporating new insights and responding to emerging challenges. This agility can be a competitive advantage, enabling organizations to stay ahead in a rapidly evolving landscape.

However, fast iteration must be balanced with the need for steady progress. Although it's tempting to rush through iterations in pursuit of quick wins, a haphazard approach can lead to technical debt, overlooked issues, and, ultimately, a lack of sustainable progress. Organizations must prioritize building a strong foundation for their AI initiatives, ensuring that each iteration contributes to a solid, scalable solution.

To achieve this balance, teams must establish clear guidelines for when to iterate rapidly and when to prioritize steady progress. This involves creating mechanisms for continuous evaluation and reflection, allowing them to assess whether their current pace aligns with the broader goals and requirements of the project. By maintaining a dynamic yet structured approach to iteration, teams can navigate the often-tricky path toward success in AI development.

An important element of this balancing act is the ability to foster a culture of experimentation while still emphasizing the importance of disciplined progress. Team members should feel empowered to explore innovative ideas and approaches, knowing that they have the support and resources to swiftly iterate. At the same time, there should be a shared understanding that every iteration should contribute to a larger strategic roadmap, avoiding the pitfalls of aimless experimentation.

Another critical element in managing and maintaining data quality is ensuring that every project has a specific way to measure success—a key performance indicator (KPI) or numerical value, which determines the success or failure of the project. Establishing clear KPIs provides a tangible benchmark against which progress can be measured, offering a straightforward metric for evaluating outcomes. These metrics should be carefully selected to reflect the project's core objectives and should be aligned with broader business goals. Whether it's accuracy, efficiency, customer satisfaction, or another measurable outcome, having these indicators in place ensures that the teams remain focused and accountable.

Additionally, KPIs facilitate transparent communication of progress and challenges to stakeholders, fostering a shared understanding of what success looks like.

Striking the right balance between fast iteration and steady progress requires a keen focus on risk management and scenario planning. Teams need to anticipate potential setbacks and calibration points, preparing to adapt their approach based on the feedback received from each iteration. This proactive approach to risk assessment ensures that rapid iteration doesn't devolve into chaotic churn but instead leads to meaningful advancements.

Ultimately, mastering the balancing act between fast iteration and steady progress demands both an artful touch and a robust framework. It requires a harmonious blend of flexibility, discipline, creativity, and structure, all guided by a steadfast commitment to delivering impactful, sustainable AI solutions.

Continuous Improvement: Setting Up Feedback Loops

As we navigate the complex landscape of AI implementation, one key strategy stands out as a critical enabler of long-term success: setting up effective feedback loops. In essence, *feedback loops* provide the mechanism for continuous improvement, allowing us to gather insights from real-world AI usage and use that data to refine and enhance our models and systems. But how do we go about implementing effective feedback loops in the context of AI?

The first step in setting up feedback loops is to establish clear mechanisms for capturing and analyzing performance data. This might involve setting up robust monitoring systems that track the behavior of AI models in real time or implementing processes for collecting user feedback and incorporating it into the development cycle. With these mechanisms in place, we can then move on to the crucial task of analyzing the data we've gathered. This step requires careful consideration of the metrics that matter most for our specific AI applications, whether it's accuracy, efficiency, fairness, or some other measure of performance. Armed with these insights, we can now take meaningful action to improve our AI systems. This might involve tweaking model parameters, refining training data, or even redesigning aspects of the AI architecture. Whatever the specific interventions may be, the key is to ensure that they are driven by the insights gleaned from our feedback loops.

The journey doesn't end here, however. Continuous improvement necessitates an ongoing commitment to iterating our AI solutions based on the feedback we receive. This might mean regularly revisiting and updating our models in response to emerging patterns and trends or proactively seeking out new opportunities to optimize performance based on user input. Ultimately, the establishment of effective feedback loops empowers us to cultivate AI solutions that not only meet their intended objectives but also evolve and improve over time. By embracing this ethos of constant refinement, we position ourselves to derive maximum value from our AI initiatives while also fostering trust and confidence among users, stakeholders, and the broader community. In the next section, we explore the critical role of tools and resources in shaping the AI journey, shedding light on the diverse array of technologies and methodologies that constitute the AI arsenal.

Tools of the Trade: Picking Your AI Arsenal

Selecting the right tools for your AI journey is akin to assembling a sophisticated arsenal. Like a skilled artisan, you must carefully curate the instruments that will enable your team to build, innovate, and continuously refine your AI solutions. In the AI realm, tools come in all shapes and sizes, each with its own unique capabilities and purposes. The first step in picking your AI arsenal is understanding the specific needs and challenges of your organization. Just as a surgeon selects the precise instruments for a delicate operation, you must identify the tools that align with your business objectives and technological infrastructure. Are you aiming to enhance customer experience through personalized recommendations? Or do you perhaps seek to optimize resource allocation and streamline processes? Understanding your goals helps guide your selection process. Once you have pinpointed your strategic ambitions, it's time to survey the vast landscape of AI tools and technologies. From machine-learning frameworks to data visualization platforms, the options can be overwhelming. Consider factors such as compatibility with your existing systems, scalability, ease of integration, and ongoing support when assessing potential tools.

Do not underestimate the importance of user-friendliness and the learning curve associated with each tool. After all, the effectiveness of your AI arsenal ultimately hinges on how well your team can wield these instruments.

As you explore the myriad offerings, keep in mind the evolving nature of AI technology. Look for tools that not only address your current requirements but also have the flexibility to adapt to future advancements. This forward-thinking approach will equip you with an agile and resilient arsenal capable of navigating the ever-changing AI landscape. Additionally, consider engaging with vendors and industry experts to gain insights into the best practices and emerging trends in AI tooling. Their expertise can help you make informed decisions and avoid common pitfalls.

Finally, assembling your AI arsenal is not a one-time affair. Continuous evaluation and optimization are crucial for maintaining a robust tool suite that serves the evolving needs of your organization. Regularly reassess the performance of your chosen tools, and be ready to swap out or upgrade components as your AI initiatives mature. Building your AI arsenal demands strategic foresight, flexibility, and a deep understanding of your organization's goals. By carefully selecting and refining your tools, you lay a firm foundation for a successful AI journey that delivers tangible value and sustains long-term innovation.

Metrics that Matter: Measuring Success on "Day Two"

Congratulations! You've made it past the initial excitement of launching your AI initiatives, but now it's time to take a step back and evaluate how well your strategies are performing. On "Day Two" of your AI journey, the focus shifts from ideation and experimentation to sustainable growth and impact measurement. But what metrics should you be paying attention to to truly assess the success of your AI endeavors?

Gone are the days when success could be measured solely by the speed of deployment or the number of models in production. Although those factors are important, they only scratch the surface of what it means to build a successful AI capability. To truly measure success, we must look at a comprehensive set of metrics that encompass not just the technical performance but also the business impact, ethical considerations, and alignment with organizational goals.

One key set of metrics that matters on "Day Two" is the business impact metrics. How is AI contributing to your organization's bottom line? Are you seeing improvements in efficiency, cost savings, revenue generation, and customer satisfaction? These tangible outcomes help demonstrate the value that AI is delivering to your business. It's important to track these metrics over time to understand the long-term impact of your AI initiatives.

Moreover, the technical performance metrics cannot be overlooked. Metrics such as model accuracy, latency, and throughput are crucial for ensuring that your AI systems are delivering the expected results reliably and efficiently. However, it's equally important to monitor these metrics in real-world scenarios and across different use cases to ensure that your AI solutions are robust and scalable.

Ethical and fairness metrics are becoming increasingly critical in the evaluation of AI success. How are you ensuring that your AI applications are not reinforcing biases or perpetuating unfair outcomes? By tracking metrics related to fairness, transparency, and accountability, you can demonstrate that your AI initiatives are not just technically sound but also aligned with ethical principles and societal values.

Additionally, measuring the effectiveness of your AI team is essential for sustainable growth. Are they able to iterate quickly and respond to changing requirements? Are they continuously learning and improving their capabilities? Tracking metrics related to team performance, skill development, and collaboration can provide insights into the health and agility of your AI team, which is crucial for your organization's long-term success.

As you embark on the "Day Two" phase of your AI journey, remember that the metrics you choose to measure will shape the narrative of your AI initiatives. Selecting the right metrics that align with your organizational objectives and ethical principles will not only guide your decision-making but also communicate the true impact of AI within your organization.

The Long Haul: Planning for Sustainability and Growth

Once your AI initiatives have transitioned from the initial development phase to day-to-day operations, it's crucial to shift focus toward ensuring the sustainability and growth of these initiatives. Although achieving short-term success is gratifying, the true measure of accomplishment lies in long-term sustainability. This section delves into the critical aspects of planning for sustainability and orchestrating growth in the AI realm.

Sustainability begins with establishing a solid foundation. Successful AI deployment requires not just technical readiness but also organizational preparedness. Companies must invest in creating a culture that embraces change and innovation and bolsters ongoing learning and adaptation. Without this foundation, even the most promising AI solutions can falter under the weight of inertia and resistance to change.

Moreover, sustaining AI initiatives involves nurturing a robust ecosystem around them. This includes cultivating partnerships with stakeholders across the business, ensuring alignment of AI outcomes with broader organizational goals, and leveraging feedback from various touchpoints to continuously fine-tune and adapt the AI strategy.

Planning for growth demands an equal measure of strategic foresight and nimbleness. Organizations must be ready to capitalize on the successes of their AI endeavors without succumbing to complacency. It is imperative to proactively anticipate scaling needs, whether in terms of handling increased data volumes, expanding AI applications to new areas, or accommodating growing user bases.

A crucial element of sustainable growth is prioritizing ethical considerations and responsible AI practices. As AI becomes deeply ingrained in business operations, the potential for unintended consequences grows. Hence, it's essential to develop governance frameworks that align with industry best practices and regulatory requirements to ensure that AI deployments remain ethical, fair, and unbiased.

Finally, the long haul also calls for vigilance against market shifts and technological evolution. Businesses must keep a watchful eye on emerging technologies to secure sustained success, the competitive landscape, and evolving customer needs. Adequate scalability and agility are indispensable to stay relevant and impactful, necessitating a constant evaluation and evolution of AI strategies.

In summary, the road to sustainability and growth in AI is paved with continuous effort, adaptability, and foresight. By fostering a culture of innovation, embracing partnerships, upholding ethical practices, and staying vigilant, organizations can not only sustain their AI initiatives but also thrive amid the ever-changing dynamics of the AI landscape.

Takeaways

- **Choosing the right metrics:** Metrics should align with organizational objectives and ethical principles to guide decision-making and communicate AI's true impact.
- **Planning for sustainability:** Emphasize long-term success by establishing a solid foundation that includes technical readiness and organizational preparedness. Foster a culture of innovation and continuous learning.

- **Nurturing a robust ecosystem:** Cultivate partnerships, ensure that your organization's AI outcomes align with your organizational goals, and leverage feedback for continuous improvement.
- **Strategic growth planning:** Capitalize on your AI successes with strategic foresight and nimbleness. Anticipate scaling needs, and expand AI applications responsibly.
- **Ethical considerations:** Prioritize responsible AI practices by developing governance frameworks that ensure ethical, fair, and unbiased AI deployments.
- **Vigilance against market shifts:** Stay informed about emerging technologies, the competitive landscape, and evolving customer needs. Ensure scalability and agility to remain relevant and impactful.
- **Continuous effort and adaptability:** Sustain and grow AI initiatives by fostering innovation, embracing partnerships, upholding ethical practices, and staying vigilant.

Reflection Questions

- How do the current metrics you use align with your organization's objectives and ethical principles, and how can you improve them to better guide decision-making?
- What steps have you taken to ensure the long-term sustainability of your AI initiatives, and how can you foster a culture of innovation and continuous learning within your organization?
- In what ways can you strengthen your partnerships and ensure that AI outcomes align more closely with your organizational goals and stakeholder expectations?
- How prepared are you to scale your AI applications responsibly, and what strategic foresight and nimbleness are required to anticipate and meet future scaling needs?
- What governance frameworks do you have in place to ensure that your AI practices are ethical, fair, and unbiased, and how can you enhance your vigilance against market shifts and emerging technologies?

Chapter 6
Beyond the Prototype: What Happens After POC?

S o, you've successfully developed a prototype for your artificial intelligence (AI) solution. Congratulations! As mentioned in earlier chapters, this is part of "Day 1," or what I affectionately call "Baby Tiger" mode. It's an exciting achievement and marks the beginning of a crucial transition phase. Now, it's time to shift gears and pivot your mindset from focusing solely on the prototype to envisioning a long-term, scalable production pilot. Why does this shift matter? Welcome to Day 2.

Shifting Mindsets: From Prototype to Production Pilot

First off, your prototype served its purpose by demonstrating the feasibility of your AI concept. Developing your hypothesis and proving it is critical to demonstrate early success. It allowed you to experiment, gather initial feedback, and validate your ideas. However, to achieve real impact, you need to think beyond the prototype. Consider the broader implications, and envision how your AI system will operate at scale in a real-world environment.

In a recent project, a manufacturing company identified a business problem that it wanted to tackle with AI. They found GitHub repository examples and used them as the foundation of their solution. They spent only a couple of weeks and were excited to demonstrate their solution to the executive board and leadership team. Good news! Their project was met with a roar of excitement. Their "baby tiger," or proof of concept, won over the leadership. Now they were given funding and time to build the solution into a production-ready application. They immediately ran into three challenges.

First, they didn't realize that the GitHub repository code they used was not secure or scalable. As they added more users, the system became unstable and slowed. They now faced the reality that they might need to rewrite the entire thing.

Second, they became aware that the system had hard-coded connections to its data sources, making it very hard to scale to the other 20+ data sources the application would need in production. It was more unplanned work.

Third, the model was providing inconsistent answers to the questions that were being asked. Every request generated a slightly different answer, and although that was not a big concern in the prototype, it became a critical challenge as the application began to scale.

The team had made promises that were much harder to keep than expected, increasing the cost and timeline for the project. Their baby tiger was growing up, and they were not ready for what was needed to tame it.

This scenario has become increasingly common in enterprises that are enthusiastic to scale pilots to production. The top concerns that became evident were security, scalability, data access and privacy, and model efficiency. Rather than wait until you get to production, the earlier you ask questions about these topics, the better.

So, how do you avoid getting caught in this scenario? It is important to shift your mindset on how you build your prototype and build a production pilot instead.

A *production pilot* is a proof of concept (POC) that intentionally considers the challenges that will be faced when the POC is deployed to production. Your production pilot isn't just about scaling up; it's about integrating your AI solution into existing workflows, systems, and processes. This shift in mindset requires a holistic approach because we often underestimate the challenges we will face due to the enthusiasm generated in the early development phases.

You'll need to consider factors such as data governance, scalability, security, and performance. Also, understanding the business and operational implications of transitioning from a prototype to a production-ready solution is vital. The earlier you can learn from other similar journeys to production, the better prepared you will be.

Your pilot is moving from a controlled environment to the complexities of real-world implementation. Whereas the prototype focused on proving that the hypothesis is possible, the production pilot emphasizes delivering measurable value and addressing the practical needs of its users and the business fairly and responsibly. Shifting your mindset isn't merely a technical transformation; it's also a cultural shift. Your team's perspective should evolve from experimental tinkering to strategic, goal-oriented implementation.

Engaging stakeholders at this stage becomes critical. By involving key decision-makers and end users, you can align the production pilot with your organizational goals and ensure its relevance to actual business needs. Understanding the importance of shifting your mindset from creating a temporary prototype to building a long-term production pilot equips you with the vision and strategic thinking needed to propel your AI solution toward meaningful, sustainable success.

Planning with the End in Mind: Visualizing a Scaled AI System

When it comes to venturing beyond the prototype and into the realm of real-world impact, it's crucial to approach the process with foresight and strategic vision. Visualizing a scaled AI system involves more than just expanding the current model or technology. It requires aligning every aspect of the organization, from infrastructure and resources to long-term objectives and priorities. The initial excitement of a successful proof of concept often blinds teams to the complexities and challenges of scaling AI solutions. However, taking the time to plan for scalability early on can be the difference between fleeting success and sustainable transformation.

Visualizing a scaled AI system encompasses not only the technical aspects of data processing and model deployment but also the broader business context within which the AI solution will operate. It entails understanding the future needs of the organization and its stakeholders and designing an AI system that can grow and adapt alongside them. This proactive and holistic approach ensures that the AI solution is not only effective in its current state but also flexible enough to evolve in response to changing requirements and opportunities.

Setting Clear Hypotheses and Goals for Your Pilot

Before embarking on any AI project, however, it's crucial to establish clear hypotheses and goals for your pilot. Doing so sets the stage for success by providing a *blueprint* for development and evaluation. A blueprint is a document that outlines your AI strategy and provides a tactical plan that outlines how to deliver the strategic plan successfully. Let's dive into this topic and explore why it's so important.

When setting a clear hypothesis, it's essential to define what you aim to achieve with your AI pilot and how you plan to measure success. Are you seeking to improve operational efficiency, enhance customer experience, or optimize decision-making processes? Clarifying your objectives not only guides your project's development process but also enables you to measure the impact of your AI solution effectively.

Additionally, it's important to articulate hypotheses about how your AI model is expected to perform. Will it accurately predict outcomes, classify data, or recommend solutions? Defining these expectations helps align your team and stakeholders around common objectives. Setting clear goals also ensures that everyone involved understands the intended pilot outcomes. Whether it's reducing error rates by a certain percentage, increasing productivity, or enhancing personalization, specific goals provide a tangible target to work toward. You must be able to measure progress and have a clear definition of what success looks like. Beyond that, clear hypotheses and goals help serve as a foundation for robust evaluation criteria. By clearly defining what success looks like for your AI pilot, you can objectively assess its performance and make informed decisions about scaling or refining the solution. Communicating these hypotheses and goals transparently fosters alignment and collaboration across teams. It empowers your stakeholders to contribute meaningfully to the project by understanding the purpose and expected impact of the pilot.

Finally, setting clear hypotheses and goals instills a sense of accountability and direction. It accelerates decision-making processes, directs resources effectively, and mitigates the risk of scope creep. Ultimately, this clarity not only streamlines the pilot phase but also lays the groundwork for future iterations and scale-up. In summary, setting clear hypotheses and goals for your AI pilot is a fundamental step that underpins your project's success. It ensures focus, alignment, evaluation effectiveness, collaboration, and accountability. By investing time and effort in this foundational stage, you pave the way for a more impactful and sustainable AI solution.

Let's now discuss some examples of metrics you can use to measure AI success.

Creating the Blueprint

One key aspect of planning with the end in mind is creating the blueprint of how an AI solution will evolve. Your blueprint should outline the envisioned progression of the AI system and identify the milestones, investments, and safety measures necessary to support its growth. By delineating the stages of ideation and experimentation, teams can anticipate the resources that will be needed and the operational impacts of scaling up their AI solution, thereby avoiding last-minute scrambles and haphazard developments.

Visualizing a scaled AI system involves engaging with cross-functional teams and stakeholders to ensure everyone is in agreement with the organization's core values and strategies. This collaborative approach facilitates the identification of potential synergies, interdependencies, and trade-offs, allowing for a more comprehensive and integrated scalability plan. Additionally, it fosters a shared sense of ownership and commitment to the long-term success of the AI solution, instilling a culture of collective responsibility and collaboration.

Ultimately, planning with the end in mind empowers organizations to anticipate and address the challenges of scaling AI solutions while leveraging the full potential of emerging technologies. By envisioning a scaled AI system from the outset, teams can architect an adaptable and resilient framework that not only meets current demands but also paves the way for future innovation and value creation.

Over the past 10 years, I have delivered hundreds of these AI executive leadership sessions. Many times, the attendees will confess that rarely, if ever, have they been in the same room, at the same time, with the other leaders in the session. AI solutions will connect cross-functional teams, and getting these leaders together early and often will ensure a higher probability of success.

Ensuring Scalability from the Start: Why It Matters

When it comes to implementing AI solutions, *scalability* isn't just a nice-to-have feature; it's an absolute necessity. As we transition from the pilot phase to production, expansion becomes crucial for ensuring that your AI systems can handle the increasing demands and complexities of real-world deployment. But why does scalability matter so much from the start? Let's delve into this vital aspect of AI implementation.

Scalability matters, because without it, even the most promising AI pilot may falter when faced with the complexities of real-world data and security challenges. When we design AI systems, we must not only consider current needs but also anticipate future growth and increased usage. Imagine a scenario where your AI solution performs exceptionally well in a controlled environment but fails miserably when subjected to a surge in user interactions or data input. This is where scalability comes into play.

Moreover, scalability ensures that your AI systems can adapt and grow along with your business. Whether it's accommodating a larger user base, handling increased computation loads, or integrating new data sources, a scalable AI system remains flexible and responsive. Without scalability, you risk being trapped in the limitations of your initial design, hindering the potential impact and value of your AI solutions.

From a technical perspective, ensuring scalability from the start allows organizations to build robust, efficient, and reliable AI architectures. It involves thoughtful considerations such as choosing the right model, designing for inclusivity, and optimizing algorithms for performance. By addressing scalability early on, teams can minimize the need for extensive rework or costly overhauls as their AI systems mature and expand.

Scalability isn't just about managing growth; it's also about future-proofing AI investments. In today's rapidly evolving technological landscape, organizations cannot afford to build AI solutions that become obsolete or inefficient within a short time span. Assess whether your infrastructure, technology stack, and operational processes are capable of supporting the scaled production deployment. Scalable AI systems are built to evolve, embracing new advancements, adapting to changing requirements, and enduring the test of time.

In conclusion, scalability matters because it empowers your AI solutions to transcend the confines of experimentation and embrace real-world challenges and opportunities. By emphasizing scalability from the start, organizations can position themselves for long-term success, resilience, and innovation in the ever-evolving domain of artificial intelligence.

Building a Strong Foundation: Key Technical Considerations

When it comes to building a strong foundation for AI initiatives, paying attention to key technical considerations is absolutely crucial. These considerations not only determine the success of your AI endeavors but also set the stage for long-term sustainability and growth. Let's dive into some essential technical aspects that play a pivotal role in laying down this much-needed groundwork.

First and foremost, robust data infrastructure forms the bedrock of any AI system. Without clean, accessible, and well-organized data, the entire AI pipeline can crumble. Therefore, investing in data governance, quality assurance, and reliable storage solutions becomes paramount at this stage. Additionally, aligning data architecture with the AI project's scalability objectives ensures that its infrastructure can support increasing volumes of data and computational demands as the AI solution evolves.

Algorithm selection also becomes another critical consideration. Different use cases call for different algorithms, and picking the right one significantly impacts the performance and efficiency of your AI application. Factors such as interpretability, speed, accuracy, and resilience to bias must be evaluated before zeroing in on an algorithm that aligns with your business's needs and ethical standards. Moreover, ensuring model explainability and interpretability shouldn't be overlooked. This becomes especially important when dealing with sensitive applications like healthcare or finance, where data must be safeguarded. The ability to understand and explain the decision-making process of AI models is vital not only for compliance but also for user trust and transparency. Security cannot be emphasized enough when discussing technical considerations for AI. Protecting data privacy, preventing unauthorized access, and safeguarding against adversarial attacks are critical aspects that must be integrated from the outset. Implementing robust security measures coupled with thorough risk assessments and compliance checks fortifies the foundation of your AI system against potential vulnerabilities.

Finally, incorporating capabilities for continuous monitoring, feedback loops, and iterative improvements prepares the project's foundation to evolve and adapt to changing requirements and challenges over time. By addressing these technical considerations early on, you're not simply building a strong foundation for your AI initiative; you're also setting the stage for innovation, responsible deployment, and sustainable growth.

Transitioning Smoothly from Pilot to Production

Transitioning from a successful pilot project to full-scale production is a crucial phase that requires careful planning, cohesive teamwork, and a clear understanding of your project's end goals. As you navigate this transition, there are several key considerations to keep in mind.

First and foremost, ensure that you have a well-defined roadmap for the transition process that outlines the necessary steps, timelines, and resources required to move from your prototype to production. It's essential to involve all stakeholders at this planning stage to align expectations and create a shared vision for the transition.

What happens when you don't involve your project's stakeholders in the planning stage? Failing to involve stakeholders in the planning stage can lead to a myriad of issues that jeopardize the success of your project. Without their input and buy-in, you risk misalignment between the project objectives and the actual needs or expectations of the end users or clients.

This can result in a lack of support for the project, unforeseen roadblocks, and, ultimately, the development of a solution that may not adequately address the real-world problems it aims to solve. Many projects are defunded due to this very challenge.

Early and frequent communication with all stakeholders is paramount to fostering a sense of ownership and ensuring that everyone is on the same page. This continuous engagement helps to surface potential concerns or ideas early in the process, allowing for timely adjustments and a more robust planning phase.

Inclusive perspectives are critical in building responsible solutions that serve everyone, as they bring diverse insights and experiences to the table. By actively seeking out and valuing these contributions, you can design more comprehensive, equitable, and effective AI solutions.

Stakeholders also provide a vested interest and inclusive perspective that can serve to help build a more robust solution.

Another critical aspect of transitioning smoothly is the evaluation of the pilot results. Take the time to analyze the data and feedback gathered during the pilot phase. It's at this point that your team can identify areas for improvement and address any challenges or limitations that might impact the scalability of your AI solution. By leveraging these insights gained from the pilot, your team can make informed decisions about the adjustments needed for successful production deployment.

Collaboration between cross-functional teams plays a pivotal role in ensuring a smooth transition. Clear communication and collaboration are paramount as various teams work together to integrate the AI solution into existing systems and processes. Establishing effective communication channels and fostering collaboration across teams helps to mitigate potential roadblocks and streamline the transition process.

Finally, empower your team with the resources and training necessary for the transition. Providing additional support, training, and skill-development opportunities will equip your team with the knowledge and capabilities required to manage the production environment effectively. Invest in building a culture of continuous learning and improvement, fostering an environment where team members feel confident in their abilities and prepared for the transition.

By carefully orchestrating the transition from pilot to production, you can minimize disruptions, optimize resource allocation, and position your AI solution for long-term success. A thoughtful and strategic approach to this crucial phase sets the stage for unlocking the full potential of AI within your organization.

Creating a Culture of Continuous Improvement

In the world of AI, the journey from prototype to production is simply the beginning. Once your AI solution is live (i.e., active), it's crucial to foster a *culture of continuous improvement* within your organization. What this means is that the culture should emphasize the value of ongoing learning, refinement, and adaptation to drive long-term success in the deployment of AI technologies. Creating a culture of continuous improvement begins with instilling a mindset embracing change and evolution. It's about encouraging a proactive approach to identifying areas for enhancement and being open to experimenting with new ideas and strategies. It requires fostering an environment where team members are empowered to voice their suggestions and bring forward innovative solutions without fear of criticism. An important aspect of this culture is promoting a safe space for experimentation, where team members can celebrate both successes and failures as learning opportunities.

Encouraging cross-functional collaboration and knowledge sharing is also essential in cultivating a culture of continuous improvement. When different teams collaborate, they bring diverse perspectives and skills to the table, enabling the generation of creative solutions and the discovery of new opportunities for improvement for all.

Another key component is establishing clear mechanisms for feedback and evaluation. Regular performance reviews and metrics tracking can help identify areas of strength and weakness, paving the way for targeted improvements. It also supports team education, where team members can learn from each other. Utilizing agile methodologies and iterative approaches can also aid in fostering a dynamic, adaptable environment where adjustments can be made efficiently.

Providing resources and incentives for ongoing education and skill development helps maintain a culture of continuous improvement. Investing in the professional growth of your employees not only benefits them individually but also adds value to the organization as those benefits are reaped across the business.

Resources and incentives for ongoing education and skills development might include training days, where the company comes together to learn a new skill, or outings, where team members travel to other companies to learn about the latest in software or hardware development.

Consider creating quarterly hackathons or short events that give employees an opportunity to learn AI and build solutions that will help them do their own jobs more efficiently. Use executive support and sponsorship to incentivize employees with high-profile praise and recognition. I have taught over 1 million people the power of learning AI by building AI in an AI Bot Builder Bootcamp. You can teach your employees how to build safe and responsible AI systems in less than four hours.

Hackathons not your company's style? Also consider setting aside time the way National Public Radio (NPR) does for some of its employees. During my time there, we called them "Serendipity Days," and they provided time for learning, building, and, most importantly, sharing what we are all learning together. Imagine giving your employees a day to learn and build whatever they want and then creating your own TED-type stage to let the most interesting and valuable ideas be presented and learned at scale.

Finally, leadership plays a vital role in driving and sustaining a culture of continuous improvement. Leaders should model a commitment to learning and improvement, setting an example for others, including their subordinates, to follow. Doing so supports the goal of open communication and inclusivity, where everyone in the company can speak their mind and bring their knowledge to the table. Leaders should communicate the importance of continuous improvement and actively support initiatives aimed at advancing the organization's AI capabilities.

In conclusion, creating a culture of continuous improvement is essential for organizations looking to derive long-term value from their AI deployments. By nurturing a work environment that encourages innovation, collaboration, feedback, and ongoing learning, organizations can ensure that their AI solutions evolve to meet the changing needs of the business and deliver sustained impact.

Evaluating Early Successes and Quick Iteration

Evaluation is a critical phase in the journey from prototype to production. Once you have deployed your AI solution in a real-world environment, it's essential to carefully assess its performance against the project's defined goals and success metrics. This evaluation process should be dynamic and iterative, enabling you to gather insights, identify areas for improvement, and make rapid adjustments.

When evaluating early successes, it's vital to measure not only the outcomes achieved but also the impact of those outcomes on the broader business objectives. Look beyond the technical performance metrics to understand how your AI solution is contributing to business key performance indicators (KPIs). These might also be known as objectives and key results (OKRs). Both paradigms require that a metric is used to measure the successfulness of a project.

Are there clear signs of positive impacts, such as improved efficiency, better decision-making, and enhanced customer experiences? By analyzing these early successes, you can gauge the alignment between your AI solution and the overarching business strategy. The key is that you must have a number to correlate to success. It must be clear to see if the project was a success or failure based on the metric selected.

Parallel to the evaluation, it is important to ensure that you create a quick cycle of development based on the feedback and data gathered during the initial deployment. The faster you can implement the feedback and update the system, the more effective the solution will be and the faster you can meet the requirements of a production launch.

This approach enables you to address any identified shortcomings or areas for enhancement swiftly. It's all about embracing a *test-and-learn mindset*, where each duplication brings incremental improvements that collectively enhance the overall performance and value of your AI solution. By fostering a culture of rapid iteration, you'll nurture an environment where continuous learning and adaptation are fundamental to success.

A culture of rapid iteration inherently fosters a commitment to continuous learning and adaptation, which are foundational to sustained success. By embracing a test-and-learn mindset, organizations encourage their teams to view each iteration as an opportunity to gain new insights, refine their approaches, and enhance their AI solutions. This iterative process not only accelerates the development of more effective and efficient solutions but also instills a sense of resilience and agility within the workforce. It encourages teams to embrace failure and improve more quickly.

Rapid iteration also cultivates an environment where experimentation and feedback are prioritized. Employees become more proactive in identifying areas for improvement and are motivated to apply their learnings from one iteration to the next. This cycle of continuous feedback and refinement ensures that AI solutions remain relevant and adaptable to changing business needs and market dynamics.

As teams repeatedly test, learn, and adapt, they develop a deeper understanding of the complexities of AI technology and its applications. This knowledge-sharing culture enhances overall organizational intelligence and equips employees with the skills and confidence to tackle future challenges. In essence, the practice of rapid iteration becomes a driving force for ongoing education and innovation, creating a robust framework for continuous improvement that is essential for long-term success in the AI landscape. Remember that this will happen for the life of the AI solution.

As mentioned earlier, you want to engage with stakeholders across the organization to gather diverse perspectives on the initial outcomes and to incorporate their feedback into the iterative process. This collaborative approach fosters a sense of shared ownership and encourages a broader range of insights and ideas for refinement. Leverage these insights to fine-tune the AI solution, ensuring that it not only meets its initial objectives but also aligns with your organization's evolving business needs and market dynamics.

You will want to leverage advanced monitoring and analytics tools such as Holistic Evaluation of Language Models (HELM) from Stanford Human-Centered Artificial Intelligence (HAI) and Azure AI Content Safety from Microsoft Azure to track the performance of your AI solution in real time.

These tools provide invaluable visibility into its behavior, uncovering patterns, anomalies, and opportunities for optimization. By continuously monitoring and analyzing the performance data, you can proactively identify potential issues and refine the AI solution before any adverse impacts occur. This proactive approach reinforces your solution's stability and reliability, instilling confidence in its ongoing operation.

Ultimately, the process of evaluating early successes and quick iterations is pivotal in shaping an AI solution that not only meets its immediate objectives but also evolves to drive sustained business value. Rapid iteration based on rigorous evaluation sets the stage for a responsive and adaptable AI solution that remains aligned with the dynamic needs of the organization and the broader market landscape. It enables your AI to scale up to meet your organization and user needs.

Finding the Balance Between Long-Term Vision and Short-Term Results

It's no secret that in today's fast-paced business environment, the pressure to deliver quick wins can sometimes overshadow the importance of long-term vision. However, finding the right balance between short-term successes and long-term goals is crucial when it comes to scaling AI solutions effectively. Let's delve into this delicate equilibrium and explore why it's essential for organizations embarking on their AI journey.

When we focus solely on short-term wins, it's easy to lose sight of the bigger picture. Although immediate victories can boost morale and demonstrate progress, they might not always align with the organization's overarching objectives.

One example of an organization focusing on short-term benefits over long-term vision is when companies see time savings translate to dollars in terms of work hours impacted by an AI solution. They see a 10X reduction in the time it takes to do certain work across the organization and get very excited about the short-term returns. They get so excited, in fact, that they announce layoffs of their workforce to reduce short-term expenses and show the benefit of AI.

What almost immediately happens is that the company realizes that AI is not a job killer but a task killer. In the world of Agentic AI, you will need humans who will be the orchestrators and choreographers of AI agents and bots. Without humans who understand the domain, the industry, and the work, success will be hard to achieve.

Agentic AI can be thought of as a team of highly skilled assistants in a bustling office. Imagine if you had a group of experts at your disposal, each specializing in different areas like scheduling meetings, analyzing data, and handling customer inquiries. These assistants are incredibly efficient and can handle tasks without needing constant supervision.

However, for them to be truly effective, you, the human manager, need to guide them, provide context, and oversee their work. Just as a manager coordinates a team to ensure that everything runs smoothly, humans play a crucial role in directing and orchestrating these AI agents to achieve the desired outcomes.

Conversely, fixating solely on a long-term vision without celebrating periodic accomplishments can lead to demotivation and a lack of momentum, leaving your team uninspired and feeling underappreciated. As we navigate this balancing act, it's important to keep in mind the evolving nature of AI technology and its potential impact on the organization's growth.

By prioritizing both short-term wins and long-term scale, businesses can maintain agility and relevance in the ever-changing landscape of AI. Achieving this equilibrium requires thoughtful planning, ongoing assessment, and an open-minded approach toward adaptations. It needs mindful, intentional leadership. It involves defining clear milestones and metrics that align with the organization's strategic goals while also allowing room for experimentation and continuous learning and recognizing the value of the workforce that will accelerate a company's success.

Additionally, fostering a culture that celebrates incremental achievements and values long-term sustainability can significantly contribute to maintaining this balance. It's about being cautious not to sacrifice tomorrow's progress for today's successes. It's a delicate dance, but finding the equilibrium between short-term wins and long-term vision will equip organizations to make informed decisions, pivot when necessary, and ultimately thrive in the AI space. In the next section, we explore how organizations can proactively prepare to tackle future challenges in scaling their AI solutions, considering the lessons learned from navigating the delicate balance between short-term wins and long-term vision.

The good news is that there are many examples of companies that have achieved this goal. One example is Finastra, the largest pure-play software vendor in financial services. Rather than realizing that it could cut staff to get immediate cost relief, Finastra opted to invest in its workforce instead. After gaining consensus through an executive steering committee led by its innovative chief executive officer (CEO), it decided to enable 300 employees with Microsoft Copilot.

Finastra didn't just hand employees a new tool enabling generative AI but took the time to teach employees a new skill of prompt engineering and the art of responsible prompting. Employees quickly began saving time by transcribing meetings, pulling intelligence from each meeting, and synthesizing next steps. They were able to do in minutes what used to take hours. The company saw time savings of 20–50 percent, enabling its employees to focus on higher-value work across the organization.

Another example is in the healthcare industry. Medigold Health is an occupational health service provider. It leveraged a productized version of OpenAI's Generative Pretrained Transformer (GPT) model through Microsoft Azure OpenAI Service to augment the ingenuity of its clinicians. Although you can implement this large language model (LLM) in many ways, the team at Medigold Health created a tool that would help clinicians with tasks that would help them increase the value they can provide to patients.

It is important to do an *AI impact audit* to identify the best use case within an organization. This audit can help organizations identify those tasks that are best suited to leverage generative AI or other AI services to gain the biggest impact. One of the most time-consuming tasks for clinicians at Medigold Health is report generation. The company decided to build several use cases to help the helpers. Medigold Health prioritized not decreasing the cost of staff doing the work but instead allowing clinicians to better serve their patients and achieve better work/life harmony through the use of AI. With use cases like AI powered-appointment bookings, appointment summaries for communication with patients and clinicians, and the generation of the right documentation in all the relevant backend systems, the company was able to enhance client and clinician experiences.

Preparing for Future Challenges in Scaling AI Solutions

Scaling AI solutions brings a myriad of challenges, both expected and unforeseen, including areas such as choosing the right model for the right problem, building for scale, and ensuring that safe and responsible practices are used to create experiences that serve everyone fairly.

Consider some of these questions as you think about the types of solutions you want to prioritize. These are the same questions that executives have been asking me in my Responsible AI Advisory services for the past decade and more recently since the release of large-scale LLMs:

- *How do I build AI systems that are helpful and not harmful?* Create AI policies that are easy to understand and have an impact on responsible use across your organization.
- *How do I ensure that I protect my customers/patients/citizens, employees, and business with the use of this new technology?* Establish clear guidelines for data use, privacy, and security. Ensure that you can measure this across the vendors you work with as well.
- *What use case should I start with?* Ensure that it is aligned with core values, minimal perceived risk, and low complexity.
- *How will the use of AI impact the workforce?* You will need to reinvent what work looks like in the age of AI.

Here are a few examples of companies that have found success in the early days of AI by embracing the effectiveness of an AI Impact Assessment that leads to the discovery of the perfect use case to deliver value in the shortest amount of time.

SmartSheet is a company that provides customers with a way to plan, capture, track, automate, and report on work at scale. It identified that the best way to create value for its customers through generative AI was to empower its employees. The company created an internal Slack chatbot powered by Amazon Q for Business, allowing employees to get the right answers to their questions at any time throughout the day, improving productivity for employees across different lines of business.

Wendy's, the quick food service company, is leveraging Google Cloud's generative AI services, Vertex AI, to create an automated and efficient drive-thru experience. Wendy's has been a long-time innovator in the quick food service industry, and it demonstrates the need for companies to have leadership in place to make no-regrets bets on the right technology to see impactful results.

The National Football League (NFL) Players Association has also led the league in innovative leadership. The NFL Players Association represents and protects professional football players and is now leveraging generative AI to help keep players safe during the off-season. Due to the massive amounts of film data being collected and evaluated for safety, health, and rule violations, AI becomes an attractive option to increase the organization's efficiency. With the help of Microsoft AI services, the association was able to reduce footage review time by 73%, creating time for staff and increasing safety for players.

As organizations embrace AI's potential to transform their operations, it becomes crucial to prepare for the hurdles that come with scaling these solutions.

As AI solutions become more integral to business operations, the complexity and potential risks associated with them also increase. Without proper preparation, organizations might face challenges such as data privacy breaches, biased outcomes, and system failures, which can undermine trust and lead to significant financial and reputational damage.

Scalable AI systems also require substantial computational resources and sophisticated infrastructure to handle the growing volumes of data and the complexity of algorithms. This necessitates robust strategies for monitoring, maintenance, and troubleshooting to ensure that these systems remain efficient and reliable. Additionally, as AI systems scale, they become more susceptible to adversarial attacks and security vulnerabilities, making it essential to implement stringent security measures.

Preparing for these hurdles involves establishing clear guidelines for data use, privacy, and security and ensuring that these guidelines are consistently applied across all vendors and partners. It also means being able to measure and monitor the impact of AI systems continuously, allowing for timely interventions when issues arise. By anticipating and addressing these challenges, organizations can harness the full potential of AI while safeguarding their stakeholders and maintaining ethical standards.

One primary consideration in preparation is comprehending the increasing complexity of AI systems as they scale. In the initial stages, a small-scale AI deployment might seem manageable, but as usage grows, so does the complexity of managing and maintaining the system. This requires robust strategies such as AI Red Teaming for monitoring, maintenance, and troubleshooting to ensure continued performance and reliability. *AI Red Teaming* broadly refers to the practice of simulating adversarial attacks to uncover risks, unexpected behavior, and biases in AI systems.

In the AI Red Teaming workshops I have delivered, it became obvious that many organizations are siloed and disconnected. When building responsible AI at scale, this can be dangerous. Here are a few lessons from some of the largest technology companies in the world on how they use AI Red Teaming to ensure success at scale.

Microsoft created an interdisciplinary team dedicated to thinking like attackers and probing the system for potential risks and failures. However, as AI has evolved into production use cases, the team is now also accountable for responsible AI outcomes. They monitor the AI systems' level of transparency, fairness, explainability, and data privacy and the robustness of the system. If you are building an AI Red Team for LLMs, Microsoft has drafted some guidance for creating your own team.

Microsoft leverages the concept of an AI Safety System to demonstrate its holistic approach to AI safety. It's not just adversarial but much more inclusive than that. The AI Safety System has four components:

- The human–AI experience
- System prompts and prompt engineering
- Model evaluation and selection
- Infrastructure scale and robustness

Google also provides guidance that it uncovered in its race to productize AI. The company developed a similar AI Red Team and shared some of the key tests its teams focus on in their AI Red Teaming efforts. Google's philosophy focuses more on adversarial attacks but provides clear guidance on the types of things to think about. The most common types of attacks the Google AI Red Team guidance mentioned are prompting attacks, training data extraction, and data poisoning.

Amazon Web Services (AWS) doesn't have specific guidance for its customers on building an AI Red Team but does provide specific guidance on building safe, scalable systems. AWS committed to the federal government and the White House to voluntarily do the following:

- Perform internal and external adversarial-style testing (also known as "red-teaming") of models or systems in areas, including misuse, societal risks, and national security concerns such as bio, cyber, and other safety areas.
- Work toward information sharing among companies and governments regarding trust and safety risks, dangerous or emergent capabilities, and attempts to circumvent safeguards.
- Develop and deploy mechanisms that enable users to determine if audio or visual content is AI-generated, including robust provenance, watermarking, or both, for AI-generated audio or visual content.
- Invest in cybersecurity and insider threat safeguards to protect proprietary and unreleased model weights.

- Incentivize third-party discovery and reporting of issues and vulnerabilities.
- Publicly report model or system capabilities, limitations, and domains of appropriate and inappropriate use, including discussion of societal risks, such as effects on fairness and bias.
- Prioritize research on societal risks posed by AI systems, including avoiding harmful bias and discrimination and protecting privacy.
- Develop and deploy frontier AI systems to help address society's greatest challenges.

With each provider, you can see some consistency in their unique approaches to scaling responsible AI. There is something to learn from all of them. At the very least, every business should be willing to ask its AI vendor questions about how it supports the safe and responsible deployment of AI services. Leaders should also be prepared to answer the same questions about their own deployments.

Here are a few best practices for you to think about as you evaluate the use of an AI Red Team in your organization:

Before testing:
- Establish a diverse and inclusive team of Red Teamers. Examine their backgrounds, educations, and domain and lived experiences.
- Think about benign and adversarial perspectives.
- Address both harms and product features for testing.
- Document and iterate on instructions to ensure consistent testing for each round. Establish standard testing procedures.

During testing:
- Test the efficacy of the AI Safety System with tests for the following:
  - Human-AI experience
  - System prompts (prompt engineering
  - Model evaluation (HELM or similar)
  - Infrastructure

- Create a list of harms and examples for model training.
- Provide guidelines to all Red Teamers in each round of testing.
- Plan and prioritize what you are most worried about with each iteration.

After each testing iteration:
- Report the results of each test:
  - Discuss top issues and the raw data related to each issue.
  - Summarize the testing plan for the next round of testing.
  - Acknowledge the team members.

General guidance:
- Get guidance and support from responsible AI advisors.
- Document and report the findings of your tests over time to ensure transparency in how your solutions have evolved.
- Use the resources freed up by generative AI solutions to invest in cyber security and AI Red Teaming efforts.

Takeaways

- Shift your mindset from a prototype focused on feasibility to a production pilot focused on integration, scalability, and business impact. Consider factors like data governance, security, performance monitoring, and operational changes early on.
- Create a detailed blueprint mapping out the stages of development, required resources, milestones, and safety measures needed as your AI system scales up. Engage stakeholders across functions in this planning process.
- Set clear hypotheses, objectives, and success metrics for your pilot to align teams, measure impact, and define goals to work toward. These should be tied to business KPIs.
- Ensure scalability from the start by choosing the right algorithms, optimizing for efficiency, robust data infrastructure, and flexibility to handle increased data volumes and users. Future-proof your solution.

- Adopt a culture of continuous improvement post-deployment by encouraging feedback loops, performance monitoring, ongoing training, and a mindset focused on constant learning and iteration. Rapidly incorporate insights to enhance your AI solution.

Reflection Questions

- Does our organization currently have a prototype mindset, or are we thinking about long-term scalability and integration from the start? What steps can we take to shift toward the latter thinking?
- Have we created a detailed blueprint for our AI solution that maps out resources, milestones, safety measures, and stakeholder engagement at each stage of scaling? If not, who can we bring together to develop this plan?
- How well have we defined success for our AI pilot in terms of clear hypotheses, measurable objectives, and relevant business KPIs? How might we improve this to ensure alignment across the organization?
- Are we designing our architecture, data infrastructure, and algorithms for scalability and future extensibility? What technical considerations do we need to prioritize to build a resilient foundation?
- How can we foster a culture focused on continuous improvement, rapid iteration, and proactive performance monitoring once our AI solution is deployed? What resources or processes may be needed to enable this?

Chapter 7

SECURE AI:
A Framework for
Deploying Responsible AI

Are you ready to embark on the journey of securing your artificial intelligence (AI)? It's truly a thrilling time to be delving into the world of AI, especially when it comes to ensuring its security and integrity. As you venture into this chapter, remember that you're not alone in this process. The importance of securing AI systems cannot be overstated, and your willingness to tackle this challenge head-on signifies your commitment to responsible and impactful AI deployment. Let's kick off this exploration with an open mind and unwavering determination.

Understanding the Move: Evaluating AI Initiatives

Evaluating AI initiatives isn't just about the technology; it's about understanding the broader impact, ethical implications, and potential risks involved. Before diving headfirst into deploying AI, however, it's crucial that you take a step back and thoroughly evaluate the initiatives at hand. This evaluation process involves a holistic approach that considers not only the technical aspects of the AI solution but also how it aligns with the organization's goals and values. One key aspect of evaluating AI initiatives is identifying the specific business problems that AI is intended to solve. By clearly defining the purpose and expected outcomes of their AI, organizations can assess whether implementing AI is truly the best course of action.

Evaluating AI initiatives also requires a deep understanding of the data that fuels the AI algorithms. It's essential to scrutinize the quality, relevance, and potential biases located within the data to ensure that the AI models are built on a solid foundation.

Understanding the data that underpins AI initiatives is a crucial aspect of their successful deployment. You must delve deeply into the data's origins, structure, and qualitative attributes to ensure that it is fit for purpose. This involves scrutinizing the data's quality and assessing its completeness, accuracy, and consistency.

Additionally, understanding the relevance of the data to the specific AI application is paramount, as irrelevant or outdated data can skew the outcomes and diminish the system's effectiveness. Potential biases within the data must also be identified and mitigated to prevent the propagation of unfairness and discrimination through AI models.

Checklist for evaluating AI initiatives

- ☐ **Define business problems:** Clearly identify the specific business problems that the AI is intended to solve. Ensure that these align with the organization's goals and values.
- ☐ **Data quality assessment:** Scrutinize the quality, completeness, accuracy, and consistency of the data used for AI. Verify its relevance to the AI application to prevent skewed outcomes.
- ☐ **Bias identification and mitigation:** Identify potential biases within the data and take proactive steps to mitigate them to ensure fairness and prevent discrimination.
- ☐ **Information architecture:** Assess and optimize the information architecture to support the data needs of the AI. This includes ensuring data privacy and security.

- ☐ **Ethical considerations:** Evaluate the societal impacts of the AI application, focusing on fairness, transparency, privacy, and data protection.
- ☐ **Organizational readiness:** Examine the readiness of the organization to embrace AI. Consider infrastructure, skills, cultural fit, and change management processes.
- ☐ **Security planning:** Integrate security considerations from the outset, involving cybersecurity professionals to anticipate and mitigate potential risks.
- ☐ **Accuracy assurance:** Implement rigorous testing and validation processes to ensure the overall performance and reliability of the AI system.
- ☐ **Interdisciplinary expertise:** Draw on expertise from various domains, including internal and external professionals, ethicists, and domain experts, to address potential risks comprehensively.

Ensuring data privacy and security is another critical dimension, as any lapses can lead to significant breaches of user trust and legal complications. By gaining a deep understanding of these various facets of the data, organizations can build more robust and reliable AI systems that align with their ethical standards and operational objectives.

Information Architecture (IA) Before Artificial Intelligence (AI)

Information architecture (IA) is often overlooked in the early stages of solution architecture. It can be frustrating having to slow down and look at how the information being fed to the machines in your organization is architected, but this is time well spent. Solutions that neglect this important step often find that the models they are building struggle to create consistent and accurate results.

Apart from the technical and data-related considerations, evaluating AI initiatives also demands a focus on ethical dimensions. This focus involves assessing the potential societal impacts of the AI application, addressing questions of fairness and transparency, and understanding the implications for privacy and data protection. Moreover, effective evaluation involves examining the readiness of the organization to embrace AI, including considerations surrounding its infrastructure, skills, cultural fit, and change management. Without comprehensive evaluation, organizations risk investing in AI initiatives that might not align with their strategic objectives, lack ethical considerations, or are not prepared to leverage and secure AI effectively. Therefore, taking the time to understand the move and rigorously evaluate AI initiatives is vital for setting the stage for responsible and successful AI deployment.

Common Pitfalls: Underestimating Security and Accuracy

Underestimating the importance of security and accuracy in AI deployment can lead to a host of challenges and risks that can undermine the entire effort. One common pitfall is the assumption that security can be addressed as an afterthought once the AI system is up and running. However, by then, potential vulnerabilities likely have already been exploited, leading to data breaches, privacy violations, or even malicious attacks.

The consequences of neglecting security and accuracy in AI deployment can be far-reaching and detrimental to a business. A significant lapse in security can lead to data breaches, resulting in the loss of sensitive customer information, financial losses, and severe damage to the company's reputation. Organizations that fail to prioritize accuracy may confront unreliable AI predictions, leading to poor decision-making, operational inefficiencies, and dissatisfied customers. The impact extends beyond immediate financial loss; it erodes trust and can result in legal ramifications and regulatory scrutiny.

The Equifax Data Breach

In 2017, Equifax, one of the largest credit reporting agencies, experienced a massive data breach that exposed the personal information of 147 million people. The breach was attributed to a failure to patch a known vulnerability in the company's web application. This oversight enabled hackers to gain access to sensitive data, including Social Security numbers, birth dates, and addresses. The repercussions were severe: Equifax faced numerous lawsuits, a substantial drop in stock value, and a settlement of up to $700 million with the Federal Trade Commission (FTC). The incident highlighted the critical importance of integrating robust security measures from the outset and maintaining continuous vigilance to prevent such catastrophic breaches.

Similarly, underestimating the need for accuracy can result in unreliable predictions, leading to suboptimal decision-making and potentially damaging outcomes. Accuracy isn't just about the correctness of individual predictions but also about the overall performance and reliability of the AI system.

Accuracy is a multifaceted concept that goes beyond simply ensuring that AI predictions are correct. It encompasses the precision, reliability, and consistency of the AI system's outputs across various scenarios and datasets. An accurate AI system must demonstrate high levels of performance in diverse and often unpredictable real-world conditions, ensuring that its predictions hold true irrespective of the context in which they are applied. This involves meticulous training on comprehensive, high-quality datasets that encapsulate the range and diversity of situations the AI might encounter.

Accuracy demands rigorous validation and testing procedures that not only verify correctness but also identify potential biases and errors. This iterative process of refinement aims to minimize false positives and negatives, enhancing the system's overall robustness. In sectors like healthcare and finance, where decisions based on AI predictions can have profound implications, the stakes for achieving high accuracy are especially high. Any deviations can lead to significant consequences, including wrongful patient diagnoses, financial missteps, or security breaches.

It is critical to recognize that achieving accuracy in AI is not a one-time effort but an ongoing commitment. As data evolves and new patterns emerge, continuous learning and adaptation are necessary to maintain the system's relevance and efficacy. This involves integrating feedback loops where user interactions and outcomes are constantly analyzed and used to improve the AI's performance. In addition to technical measures, fostering a collaborative environment where data scientists, domain experts, and ethicists work together can significantly enhance the accuracy and reliability of AI systems.

For example, in a healthcare setting, inaccurate AI predictions can lead to misdiagnoses or inappropriate treatment plans, endangering patient safety and health outcomes. Similarly, in financial services, an AI system that fails to predict market trends or detect fraudulent transactions accurately can result in significant financial losses and erode client confidence.

In the field of autonomous driving, inaccuracies in object detection or path planning can cause accidents, compromising passenger safety and public trust in the technology. These scenarios illustrate that accuracy isn't just a technical requirement; it's a foundational element that directly influences the effectiveness and dependability of AI systems.

Overlooking the impact of bias on security and accuracy can introduce harmful biases into the AI system, leading to unfair treatment of individuals or groups damaging the inclusivity that is needed in such a project. This can result in ethical and legal implications, damaging the reputation of and trust in both the AI system and the organization deploying it.

It's crucial to recognize that these pitfalls are not merely technical issues; they have significant real-world consequences and can affect how your organization is viewed by its users and stakeholders, causing a detrimental financial issue for your company.

Therefore, deploying responsible AI requires a comprehensive approach to address security and accuracy from the outset, integrating them into every stage of the AI lifecycle. It involves rigorous testing and validation processes that go beyond traditional software development practices. It also means drawing on interdisciplinary expertise to anticipate and mitigate potential risks, including input from both internal and external cybersecurity professionals, ethicists, and domain experts.

Deploying responsible AI checklist

- ☐ **Fairness:** Evaluate potential biases and unintended impacts on diverse populations. Mitigate unfair outcomes.
- ☐ **Reliability and safety:** Rigorously test to ensure accurate and consistent results that avoid harm. Build in safeguards.
- ☐ **Privacy and security:** Protect user data through encryption, access controls, and other privacy-enhancing methods.
- ☐ **Inclusiveness:** Seek wide representation in training data. Design for accessibility. Provide transparency to build trust.
- ☐ **Transparency:** Communicate system limitations and how AI decisions are made. Enable human review of outcomes.
- ☐ **Accountability:** Assign roles and responsibilities for AI systems. Audit and document processes thoroughly.
- ☐ **Human agency and oversight:** Keep humans in the loop. Allow user feedback and control. Set clear human governance.
- ☐ **Competence:** Train AI teams on responsible AI principles and best practices in design and development.
- ☐ **Awareness and communication:** Conduct impact assessments and risk analysis. Communicate results to users and stakeholders.
- ☐ **Systemic and societal influence:** Consider broader economic, political, and social impacts of the AI system.

This robust framework has been documented in the Responsible AI Standard that was released by Microsoft as early as 2018; it continues to evolve through the scaled application of AI across the Microsoft ecosystem.

Ultimately, underestimating the critical importance of security and accuracy in AI deployment is an extremely perilous mistake that can jeopardize the success, credibility, and impact of AI initiatives and your company overall. By acknowledging and proactively addressing these challenges, organizations can enhance the trustworthiness, reliability, and positive impact of their AI systems and their success.

Scaling Responsibly: Real-Time Performance at Scale

When it comes to deploying responsible AI, *scaling responsibly* is a critical factor. Scaling responsibly is crucial in deploying responsible AI because it ensures that the AI system can handle real-time performance demands while maintaining accuracy, speed, and ethical standards.

As organizations transition from proof-of-concept to production, they face several challenges, including processing large data volumes swiftly and serving a vast user base without compromising quality. Responsible scaling involves integrating advanced technologies seamlessly into existing infrastructures, safeguarding against potential risks, and prioritizing the development of adaptable and efficient AI systems. This approach helps maintain security and compliance, which are critical to gaining user trust and supporting seamless operations.

Achieving real-time performance at scale requires a robust infrastructure, continuous monitoring, and optimization to address potential bottlenecks. Organizations must invest in scalable hardware and software solutions, reliable networks, and design frameworks for interoperability and resilience.

Understanding user behaviors and needs is also essential to forecast requirements and prevent system overloads, which can lead to user dissatisfaction and loss of market share. Collecting and analyzing diverse datasets enhances user experiences and system performance. However, this must be done cautiously to avoid privacy infringements and biases.

Responsible scaling also means future-proofing AI deployments by anticipating technological advancements and market shifts, ensuring adaptability and effectiveness over time. Integrating ethical considerations into every decision, from algorithm selection to governance mechanisms, is vital. By focusing on responsible and sustainable scaling, organizations can future-proof their AI initiatives, drive positive impact, and uphold real-time performance while navigating the complexities of AI deployment. Scaling responsibly requires a comprehensive approach encompassing technical expertise, ethical integrity, and a commitment to continual improvement.

Scaling responsibly means not only embracing advanced technologies but also integrating them seamlessly into existing infrastructures while safeguarding against potential risks. Organizations must prioritize the development and deployment of AI systems that can adapt and perform efficiently as demands grow without sacrificing security or compliance.

Real-time performance at scale necessitates a robust infrastructure and architecture, along with continuous monitoring and optimization to mitigate potential bottlenecks and ensure seamless operations. It involves leveraging scalable hardware and software solutions, investing in reliable networks, and designing a framework for interoperability and resilience. Maintaining real-time performance at scale also requires a deep understanding of user behaviors, preferences, and needs so that your organization can forecast the requirements of your AI framework.

Imagine this scenario unfolding during a critical phase, such as a high-profile product launch or a peak business period. The influx of users, driven by curiosity and necessity, flock to your AI-powered platform, expecting swift and accurate responses. However, the sudden surge in demand exposes the limitations of your framework.

The system, unable to scale in real time, begins to falter. Response times elongate, errors proliferate, and the once seamless user experience disintegrates into frustration and disappointment.

The immediate consequence is a flood of negative feedback. Social media channels buzz with complaints, forums light up with criticisms, and your customer support is inundated with irate users seeking explanations and resolutions.

The reputation you painstakingly built over the years starts to erode in mere hours. Users, disillusioned by the subpar performance, begin to explore alternative platforms that can meet their needs efficiently, resulting in a tangible loss of market share. In the longer term, the financial repercussions become evident.

The initial investment in AI deployment, which promised a significant return, now faces scrutiny as the expected revenue fails to materialize. Marketing campaigns aimed at showcasing your cutting-edge capabilities now serve as reminders of the system's failure. The loss of user trust translates to declining engagement metrics, reduced conversions, and, ultimately, a dip in overall revenue.

To make things worse, the resources required to address and rectify these issues—be it through system upgrades, compensations, or damage control—further strain the company's financial health.

The failure to scale responsibly not only jeopardizes immediate user satisfaction but also inflicts lasting damage to the company's market position and financial stability. It underscores the critical need for robust, scalable infrastructures that can adapt to unpredictable demands while maintaining performance, security, and compliance.

By collecting and analyzing diverse datasets, organizations can harness such insights to enhance user experiences and optimize system performance. For instance, by analyzing diverse datasets, an e-commerce platform can tailor its recommendations to reflect the preferences and buying behaviors of different customer segments, leading to a more personalized shopping experience.

Similarly, a healthcare provider can utilize patient data to identify trends and improve the accuracy of diagnoses and treatment plans, thus enhancing patient outcomes. In the field of transportation, analyzing traffic patterns and commuter behavior enables the optimization of public transit systems, reducing congestion and improving efficiency. These examples demonstrate how a data-driven approach can lead to significant improvements in user satisfaction and operational effectiveness.

However, this process must be approached with caution to avoid infringing on the user's privacy rights or perpetuating biases.

As the digital landscape evolves, responsible scaling also entails *future-proofing AI deployments*, which involves anticipating technological advancements and market shifts to ensure that systems remain adaptable and effective in the long term. Ethical considerations should be woven into the fabric of every decision, from selecting algorithms to establishing governance mechanisms.

Ethical considerations play a crucial role in every stage of AI development and deployment. By integrating ethical principles into the process of selecting algorithms, organizations ensure that the technology operates fairly and transparently, minimizing the risk of biased outcomes. This thoughtful approach prevents potential harm and fosters trust among users, stakeholders, and society at large.

Establishing robust governance mechanisms grounded in ethical principles helps maintain accountability and oversight. It ensures that AI systems adhere to legal and societal norms, protecting users' rights and safeguarding privacy. This foundation of ethical governance aids in identifying and mitigating risks, promoting responsible innovation, and sustaining the long-term viability of AI initiatives.

In essence, embedding ethical considerations into decision-making helps align AI technologies with human values, ensuring they serve the greater good while mitigating negative impacts. This holistic approach is essential for fostering a sustainable and trustworthy relationship between AI systems and the communities they serve.

By setting up a foundation focused on responsible and sustainable scaling, organizations can future-ready their AI initiatives and drive positive impact across various domains. Responsible scaling positively impacts business domains by ensuring robust infrastructures that adapt to unpredictable demands, enhancing user satisfaction and financial stability.

Data analysis aids in optimizing experiences and performance across sectors like e-commerce, healthcare, and transportation. Ethical considerations in AI development prevent biases and foster user trust. Inclusive testing ensures that AI solutions serve diverse user needs, promoting accessibility and equity. Balancing excitement with prudence during AI deployment avoids disillusionment, guiding organizations toward sustainable and impactful integration.

Ultimately, scaling responsibly requires a comprehensive approach that encompasses technical prowess, ethical fortitude, and a commitment to continual improvement of your AI framework. With careful planning, execution, and ongoing refinement, organizations can uphold real-time performance at scale while navigating the complexities of responsible AI deployment.

Inclusive Testing: The Validation Crucible

Inclusive testing isn't just about finding bugs and glitches. *Inclusive testing* is about understanding how different users interact with your AI solution and ensuring that it works for everyone. It's the *validation crucible*, where your solution is put through the ultimate test to see if it truly stands up to the diverse needs and behaviors of real users. Inclusive testing goes beyond traditional QA processes— it's about embracing and accommodating diversity in all its forms. When we talk about diversity, we're not just referring to race or gender. We're speaking about diverse abilities, cultures, and contexts. Think about it this way: if your AI solution can't meet the needs of a wide range of users, it's not really a solution at all, is it? The validation crucible is where you discover whether your AI solution is empowering or excluding.

So, how do you create an inclusive testing environment? You start by assembling a diverse team of testers who can provide valuable insights from various perspectives. These testers should represent different demographics, cultural backgrounds, and accessibility needs. By doing so, you'll be able to uncover issues and limitations that might otherwise go unnoticed in your AI.

In addition, inclusive testing also involves using realistic and representative datasets that reflect the diversity of your user base. Ensure that your test scenarios encompass a wide range of use cases and real-world situations. This helps to identify any biases or gaps in your

AI model's performance. By acknowledging and addressing these challenges during the validation process, you can refine and enhance your AI solution to be more inclusive and equitable. Additionally, consider leveraging assistive technologies and tools to accommodate users with various needs and preferences. This could involve screen readers, voice recognition software, and other accessibility features that enable a more inclusive user experience. Remember, validation is not just a box to check—it's an ongoing commitment to ensuring that your AI solution is accessible and beneficial to all. Through the validation crucible, you have the opportunity to make meaningful strides towards creating technology that serves everyone. So, embrace inclusivity in your testing practices, and let the validation crucible guide you toward a more equitable and effective AI solution.

Balancing Excitement with Prudence: The Hype Cycle

The *hype cycle* is a critical phase in your journey of AI deployment. It's where excitement meets practicality, and expectations meet reality. In this phase, your enthusiasm generated by the potential of AI must be balanced with a prudent understanding of its challenges and limitations.

As organizations embrace AI, it's crucial to navigate the hype cycle effectively. The initial peak of inflated expectations can create a sense of boundless opportunity, but it's essential not to get swept away by unbridled optimism. There is no denying that AI has the potential to transform businesses and industries, but it's equally important to approach this transformation with caution. This stage calls for a deep examination of what AI can realistically achieve and the obstacles that lie ahead. Organizations must temper their initial exuberance with a sober consideration of the complexities involved. By doing so, they can avoid falling into the trough of disillusionment that follows the initial hype. It's imperative to recognize that the true impact of AI comes from its responsible and sustainable deployment rather than from overblown promises.

As the initial fervor gives way to a more measured perspective, organizations can then recalibrate their strategies, leveraging AI for genuine value. They will start to recognize the nuanced interplay between ambition and feasibility, understanding that the journey ahead involves both triumphs and setbacks. Embracing this mindset enables them to transition through the hype cycle with a sense of purpose and realism. This phase demands thoughtful leadership that steers the organization with a steady hand, avoiding the pitfalls of undisciplined enthusiasm while capitalizing on the genuine potential of AI. Leaders must ensure that the hype cycle serves as a catalyst for informed decision-making, leading to a balanced and sustainable AI deployment. Navigating the peaks and valleys of the hype cycle isn't just an exercise in managing expectations; it's an opportunity to cultivate a culture of discernment and prudence. By embracing this balance, organizations can set the stage for successful and impactful integration of AI into their operations, steering clear of the hype-driven perils that often lead to disappointment and setbacks.

To ensure that your organization's hype cycle serves as a catalyst for informed decision-making, as a leader, you might create/leverage these tools:

- **AI capability assessment framework:** A structured way to evaluate AI readiness across factors like data, infrastructure, skills, use cases, and culture.
- **AI ethics checklist:** A checklist to assess ethical considerations around fairness, bias, transparency, privacy, and security for any AI project.
- **AI pilot intake process:** A standardized process to evaluate, prioritize, and select AI pilot projects based on clear criteria.
- **AI vendor due diligence checklist:** A list of questions to assess AI vendors across technology, team, experience, ethics, and services.

- **AI success metrics dashboard:** A set of quantifiable metrics to track progress and outcomes for AI pilots and deployments. Could include business KPIs, technical metrics, and stakeholder feedback.
- **AI education modules:** Short modules covering AI basics, applications, implementation challenges, and responsible practices to build a common knowledge base.
- **AI governance policy template:** A template policy outlining processes, standards, roles, and responsibilities required for accountable and ethical AI development.
- **AI adoption forecasting model:** A data model to forecast realistic timelines for mainstream AI adoption based on technology maturity, market dynamics, and internal readiness.
- **AI pilot post-mortem template:** A standard set of questions to conduct a retrospective analysis of AI pilots to capture lessons learned.

We have templates for these tools available at https:// responsibleaibook.com.

Intentionality in Production: Following a Robust Process

In the fast-paced world of AI deployment, it's tempting to rush into production without thoroughly considering the impact and implications of your creations. However, *intentionality in production* is crucial for ensuring that the deployment process follows a robust approach aligning with ethical and responsible principles. Before advancing to the production phase, it's imperative to take a step back and carefully assess the potential consequences and benefits of integrating AI solutions into real-world scenarios. This involves not only evaluating the technical performance of the AI models but also examining their broader societal impacts. An intentional approach means considering the diverse perspectives and stakeholders who will be affected by the deployment of AI systems.

So, what could potentially happen if you don't carefully assess your AI's potential consequences and benefits?

Financial consequences:

- Poor return on investment if AI projects don't generate predicted cost savings or revenue growth. Could waste significant budget.
- Penalties, lawsuits, and fines for breaching regulations related to safety, privacy, security, or responsible AI principles.

Brand and reputation damage:

- Consumer distrust or backlash if an AI system makes unethical, biased, or dangerous decisions.
- Public criticism from advocacy groups, regulators, and influential voices.
- Reduced brand value and loyalty if customers view the company negatively due to irresponsible AI.

Operational disruption:

- Inaccurate or biased AI leading to wrong decisions and poor outcomes.
- AI systems behaving erratically or unreliably once deployed.
- Integration challenges with existing business processes and workflows.

Loss of competitive advantage:

- Competitors may surpass the company in leveraging AI responsibly and effectively.

- Outdated systems may need replacement if AI regulation standards increase.
- Lagging progress on AI talent development.

To avoid these pitfalls, a rigorous assessment of ethical, legal, financial, and operational considerations is essential *before* deploying any AI system. Ongoing governance is required as well. The benefits of AI come from deliberate, strategic adoption, not hasty implementation.

One key aspect of following a robust process is establishing clear guidelines and best practices for deploying AI in production. This includes defining criteria for assessing the readiness of AI solutions for deployment, such as comprehensive testing protocols, accuracy benchmarks, and data privacy measures. It's important to cultivate a culture that prioritizes transparency and accountability throughout the production pipeline, ensuring that all team members are aligned with the goal of responsibly integrating AI into the organization's operations.

Transparency and accountability are the bedrock of trust, both within the organization and among its external stakeholders. When all team members are aware of the guiding principles and ethical standards expected in AI development, they are better equipped to make informed decisions that align with the company's values. This alignment fosters a cohesive work environment where the goals of responsible AI integration are shared and actively pursued.

By maintaining transparency, organizations can more effectively demonstrate their commitment to ethical practices, thereby gaining the confidence of users, clients, and regulatory bodies. This trust is essential for fostering collaboration, innovation, and long-term success in the rapidly evolving field of AI.

Furthermore, carrying out thorough risk assessments and impact analyses before moving into production can help uncover any potential ethical, legal, or operational challenges that might arise. By systematically identifying and addressing these risks, organizations can steer clear of unintended negative consequences and foster a more secure and resilient AI deployment process. Additionally, incorporating feedback loops into the production pipeline enables continuous monitoring and evaluation of AI systems in real-world settings, empowering organizations to adapt and refine their approaches based on ongoing insights and user experiences.

Ultimately, intentionality in production demands a holistic view that goes beyond technical capabilities, taking into account the ethical and societal ramifications of deploying AI. It calls for close collaboration between multidisciplinary teams, including ethicists, domain experts, and end users, to ensure that their AI solutions are developed and deployed with careful consideration for their broad-reaching impacts. By embedding intentionality into the production process, organizations can uphold their commitment to responsible AI deployment and contribute to building trust and confidence in the transformative power of AI technology.

The Power of Diverse Perspectives: Building for All Users

In the AI world, building for users isn't just about creating a product that looks good or functions well. It's about understanding the diverse perspectives and needs of the people who will be affected by the AI systems being built. You cannot afford to build in isolation, assuming that your experiences and viewpoints represent everyone. Instead, you need to actively seek out and embrace the rich diversity of the human experience. By doing so, you can create AI systems that truly serve and empower all users.

When I talk about *diverse perspectives*, I'm not just talking about ethnicity or gender. Although these are crucial aspects of diversity, they go beyond that, including considering different cultural backgrounds, abilities, socioeconomic statuses, and more. You must engage with diverse communities and stakeholders throughout your entire AI development process. From the initial design phase to testing and deployment, incorporating diverse perspectives enriches your entire AI development. By welcoming a wide range of feedback, you gain valuable insights into how your AI solutions can best meet the unique needs of various user groups.

Furthermore, embracing diverse perspectives helps you identify and mitigate potential biases within the AI system. Bias can unwittingly creep into AI algorithms and decision-making processes, leading to unintended discriminatory outcomes. However, by actively seeking diverse viewpoints, you can challenge and uncover these biases, ensuring that your AI solutions are fair and inclusive to all. Besides, building for users with diverse perspectives fosters trust and credibility in AI. Users want to feel represented and understood by the technologies they interact with, especially when AI influences their critical decisions. By showing a genuine commitment to respecting and valuing diversity, you demonstrate that your AI solutions prioritize inclusivity and equity. It engenders trust among users, fostering stronger engagement and adoption of AI solutions. Ultimately, by building for users with diverse perspectives, you advance towards a future where your AI contributes positively to society, respects individuals' dignity, and brings about meaningful, impactful change.

Red Teaming AI: The SECURE AI Framework

The SECURE AI Framework eliminates the guesswork related to building and maintaining secure and safe AI systems. It was crafted to guide leaders in growing their businesses responsibly with AI.

S—Secure

Focus on creating a solid foundation for your AI systems by prioritizing cybersecurity. Protect your data and algorithms from breaches, unauthorized access, and other threats. This ensures that your customers' and stakeholders' trust in your AI-driven solutions remains uncompromised.

Connection to growth: Securing your AI systems protects your business reputation, mitigates legal risks, and establishes a reliable infrastructure for scaling your AI solutions.

E—Ethical

Develop AI solutions guided by ethical principles. Avoid harm, ensure fairness, and promote inclusivity. Commit to transparency in AI decision-making processes so stakeholders understand how AI supports business decisions.

Connection to growth: Ethical AI fosters customer loyalty and builds a brand image centered on trust and responsibility, which can differentiate your business in competitive markets.

C—Compliant

Ensure that your AI initiatives adhere to local, national, and international regulations and industry standards. Stay informed about evolving legal frameworks related to AI to avoid penalties and maintain credibility.

Connection to growth: Compliance minimizes risks and liabilities, enabling you to expand into new markets confidently and attract clients who value regulatory adherence.

U—Unbiased

Actively address biases in your AI systems to prevent discrimination and ensure equity. Regularly evaluate data sources, algorithms, and outputs to identify and mitigate potential biases.

Connection to growth: By creating unbiased AI, you broaden your market appeal, enhance user satisfaction, and demonstrate your commitment to inclusivity, which can attract diverse customer bases.

R—Red Team

Implement a Red Team approach to actively stress-test your AI systems. Encourage diverse teams to simulate attacks, identify vulnerabilities, and explore unintended consequences of your AI solutions.

Connection to growth: Red Teaming strengthens your AI's resilience, builds trust through proactive risk management, and positions your business as a leader in responsible AI innovation.

E—Explainable

Ensure that your AI systems are understandable to both technical and non-technical stakeholders. Provide clear explanations for how decisions are made, emphasizing transparency and accountability.

Connection to growth: Explainable AI empowers leaders to make informed decisions, increases stakeholder buy-in, and enhances customer confidence in your solutions.

A—Accountable

Establish clear accountability for AI outcomes by defining roles, responsibilities, and escalation processes within your organization. Own your successes and mistakes openly.

Connection to growth: Accountability builds trust with customers, partners, and regulators, creating a resilient foundation for long-term growth.

I—Iterative

Adopt a continuous improvement mindset. Regularly revisit and refine your AI systems based on user feedback, performance data, and advancements in technology.

Connection to growth: Iterative development keeps your AI solutions relevant, adaptive, and ahead of the curve, ensuring sustained innovation and competitiveness.

As part of this framework, *Red Teaming*, as discussed previously, is a term originating from military strategy and is a process in which a group of individuals with alternative viewpoints or roles intentionally challenge the core assumptions and beliefs of an organization. In the context of deploying responsible AI, Red Teaming becomes an essential part of the SECURE AI Framework. This practice involves creating a dedicated team to identify potential vulnerabilities, biases, and ethical concerns associated with AI systems, including those that might go unnoticed during traditional testing and validation processes. Red Teaming is crucial for uncovering blind spots and ensuring that AI models are robust, reliable, and aligned with ethical standards.

One key aspect of Red-Teaming AI is simulating adversarial attacks and scenarios that might exploit weaknesses in the AI system. You want to ensure that your AI is secure, and so do its users. By taking on the role of simulated adversaries, the Red Team can proactively identify security gaps, privacy risks, and potential avenues for exploitation. This proactive approach enables organizations to preemptively address and mitigate potential threats before they manifest into real-world issues. Additionally, Red Teaming helps evaluate the impact of AI decisions on different user groups and identify any unintended consequences that may result from algorithmic decision-making.

The SECURE AI framework emphasizes the importance of integrating Red Team practices throughout the development and deployment lifecycle of AI systems. This involves establishing clear guidelines for Red Team activities, defining the scope of assessments, and ensuring that diverse perspectives are included within the Red Team to comprehensively assess the AI model's performance and ethical implications. Moreover, organizations must provide the necessary resources and support to empower their Red Team in challenging assumptions, exploring alternative pathways, and raising critical questions that push the boundaries of conventional thinking.

Here are some examples of what a Red Teaming effort might include:

- Inject adversarial inputs to identify vulnerabilities in the model.
- Manipulate prompts or queries to test for unintended or harmful outputs.
- Test for biases by evaluating the AI's behavior with different demographic groups.
- Simulate edge cases to identify failures in fairness or inclusivity.
- Test for data leakage to ensure the AI doesn't reveal sensitive information.
- Attempt to access or corrupt the model through security penetration tests.

- Evaluate compliance with ethical standards using morally ambiguous scenarios.
- Roleplay malicious users to identify potential exploitation risks.
- Test the AI's response to misinformation or misleading queries.

By incorporating Red Teaming into the SECURE AI Framework, organizations can instill a culture of continuous improvement and vigilance in their AI initiatives. Red Teaming promotes a proactive and holistic approach to AI security, moving beyond conventional testing methodologies to actively identify and address potential vulnerabilities and ethical considerations. Ultimately, the integration of Red Teaming within the SECURE AI Framework serves as a vital safeguard, fostering confidence in the ethical deployment of AI and enhancing overall resilience against emerging threats and challenges.

Blueprint for Success: Avoiding AI Pilot Purgatory

Have you ever felt like your AI initiatives are stuck in an endless loop of pilots and proofs of concept? You're not alone. Many organizations find themselves caught in what feels like AI pilot purgatory—the place where exciting ideas go to get endlessly tested and refined but never quite make it to prime time. In this section, I'll discuss a blueprint for success that can help you break free from this cycle and move your AI initiatives forward with confidence.

The key to avoiding this purgatory is to approach your initiatives with a clear plan and a focus on real-world impact. It begins with setting clear objectives for your AI projects and aligning them with your business goals. By defining success criteria up front, you can better assess when a pilot has achieved its intended purpose and is ready to progress to the next stage.

It's also crucial to involve stakeholders from across the organization early in the process to gain their input. This input can provide valuable insights into the potential challenges and opportunities of deploying AI solutions in the real world. This collaborative approach also helps build organizational support for the initiative and ensures that it addresses the genuine needs of the business.

Another critical aspect of the blueprint for success is establishing scalable and secure technology infrastructure, as I mentioned before. It means evaluating the technical requirements for a successful deployment and integrating the necessary safeguards for data security and model performance. By proactively addressing these considerations, you can avoid the common pitfalls that often derail AI initiatives in production. Examples include the following:

- **Lack of clear objectives:** Without defined goals and measurable success criteria, AI initiatives can lack focus and fail to deliver value.
- **Poor data quality:** Incomplete, inaccurate, or biased data undermines AI performance and leads to unreliable outcomes.
- **Insufficient stakeholder buy-in:** Failing to engage key stakeholders early can result in resistance and misalignment with organizational priorities.
- **Underestimating costs:** Overlooking the full scope of AI-related costs, including infrastructure, talent, and ongoing maintenance, can strain resources and derail progress.
- **Overestimating AI capabilities:** Unrealistic expectations about AI's capabilities can lead to disappointment when systems fail to meet exaggerated goals.
- **Ignoring ethical and compliance standards:** Neglecting fairness, transparency, or legal requirements (e.g., General Data Protection Regulation [GDPR], California Consumer Privacy Act [CCPA], etc.) can lead to reputational damage and regulatory penalties.
- **Failure to plan for scaling:** Many AI initiatives succeed in pilots but fail to scale effectively, limiting their impact across the organization.

To further solidify your foundation for success, it's essential to monitor and measure the impact of your AI initiatives rigorously. Implementing robust tracking and evaluation mechanisms enables you to gather meaningful insights about how the AI solutions are performing in real-world scenarios and whether they are delivering the expected value. This ongoing assessment provides the opportunity to adapt and refine the initiatives as needed, ensuring continuous improvement and sustained success.

Finally, adopting a mindset of scalability and sustainability right from the beginning can prevent AI pilot purgatory. Thinking beyond the initial pilot phase and considering how the AI solution will evolve and grow over time can help you avoid getting stuck in a perpetual testing loop. By following this blueprint for success, you can navigate past purgatory and steer your AI initiatives toward impactful and sustainable outcomes.

Takeaways

- **Evaluate AI initiatives holistically:** Assess not just the technology but the broader business impact, ethical implications, risks, and organizational readiness. A comprehensive evaluation sets the stage for responsible and successful AI adoption.
- **Prioritize security and accuracy from the outset:** Underestimating these factors can lead to catastrophic risks and failures when AI is deployed. Integrate security, rigorous testing, and validation processes from the beginning.
- **Scale AI solutions responsibly:** Ensure that infrastructures are robust, monitor systems continuously, and optimize performance to maintain security, compliance, and experience as user demands grow.
- **Pursue inclusive testing practices:** Incorporate diverse perspectives into testing to uncover biases and gaps. This enables building AI that works equitably for all user groups.
- **Balance AI excitement with practicality:** Navigate the hype cycle by tempering initial enthusiasm with a prudent assessment of limitations and real-world feasibility. This results in strategic adoption.

Reflection Questions:

- How can we create a comprehensive framework to evaluate AI initiatives across technical, business, ethical, and risk factors before moving forward?
- What security, testing, and validation practices must be incorporated from day one in our AI development process?
- How do we ensure that our technology infrastructure and architecture can scale responsibly as our AI solutions expand to larger user bases?
- What does an inclusive testing environment look like for our organization? How can we bring in diverse perspectives?
- Is our current AI strategy guided more by enthusiasm or practical feasibility? How can we achieve a better balance?

Chapter 8
Architecting AI: Designing for Scale and Security

When architecting an artificial intelligence (AI) system, it can be tempting to focus solely on dazzling capabilities and advanced algorithms. But as one healthcare company learned the hard way, failing to prioritize scalability and security from the start can lead to disastrous outcomes. After rushing to deploy its flashy new AI chatbot, the company experienced crippling outages and data breaches that sank consumer trust and halted operations indefinitely.

This chapter provides indispensable lessons to avoid such fates by outlining strategies for architecting robust, enterprise-grade AI. It starts by stressing the importance of fully understanding business needs and goals. This knowledge then informs a scalable architecture that smoothly accommodates growth through optimized data pipelines, flexible infrastructure, and stringent monitoring. The chapter also underscores baking security into each architectural layer, from access controls to encryption. Additionally, it covers responsible AI principles, evaluation of architecture options, and revealing case studies of real-world implementations.

By clearly delineating these essential topics, this chapter provides a practical playbook for architecting AI that drives transformative value while sustaining scalability, security, and ethics. Companies that heed its lessons will be poised to launch AI that withstands the tests of time rather than crumble at the first signs of trouble.

Getting Ready to Scale: The Basics of AI Architecture

Understanding your unique requirements is crucial before diving into the architecture of your AI system. When it comes to scaling your AI, taking the time to thoroughly understand your organization's needs and goals sets a strong foundation for designing an effective and efficient architecture. Every business has its own set of challenges, opportunities, and priorities, and these should guide the architecture of your AI system. It means considering factors like the volume and variety of your data, the specific use cases for AI within your organization, and the desired outcomes you hope to achieve with AI. By examining these aspects, you can pinpoint the exact areas where AI can add the most value and then design an architecture tailored to meet those needs.

Understanding your unique requirements also involves assessing the scalability potential of your current systems. You must be aware of existing infrastructure and technologies, as well as any limitations they might have when it comes to accommodating the growth and demands of your AI initiatives. This proactive approach ensures that the AI architecture you build integrates seamlessly with your current systems while allowing for future expansion. Employing best practices to understand your requirements for AI architecture means involving a cross-functional team that represents diverse perspectives within your organization. This collaborative effort can reveal insights and considerations that might not have been apparent when viewed from a single departmental lens. Let's look at a few examples.

A retail company developing an AI-driven recommendation engine benefits greatly from a cross-functional team where marketing offers customer segmentation insights, IT ensures scalability and compliance, customer service highlights user pain points, and finance evaluates return on investment (ROI). This diverse collaboration reveals critical insights that a single department might miss, resulting in a solution that balances customer needs, technical feasibility, and financial impact.

In a hospital implementing AI for radiological diagnostics, a cross-functional team brings together radiologists to validate clinical accuracy, compliance experts to ensure adherence to regulations, IT professionals to integrate with electronic health record (EHR) systems, and patient advocates to address trust and usability concerns. This collaboration ensures that the tool is effective, compliant, and patient-centered, which would be difficult to achieve without these varied perspectives.

A manufacturing company leveraging AI for supply chain optimization involves operations to pinpoint bottlenecks, procurement to identify vendor challenges, data science to design predictive models, and sustainability teams to incorporate environmental goals. This cross-functional effort surfaces interdependencies and broader impacts that might not be apparent in isolation, enabling a more robust and sustainable AI solution.

Additionally, this approach fosters a deeper understanding of the impacts and implications of AI architecture across the entire organization, leading to more comprehensive and robust solutions. Ultimately, by embracing the importance of understanding your unique requirements, you pave the way for an AI architecture that not only meets the current needs of your business but also positions you for scalable growth and success in the future.

Designing with Growth in Mind: How to Scale Your AI System

To truly harness the power of AI, it's essential to design your system with growth in mind. Scaling your AI system is about more than just adding more resources; it requires thoughtful consideration and strategic planning to ensure that your AI can handle increasing data volumes, new functionalities, and evolving business needs. How do you navigate these challenges, you ask?

First, it's crucial to understand the current limitations and bottlenecks within your AI architecture. Identifying these pain points helps you prioritize where to make improvements as you scale. This might involve optimizing data storage and processing, streamlining communication between different components, or reevaluating the overall system design.

Once you've identified areas for improvement, it's time to focus on choosing the right tools and technologies to support your AI system's growth. Consider factors such as scalability, performance, flexibility, and compatibility with your existing infrastructure. Whether it's leveraging cloud services, adopting microservices architecture, or deploying containerization, selecting the tools that best fit lays a solid foundation for accommodating future expansion.

Checklist for identifying areas for improvement in your AI architecture

- [ ] **Conduct thorough audits.** Review every component of your current architecture to identify limitations or bottlenecks that impact scalability, performance, or efficiency.
- [ ] **Profile workloads.** Use tools like cProfile to analyze where your AI systems spend time and resources. This reveals optimization opportunities.
- [ ] **Monitor extensively.** Implement robust monitoring across all layers of the stack to surface issues early. Log aggregation is key.
- [ ] **Diagnose pain points.** Speak with data scientists, engineers, and other users to learn where they encounter friction or setbacks in the architecture.
- [ ] **Simulate future demands.** Model expected business growth, and run load tests to determine where your architecture may strain under increased volumes.
- [ ] **Visualize dependencies.** Create architecture diagrams to clearly map integration points and dependencies that could create cascading issues.

- ☐ **Assess technical debt.** Review systems for lingering issues resulting from expedient solutions. These "shortcuts" often accumulate into major obstacles.
- ☐ **Compare options.** Regularly research new tools and paradigms that may better meet your evolving architecture needs. Avoid stale tech stacks.
- ☐ **Prioritize agility.** Evaluate how quickly your architecture can adapt to new demands or innovations. Agility is key in a rapidly changing AI landscape.
- ☐ **Strengthen foundations.** Revisit core components like data pipelines and infrastructure provisioning that underpin the entire architecture. Shaky foundations lead to problems down the line.

After addressing the technical aspects, don't overlook the importance and significance of operational considerations. As your AI system expands, monitoring, management, and maintenance become increasingly complex as more considerations become involved. It's essential to establish robust processes for system monitoring, automating routine tasks, and implementing efficient change management practices. Moreover, security must remain at the forefront of your expansion efforts. With growth comes increased exposure to potential threats, making it imperative to bake security measures into every layer of your AI architecture. This encompasses securing data at rest and in transit, enforcing access controls, implementing encryption, and staying vigilant against emerging cyber risks. Additionally, building redundancy and failover mechanisms into your system can fortify its resilience against disruptions.

Finally, fostering a culture of continuous improvement and innovation is key to successfully scaling your AI system. Embrace an agile mindset that encourages experimentation, feedback, and adaptation to aid in that improvement and innovation. Encourage collaboration between data scientists, developers, and operations teams to iteratively improve the system. Learning quickly from failures and promptly updating the solution will ensure long-term stability.

By staying adaptable and forward-thinking, you can ensure that your AI system not only meets current demands but also evolves to meet future challenges. Designing with growth in mind is about more than expanding capacity; it's a strategic endeavor that positions your AI system to thrive amidst a dynamic landscape of technological advancements and business transformations. This means it is important to strategically prepare your AI system to evolve as your business needs evolve.

By approaching scaling with thoughtful consideration and deliberate planning, you can propel your AI system toward a future of limitless possibilities.

Choosing the Best Architecture for Your Needs

As you consider the architecture for your AI system, it's essential to weigh the various tools available to ensure that you pick the right one for your specific needs. The world of AI architecture is vast and varied, with numerous frameworks, libraries, and platforms from which to choose. Each tool comes with its strengths and weaknesses, and understanding these nuances is crucial for making an informed decision.

You must evaluate the pros and cons for each when doing so. One key consideration when evaluating AI architecture tools is their compatibility with your existing infrastructure. You must ask yourself the following:

☐ How will the selected tools integrate with your current technology stack?

☐ Are there any potential conflicts or challenges that may arise during implementation?

☐ Will the tool conflict with other components at the application layer? Different design patterns like SOA vs. microservices can clash.

☐ Does the tool require specific hardware optimizations like GPUs or TPUs that you lack? Lacking prerequisite infrastructure blocks adoption.

☐ Is the tool compatible with orchestration frameworks you utilize, like Kubernetes? If not, substantial integration work is needed.

☐ Can your current network topology and security controls support the tool's connectivity demands? Incompatible networks prompt redesign.

☐ Does your governance processes permit the adoption of the tool? Compliance, risk tolerance, and other factors may restrict viable options.

Performance and scalability are also paramount factors to consider. You'll want to assess how each tool performs under varying workloads and determine whether it can easily scale alongside your business growth. Some simply might not be able to handle the workload (You can find a downloadable checklist on the book's website `https://responsibleaibook.com`).

Beyond pure functionality, the ecosystem surrounding an architecture tool heavily influences its ease of adoption. Tools with strong community support and comprehensive documentation empower users to integrate and operate the technology successfully. Architects should weigh these ecosystem factors when evaluating options.

Vibrant user communities provide several advantages:

- Troubleshooting forums to tap collective knowledge when facing issues.
- Mature open-source projects with robust contributor bases to showcase best practices.
- Conferences and meetups to learn directly from experienced practitioners.
- Responsive support channels to get timely answers to questions.
- Customizable templates and examples tailored to your use cases.
- Robust third-party integrations and plugins built by community members.
- Thriving communities accelerate learning curves and reduce friction when adopting new tools. Without community support, users face isolated struggles to resolve integration challenges.

Comprehensive documentation is equally important:

- Well-documented API references help engineers leverage capabilities correctly.
- Concept guides explain key paradigms for smooth onboarding.
- Step-by-step tutorials enable quickly building initial proofs of concept.
- Sample configurations provide templates for optimal tool setup.
- Administration manuals aid IT teams in monitoring and managing the technology.
- Release notes highlight version compatibility considerations.
- Strong documentation prevents organizations from adopting tools blindly. It empowers self-sufficient discovery and education. It encourages a culture of learning by doing.
- By evaluating ecosystem factors like community activity and documentation maturity, architects choose tools that offer built-in on-ramps to successful usage and continuous learning. With engaged communities and robust resources, teams can unlock the full value these technologies provide.

Evaluating the tool's security features is also vital, as data protection and privacy are non-negotiable in the realm of AI. Without them, you run the risk of exposing sensitive customer data, proprietary business information, or compliance with industry regulations like the General Data Protection Regulation (GDPR) or the Health Insurance Portability and Accountability Act (HIPAA). Look for tools with robust security measures and a track record of safeguarding sensitive information. Examples include an AI chatbot platform with end-to-end encryption to protect customer interactions, a fraud detection system that anonymizes data to prevent leaks, and an AI-driven analytics tool certified to meet ISO 27001 security standards.

It is also important to consider the long-term implications of these features. Questions to ask yourself include the following:

☐ Will the chosen tool be adaptable for future advancements in AI technology?

☐ Can the chosen tool evolve and stay relevant as your AI's landscape continues to shift?

☐ Does the tool integrate seamlessly with your existing systems and workflows?

☐ How scalable is the tool as your data volume and user base grow?

☐ What is the vendor's commitment to ongoing updates, support, and innovation?

☐ Does the tool allow for customization to meet your organization's unique requirements?

☐ How transparent is the tool in terms of its decision-making processes and outputs?

☐ What is the cost of ownership over time, including potential upgrades, maintenance, and training?

☐ Does the tool comply with current regulatory requirements, and how quickly can it adapt to new regulations?

☐ What mechanisms are in place to detect and mitigate biases in the tool's outputs?

☐ How easy is it to switch providers if the tool no longer meets your needs in the future?

Finally, cost and licensing models cannot be overlooked. In this context, *cost* and *licensing models* refer to the pricing structure and terms of use associated with AI tools or platforms. These models outline how organizations pay for the tool, what they get in return, and the rules governing its use.

Examples include:

- **Subscription-based models:** Recurring fees (monthly or annually) for access to the tool, often tiered based on features, data limits, or users
- **Pay-as-you-go models:** Charges based on actual usage, such as the number of API calls or data processed
- **Perpetual licensing models:** A one-time fee for indefinite use of the tool, often with optional fees for upgrades or support

- **Open-source models:** Free tools that may have costs associated with premium features, support, or customization
- **Enterprise agreements:** Custom contracts tailored to large organizations, often including bulk discounts and specialized support

Understanding these models ensures that you can anticipate both the upfront and ongoing financial obligations, assess the scalability of the tool within budget constraints, and determine whether the licensing terms meet your organization's operational and legal needs.

Understanding the financial implications and constraints associated with each architecture tool will contribute to a well-informed decision-making process. By carefully assessing these factors and conducting thorough research, you can confidently select the architecture tools that align with your organization's unique requirements and set the stage for a successful AI implementation.

Managing Your AI After Deployment

So, you've deployed your AI system, and it's up and running, making an impact on your business operations. The work doesn't stop there, however. In fact, your work is just beginning. Managing your AI after deployment ensures its continued success and effectiveness. One key aspect of managing your AI system post-deployment is monitoring its performance and making any necessary adjustments. This involves regularly reviewing the data inputs and outputs, identifying any anomalies or discrepancies, and taking proactive steps to address all of them. Having a robust monitoring and maintenance plan in place will keep your AI running smoothly.

Staying on top of the latest developments in AI technology and research is essential for managing your AI after deployment. As the field of AI continues to evolve rapidly, keeping abreast of new algorithms, techniques, and best practices helps ensure that your AI system remains cutting-edge and competitive. You must also monitor and maintain its ethical and responsible use. That includes regularly evaluating your AI's impact on various stakeholders and then making adjustments as needed to ensure fairness, transparency, and accountability in its operation. Fostering a culture of continuous improvement within your organization is another key to managing your AI after deployment. Encouraging feedback from users and stakeholders, gathering frontline insights, and leveraging these inputs to refine and enhance your AI system contribute to its ongoing success.

Remember, managing your AI after deployment isn't solely a technical task. It requires collaboration across various teams within your organization. Effective communication and coordination between data scientists, engineers, IT professionals, and business leaders are essential for addressing any issues that arise, in addition to driving ongoing AI system improvements. Finally, documenting and analyzing the performance of your AI system post-deployment enables you to make informed decisions about future enhancements and optimizations.

Establishing a feedback loop enables you to collect insights from real-world usage, enabling continuous improvements to your AI system and ensuring that it remains effective and efficient over time.

Locking It Down: Building Cybersecurity into Your AI

In today's digital landscape, where data is the new oil and AI is the engine powering innovation, cybersecurity has never been more grave. As organizations integrate AI into their operations, they must prioritize building robust cybersecurity measures to safeguard sensitive data and ensure the integrity of their AI systems. This section explores the essential principles and strategies for effectively locking down your AI through your cybersecurity practices.

Building cybersecurity into your AI begins with understanding the unique vulnerabilities that AI systems face. From adversarial attacks to data poisoning, AI systems are susceptible to a range of sophisticated threats requiring proactive defense measures. By integrating security protocols into every stage of your AI's lifecycle, from data collection and model training to deployment and maintenance, organizations can create a comprehensive shield against cyberthreats.

Imagine that your company deploys an AI-powered facial recognition system to enhance security at office entrances. One day, an intruder subtly alters their appearance using adversarial techniques—changing minute details on their face to trick the AI into thinking they are an authorized employee. By proactively integrating adversarial training into your AI development, your system learns to recognize these manipulative tactics, preventing unauthorized access and safeguarding your premises.

Or maybe your organization relies on an AI system to predict market trends and guide investment strategies. What if a malicious actor injects false data into your training pipeline, skewing predictions and leading to costly decisions? By embedding data validation checks and source authentication protocols at the data collection stage, you can block these attacks before they infiltrate your model, protecting your financial forecasts and maintaining investor confidence.

What if your company is revolutionizing transportation with AI-powered autonomous vehicles? Now picture a hacker exploiting vulnerabilities in the vehicle's decision-making algorithms, potentially causing it to misinterpret road signs or traffic conditions. By incorporating encrypted communications, regular updates, and rigorous testing throughout the AI lifecycle, you ensure that your vehicles stay resilient against cyberthreats, protecting passengers and maintaining trust in your innovation.

At the heart of AI cybersecurity lies the concept of *secure AI architecture*, which entails designing AI systems with built-in security controls and mechanisms to mitigate potential risks. Incorporating encryption, access control, and anomaly detection into the fabric of AI infrastructure fortifies its resilience against unauthorized access and malicious activities. Moreover, continuous monitoring and auditing are pivotal in identifying and addressing any security gaps emerging over time.

Securing AI also fosters a culture of awareness and accountability among stakeholders. Educating personnel about best practices for handling AI-related data, as well as implementing stringent authentication and authorization protocols, empowers organizations to establish a human firewall against cyberthreats. Additionally, transparent communication with end-users regarding data privacy and security builds trust and confidence in the AI systems they interact with.

Human firewall is a term that describes teaching your team to follow cybersecurity best practices. In doing so, your teams can aid in scam prevention, phishing attempts, malware infections, and other forms of cyber espionage. This human firewall also complements your security department's regular firewall in protection.

Furthermore, the convergence of AI and cybersecurity presents an opportunity for leveraging AI itself as a powerful tool for threat detection and response. By deploying AI-driven threat intelligence and predictive analytics, organizations can stay ahead of ever-evolving cyberthreats and proactively defend their AI systems against future potential breaches. Ultimately, successful cybersecurity integration into AI hinges on a multidimensional approach that encompasses technical, organizational, and cultural domains By weaving a strong cybersecurity fabric into the very DNA of AI, organizations can unleash the full potential of their AI initiatives while safeguarding against the perils of the digital realm.

Defense Mechanisms: Prompt Defense Strategies for AI Systems

As the field of AI continues advancing, it's essential to prioritize prompt defense strategies for AI systems. In an era fraught with evolving cyberthreats and vulnerabilities, ensuring the security and resilience of your AI systems is paramount. Defense mechanisms play a fundamental role in safeguarding AI from potential attacks and unauthorized access. Prompt defense strategies encompass a range of proactive measures designed to identify, mitigate, and respond to security threats quickly and effectively. It's essential that your organization adopt a multilayered approach to defense, integrating robust security protocols at every stage of the AI lifecycle. From initial development and deployment to ongoing operation, prompt defense strategies must be woven into the fabric of AI systems.

One central component of prompt defense is the implementation of real-time monitoring and threat detection mechanisms. By leveraging advanced technologies such as machine learning and anomaly detection, AI systems can proactively identify and thwart potential security breaches. Additionally, fostering a culture of security awareness and accountability among stakeholders aids in prompt defense. It involves providing comprehensive training and resources to enable individuals to recognize and respond to security threats in real time or creating your human firewall.

Furthermore, incident response frameworks are instrumental in addressing security breaches swiftly and minimizing their impact. Establishing clear escalation protocols, automated response mechanisms, and regular simulation exercises can bolster the agility of defense strategies. Incorporating threat intelligence and information sharing also enhances the efficacy of prompt defense mechanisms. By staying abreast of emerging threats and vulnerabilities, AI systems can adapt their defenses accordingly.

In addition, collaborating with industry peers and security experts fosters a collective defense approach, reinforcing the overall resilience of AI ecosystems. As AI continues to permeate diverse domains, including finance, healthcare, and transportation, prompt defense strategies are indispensable in upholding the integrity and trustworthiness of these systems. Recognizing the interconnected nature of cyberthreats, organizations must prioritize cooperative efforts to fortify collective defenses. For example, financial institutions collaborate through networks like the Financial Services Information Sharing and Analysis Center (FS-ISAC) to share data on emerging cyberthreats, including fraud schemes targeting AI-driven fraud detection systems. This collective effort strengthens the industry's ability to identify and respond to threats faster than any single organization could.

In transportation, automotive companies involved in developing autonomous vehicles participate in groups like the Automotive Information Sharing and Analysis Center (Auto-ISAC). By exchanging threat intelligence and collaborating on cybersecurity frameworks, these companies collectively work to secure AI systems against hacking attempts that could compromise passenger safety.

In retail, major e-commerce platforms and payment processors collaborate to counteract threats like AI-powered bots targeting inventory systems or fraudulent transactions. Shared insights and technologies, such as machine learning models trained on common attack patterns, enhance the resilience of the entire sector.

Looking ahead, innovations in areas such as autonomous threat response and homomorphic encryption hold promise for further bolstering prompt defense strategies for AI systems. By continuously refining and evolving defense mechanisms, the AI community can navigate the evolving threat landscape with confidence and resilience.

Implementing Best Practices: The Responsible AI Architecture Playbook

As you continue your journey toward architecting AI systems designed for scale and security, it's of paramount importance to ensure that responsible and ethical considerations are integrated into the very fabric of your architecture. In this section, we delve into the crucial strategies and best practices that constitute what is known as the *Responsible AI Architecture Playbook*. I created this playbook for my clients to help them navigate the matrix of skills needed to lead projects successfully. The playbook provides a comprehensive framework for implementing AI architectures that not only prioritize scalability and security but also uphold ethical standards and promote responsible AI practices. It encompasses a wide range of considerations, including data privacy, transparency, accountability, and fairness, all of which play instrumental roles in shaping a responsible and sustainable AI infrastructure.

In this section, we will explore how to address these considerations at every stage of AI architecture design, from data collection and model development to deployment and ongoing maintenance. We'll also discuss the adoption of industry best practices and standards, such as those outlined in ethical guidelines and regulatory frameworks, to create a robust foundation for responsible AI architectures. By leveraging these concepts and guidelines presented, you can align your AI architecture with ethical principles and build trust among stakeholders, fostering responsibility and integrity within your organization. Ultimately, the *Responsible AI Architecture Playbook* aims to empower you to architect AI systems that not only excel in terms of scalability and security but also demonstrate a steadfast commitment to ethical and responsible AI innovation.

The Responsible AI Architecture Playbook

Creating AI systems that prioritize scalability, security, and ethical responsibility is essential in today's rapidly evolving technological landscape. The *Responsible AI Architecture Playbook* provides a step-by-step framework for leaders to ensure that their AI systems are built with integrity and responsibility at their core. The following is a comprehensive guide to implementing responsible AI architecture at every stage of its lifecycle. You can download this playbook on the books website `https://responsibleaibook.com`.

Step 1: Establish ethical foundations
☐ **Define ethical principles.** Begin by aligning your AI strategy with core ethical principles, such as fairness, transparency, accountability, and privacy.

☐ **Create an ethical AI charter.** Develop an organizational charter outlining your commitment to responsible AI practices, with input from cross-functional teams and stakeholders.

☐ **Foster a culture of responsibility.** Provide training and resources to ensure your team understands the ethical implications of AI development and deployment.

Step 2: Responsible data collection

☐ **Ensure data privacy.** Implement robust policies to collect, store, and process data in compliance with regulations like GDPR and CCPA.

☐ **Eliminate bias.** Evaluate datasets for potential biases and ensure diverse representation to prevent unfair outcomes.

☐ **Secure consent.** Obtain explicit consent from data subjects and provide clear explanations of how their data will be used.

Step 3: Design transparent and explainable models

☐ **Incorporate explainability features.** Use tools and techniques to ensure models can provide understandable outputs and decisions.

☐ **Document model decisions.** Maintain a record of decision-making processes, including algorithms and training data used.

☐ **Regularly evaluate transparency.** Test models with diverse stakeholders to ensure that decisions are clear and comprehensible.

Step 4: Build accountability mechanisms

☐ **Assign clear ownership.** Identify roles and responsibilities for managing ethical risks and addressing issues throughout the AI lifecycle.

☐ **Conduct ethical audits.** Regularly review AI systems for compliance with ethical standards and organizational goals.

☐ **Implement feedback loops.** Enable users and stakeholders to report issues and provide input for continuous improvement.

Step 5: Ensure fairness in AI outputs

☐ **Audit for bias.** Continuously assess models for potential biases, particularly those affecting underrepresented groups.

☐ **Test across demographics.** Validate performance across different populations to ensure equitable outcomes.

☐ **Iterate to improve fairness.** Adjust algorithms and datasets based on audit findings to address disparities.

Step 6: Embed security at every level

☐ **Adopt security by design.** Integrate security protocols from the ground up, including encryption, secure APIs, and access controls.

☐ **Safeguard against adversarial threats.** Use adversarial training to protect against malicious attacks and data manipulation.

☐ **Monitor and respond.** Deploy monitoring tools to detect and address security vulnerabilities in real time.

Step 7: Align with industry standards and guidelines

☐ **Adopt ethical frameworks.** Incorporate established ethical AI guidelines from organizations like IEEE, NIST, and AI4People.

☐ **Comply with regulations.** Stay updated on regulatory requirements relevant to your industry and location.

☐ **Collaborate with peers.** Engage in industry forums and partnerships to share best practices and stay ahead of emerging challenges.

Step 8: Plan for ongoing maintenance and governance

☐ **Establish governance frameworks.** Create policies for continuous oversight of AI systems, including updates and retraining schedules.

☐ **Monitor impact.** Regularly evaluate the societal and organizational impact of AI deployments.

☐ **Adapt to change.** Stay flexible, and update your systems as new ethical considerations and regulations arise.

Step 9: Build stakeholder trust

☐ **Communicate transparently.** Share your organization's responsible AI efforts with stakeholders through reports, presentations, and public statements.

☐ **Engage stakeholders.** Involve customers, employees, and partners in discussions about AI's ethical implications.

☐ **Demonstrate accountability.** Respond promptly to concerns and take corrective action when necessary.

Step 10: Measure success and iterate

☐ **Define success metrics.** Establish KPIs for ethical performance, scalability, and security.

☐ **Review and refine.** Regularly assess progress against these metrics, and adjust strategies as needed.

☐ **Celebrate milestones.** Recognize and share successes to reinforce the importance of responsible AI practices within your organization.

By following the steps outlined in the *Responsible AI Architecture Playbook*, leaders can ensure that their AI systems are not only scalable and secure but also uphold the highest standards of ethical responsibility. This approach fosters trust, aligns with organizational values, and sets the stage for long-term success in the era of AI innovation.

Real-World Applications: Case Studies in Scalable, Secure AI

In this section, I discuss real-world examples of scalable and secure AI applications that have made a meaningful impact. One fascinating case study is the implementation of AI-driven cybersecurity systems in large financial institutions. These systems utilize scalable AI architecture to continuously monitor and analyze massive volumes of network traffic and user behavior, detecting and responding to potential security threats in real time. By leveraging scalable AI, these institutions have been able to stay ahead of rapidly evolving cyberthreats and ensure the security of sensitive financial data.

Another compelling example is the use of secure and scalable AI in healthcare. Advanced AI algorithms are being applied to analyze medical images, identify patterns, and assist in diagnosis, leading to more accurate and timely patient care. The scalability of these AI systems enables processing large datasets and accommodating the growing demand for medical imaging analysis while robust security measures protect patient privacy and ensure compliance with healthcare regulations.

The transportation industry has also seen a transformative impact from scalable and secure AI. Autonomous vehicles rely on AI algorithms for real-time decision-making, navigation, and collision avoidance, demonstrating the power of scalable AI in enabling safe and efficient transportation solutions.

All of these case studies demonstrate how scalable and secure AI is not just a theoretical concept but a tangible reality with significant implications across various sectors. As technology continues to advance, the potential for scalable and secure AI applications will only expand, opening doors to new frontiers in innovation and problem-solving. By studying these real-world examples, you gain valuable insights into the practical implementation of scalable and secure AI, inspiring further exploration and development in this exciting field.

Looking Forward: Future Trends in Scaling and Securing AI

As the boundaries of AI are pushed and you witness its increasingly pervasive impact across industries, it's important to consider the future trends that will shape the scaling and securing of AI systems. One prominent trend on the horizon is the evolution of *edge AI*, where processing and decision-making capabilities are pushed closer to the data source, reducing latency and enhancing privacy by minimizing data transfer. This shift toward edge AI will demand new architectural paradigms that can efficiently manage and secure distributed AI systems. Additionally, with the proliferation of Internet of Things (IoT) devices, scalable and secure AI architectures will need to seamlessly integrate with these devices, enabling intelligent decision-making at the edge. As the boundaries between physical and digital worlds blur, AI architectures must evolve to accommodate this interconnected landscape.

Another crucial trend is the increasing emphasis on automated security measures within AI architectures. With the growing complexity and scale of AI systems, the traditional manual approaches to security management are no longer sufficient. Future AI architectures will incorporate sophisticated autonomous security mechanisms that can adapt to dynamic threats and vulnerabilities in real time. These autonomous defenses will leverage AI and machine learning to proactively identify and mitigate security risks, ensuring continuous protection without human intervention.

The rise of quantum computing also presents a compelling future trend in scaling and securing AI. Quantum computing has the potential to revolutionize AI by exponentially accelerating complex computations, opening new frontiers for AI applications. However, this unprecedented computing power also poses significant security challenges, as traditional encryption methods may become obsolete in the face of quantum-enabled attacks. Future AI architectures will need to integrate quantum-resistant encryption and authentication mechanisms to safeguard against emerging threats in the quantum era.

Finally, ethical considerations will play an increasingly pivotal role in shaping the future of AI scaling and security. As AI systems become more deeply embedded in society, concerns regarding fairness, accountability, and transparency will drive the development of responsible AI architectures. Future AI systems will be designed with built-in mechanisms for ensuring equitable treatment, explicability of decisions, and traceability of algorithmic processes. It is evident that the future of scaling and securing AI holds immense promise and complexity, requiring continued innovation and adaptability to navigate the evolving technological landscape.

Takeaways

- Architecting for scale requires planning for growth from the outset by optimizing data pipelines, using flexible infrastructure, and implementing robust monitoring.

- Security must be baked into every layer of an AI architecture through access controls, encryption, adversarial training, and ongoing vigilance.
- Responsible AI principles like transparency, accountability, and fairness should be embedded throughout the architecture process.

Reflection Questions:

- How can we design our AI architecture to seamlessly scale up as our business grows? What are the current bottlenecks?
- What are the unique security vulnerabilities in our AI systems? How can we implement stronger safeguards?
- How can we ensure that our AI architecture aligns with ethical values? What mechanisms can promote transparency and accountability?

Part III

The AI Journey: Navigating Challenges and Embracing Change

Chapter 9

Why Change Is the Only Constant in AI

A
I is an ever-evolving field, and staying updated with the latest trends is vital to remaining relevant in the field. As technology continues to advance rapidly. AI's landscape is constantly shifting. New developments, breakthroughs, and innovations are emerging at lightning speed, shaping the way businesses approach and implement AI solutions. The rapid evolution of AI brings about both exciting opportunities and daunting challenges. Keeping up with these changes isn't just advisable—it's imperative for organizations and professionals in the AI domain so they don't get left behind.

One of the key reasons why change is the *only* constant in AI is the continuous improvement in algorithms and models. What may be considered cutting-edge today could become obsolete by tomorrow, making it essential for AI practitioners to constantly refine their knowledge and skills. Additionally, the interdisciplinary nature of AI means that it's influenced by advancements in various fields, including computer science, mathematics, and neuroscience. Furthermore, the ethical and regulatory considerations surrounding AI are continuously evolving, requiring AI practitioners to adapt and respond to changes in laws, standards, and best practices. Embracing change isn't just about keeping pace with the latest technology; it's also about cultivating a mindset that thrives on innovation and adaptation. Those who remain stagnant in their approaches risk falling behind, whereas those who embrace change can lead the way in shaping the future of AI.

However, it's important to recognize that embracing change doesn't mean blindly following every new trend or technology. Rather, it involves critically evaluating emerging developments and then determining their relevance and potential impact on your specific AI initiatives. This discerning approach enables you to identify and leverage the changes that will truly drive value for your organization and the broader AI community. Ultimately, understanding why change is the only constant in AI empowers individuals and organizations to navigate the dynamic and unpredictable nature of this field with confidence and agility.

Embracing Uncertainty with Open Arms

In the fast-paced world of AI, uncertainty is a constant companion. The landscape is ever-evolving, and the only way to stay ahead is to embrace this uncertainty with open arms. It's essential to understand that in the AI realm, there are often no clear predefined paths to success. Instead, it's about navigating a terrain of unknowns and surprises, which can be both exhilarating and intimidating. The key is to cultivate an agile mindset that thrives in the face of uncertainty. Embracing uncertainty means acknowledging that not all outcomes can be predicted or controlled. You must learn to be comfortable with ambiguity and remain open to unexpected twists and turns along the AI journey.

Rather than fearing uncertainty, successful AI leaders view it as an opportunity for growth and innovation. Embracing uncertainty also requires a willingness to challenge conventional thinking and explore uncharted territories. It means recognizing that the unknown holds vast potential for discovery and advancement.

This mindset encourages AI teams to stay flexible and adapt as new information emerges.

By embracing uncertainty, AI leaders empower their teams to think creatively and experiment boldly, fostering a culture of adaptability and resilience. Embracing uncertainty with open arms isn't about abandoning strategic planning; rather, it's about infusing plans with the flexibility and agility needed to thrive in an uncertain environment. It encourages proactive risk management and scenario planning while maintaining a focus on the larger mission.

When teams are open to uncertainty, they become more adept at recognizing emerging opportunities and adapting strategies accordingly. This approach positions organizations to weather turbulence and capitalize on unforeseen breakthroughs, ultimately propelling them further along their AI journey. In essence, embracing uncertainty with open arms equips AI leaders and their teams with the mindset and tools needed to navigate the ever-shifting landscape of AI with confidence and creativity.

Identifying Roadblocks Early

In the fast-paced world of AI, identifying potential roadblocks early in the process is key for ensuring successful outcomes. Roadblocks can come in many forms—from technical challenges to ethical considerations—and having the foresight to anticipate these issues can save valuable time and resources. The following lists some of the roadblocks that can either limit or stop your AI's success:

- **Data quality issues:** Poor quality or biased data can significantly impact the performance and reliability of AI systems. Organizations can proactively identify and address potential data-related roadblocks by conducting thorough data audits and implementing robust data governance practices. Here are some ways this can happen:
  - It can lead to poor training of the models. If the training data is of low quality or contains biases, the models will learn from those faulty patterns and exhibit poor performance when

deployed. This can result in outcomes that are inaccurate, unreliable, or discriminatory.

- It undermines the trust and adoption of AI. If stakeholders and end users do not trust the outputs and recommendations from an AI system, they will be unlikely to adopt and utilize it. Low-quality or biased data contributes to a lack of trust.
- It increases risk and liability. Biased or poor-quality data heightens the risks of models making unfair, unethical, or illegal decisions. This results in higher liability for companies deploying AI systems.
- It requires more effort to fix retrospectively. It is much harder to fix data-quality issues after model development than to address them proactively. This can significantly delay deployments and increase costs.

- **Regulatory compliance:** The constantly evolving landscape of AI regulations and privacy laws requires organizations to stay abreast and compliant. Organizations can proactively mitigate this risk of regulatory roadblocks by engaging with legal experts. Regular compliance audits and legal counsel will help address evolving regulatory requirements.
- **Technical limitations and bottlenecks:** Identifying potential infrastructure and technical constraints can help organizations proactively plan for necessary upgrades or enhancements. Thorough assessments of infrastructure and planning for upgrades will mitigate technical roadblocks.
- **Cultural and organizational resistance:** By fostering open communication and promoting a culture of innovation and collaboration, organizations can address resistance early on and work toward achieving buy-in from all stakeholders. Promoting transparency and collaboration will help gain buy-in across the organization.
- **Ethical implications of AI:** Identifying potential ethical dilemmas before they manifest helps organizations navigate the delicate balance between technological advancement and responsible deployment. Impact assessments and ethical oversight procedures will address potential ethical dilemmas.

- **Financial constraints:** By conducting comprehensive cost–benefit analyses and budgeting for unforeseen expenses, organizations can minimize the impact of financial roadblocks.

Ultimately, by diligently identifying roadblocks early in their AI journey, organizations can position themselves to tackle challenges proactively and pave the way for successful AI deployment.

Turning Challenges into Opportunities

When it comes to navigating the complex AI landscape, challenges are an unavoidable reality. However, these challenges shouldn't be viewed as roadblocks but rather as opportunities for growth and innovation. By shifting your perspective, you can leverage these challenges to drive positive change and propel your initiatives forward. One of the most powerful ways to turn challenges into opportunities is through problem-solving and creative thinking. When faced with obstacles, it's essential to approach them with a solution-oriented mindset, involving identifying the root causes of the challenges and brainstorming innovative strategies to address them. In doing so, you not only overcome the immediate obstacles but also lay the foundation for more robust and resilient AI systems.

Another way of transforming challenges into opportunities is fostering a culture of adaptability and agility within your AI team. Embracing change and uncertainty enables your team to pivot and adjust their approach in response to challenges, ultimately strengthening your ability to navigate complex landscapes and seize new opportunities. It's important to encourage a growth mindset among team members, empowering them to view challenges as gateways to learning and improvement.

Such challenges will often reveal untapped potential and areas for improvement within your AI systems. By carefully analyzing the nature of these challenges, uncovering valuable insights that drive continuous enhancement and optimization is possible. This process not only leads to more sophisticated AI solutions but also cultivates a culture of introspection and evolution.

Finally, collaboration plays an essential role in transmuting challenges into opportunities. By fostering open communication and knowledge sharing, teams can pool their diverse skills and expertise to tackle obstacles from multiple angles. Leveraging collective team intelligence enables your organization to generate innovative solutions and identify growth opportunities that may have otherwise gone unnoticed. In essence, turning challenges into opportunities requires a proactive, collaborative, and adaptable approach. By embracing adversity as a catalyst for progress, you harness AI's full potential and lead your organizations toward sustainable success.

Building a Resilient AI Team

Building a resilient AI team is essential for navigating the ever-changing AI landscape. In this digital age, the success of any AI initiative hinges not just on cutting-edge technology but also on the strength and adaptability of the team behind it. A resilient AI team is one that can weather challenges, pivot when necessary, and continuously learn and grow in the face of adversity. So, how do you go about building such a team? It begins by fostering a culture of collaboration and diversity. Your team should be composed of individuals from varied backgrounds, with each bringing a unique perspective to the table. Embracing diversity of thought and experience can lead to more creative problem-solving and innovation.

In addition, communication is key in team building. Encouraging open dialogue and feedback within your team can help foster a supportive environment where ideas can be freely exchanged and evaluated. Building such trust among team members is crucial for your team's resilience. When team members trust each other, they are more likely to collaborate effectively, share knowledge, and support one another throughout any challenges.

Another aspect of building a resilient AI team is investing in continuous learning and development. The AI field is constantly evolving, so it's essential for team members to stay updated with the latest advancements and best practices. This can be achieved through regular training, workshops, and access to resources that promote ongoing education. Providing opportunities for cross-training and skill-building can also enhance the versatility of your team and prepare them to adapt to changing roles and responsibilities.

Finally, a resilient AI team is adaptable and agile. Encouraging a flexible mindset and empowering team members to embrace change and navigate uncertainty is pivotal. This involves being open to iterating on strategies, embracing new technologies, and adjusting goals based on evolving circumstances. By cultivating these qualities within your team, you can better position them to handle the challenges and changes that come with the dynamic nature of AI.

In conclusion, building a resilient AI team requires an intentional approach focusing on nurturing a collaborative, diverse, well-informed, and adaptable workforce. Such a team will not only weather the ebb and flow of AI advancements but also thrive in the face of uncertainty, driving meaningful and sustainable impact in the world of AI.

Here is a checklist of tools and resources that could help you build better AI teams:

- ☐ **A continuous learning program:** Create a structured curriculum covering ethics, bias mitigation, the latest AI advances, and so on, with workshops, courses, and certifications.
- ☐ **An AI ethics framework:** Develop a detailed framework outlining ethical AI practices, impact assessments, and oversight procedures.
- ☐ **A team collaboration portal:** Build an online portal for sharing ideas and resources and discussing projects across teams.
- ☐ **An AI leadership guidebook:** Create a guidebook summarizing best practices for leading AI teams, case studies, and advice from experts.
- ☐ **A risk assessment checklist:** Design a comprehensive checklist to identify potential risks across bias, security, regulations, and so on in AI systems.

- ☐ **An AI partnership toolkit:** Build a toolkit with templates and resources to foster partnerships with academia, government, and other stakeholders.
- ☐ **An AI innovation lab:** Launch a dedicated innovation lab for research and development (R&D), hackathons, and design sprints to spark creativity.
- ☐ **A strategic foresight report:** Publish regular reports anticipating future AI trends, regulations, and risks to inform strategy.
- ☐ **An AI speaker series:** Host talks and panels with internal and external experts to exchange insights.
- ☐ **A mentorship program:** Set up a mentorship program between senior and junior AI team members to facilitate knowledge transfer.
- ☐ **An AI adaptation plan:** Create a detailed plan to pivot initiatives and reskill teams in response to AI advances.

Adapting Your Strategy on the Fly

In the dynamic AI landscape, being able to adapt your strategy on the fly is not just a valuable skill; it's a necessity. The pace at which technology evolves and market demands shift requires a level of flexibility that goes beyond traditional business practices. Adapting your strategy on the fly means having the agility to pivot when new information arises or unexpected obstacles surface. It's about empowering your team to embrace change and make decisions in real time without losing sight of the overarching goals.

One of the keys to successfully adapting your strategy on the fly is fostering an environment that encourages open communication and rapid decision-making. This means creating a culture where diverse perspectives are valued and where individuals feel empowered to voice their ideas and concerns. It's about instilling a mindset that views change as an opportunity for growth rather than a threat.

As a leader, it's crucial to lead by example, demonstrating your own ability to adapt and showing resilience in the face of uncertainty. Adaptation requires a balance of proactive planning and reactive response. It's not about simply throwing caution to the wind but rather about being prepared to adjust your course when necessary. This may involve regularly reassessing your priorities, staying attuned to emerging trends, and iterating on existing processes.

Embracing feedback from team members and stakeholders can provide invaluable insights that inform your adaptive strategies. In a rapidly evolving field like AI, being able to adapt your strategy on the fly also involves harnessing the power of data-driven decision-making. Leveraging real-time analytics and predictive modeling can help you anticipate changes and optimize your approach accordingly. Moreover, embracing automation and AI-driven tools can streamline processes, freeing up resources to focus on strategic adaptations.

Ultimately, adapting your strategy on the fly is about maintaining a dynamic equilibrium between stability and innovation. It's about fostering a culture of continuous improvement and remaining agile in the face of constant change. By recognizing the need for adaptability and integrating it into your organizational DNA, you can position your team to thrive in an ever-shifting landscape.

The Role of Continuous Learning

Continuous learning is the cornerstone of success in the AI world. As technology evolves rapidly, staying relevant and competitive requires a commitment to ongoing education and skill development. In this AI realm, remaining relevant and competitive is particularly critical, as new techniques, algorithms, and best practices emerge regularly. Embracing continuous learning means acknowledging that there will always be something new to discover and integrate into your AI journey.

One of the key benefits of continuous learning is the ability to adapt to change more effectively. By staying abreast of the latest AI developments and trends, you can anticipate shifts in the landscape and proactively adjust your strategy. This agility is invaluable in navigating the challenges of a dynamic industry, enabling you to pivot with confidence as new opportunities arise and potential pitfalls loom on the horizon.

Furthermore, continuous learning fosters a culture of innovation within your AI team. When individuals are encouraged to expand their knowledge and explore new ideas, they are encouraged to bring fresh perspectives and creative solutions to the table. This not only enhances the quality of your AI initiatives but also cultivates a collaborative environment where diverse insights drive progress.

In addition, continuous learning empowers your team to address complex problems with confidence and expertise. As they deepen their understanding of AI principles and applications, they become better equipped to tackle intricate challenges, pushing the boundaries of what is achievable and propelling your AI journey forward.

Also, embracing continuous learning demonstrates a proactive commitment to ethical and responsible AI practices. By keeping abreast of the latest developments in AI ethics and regulations, your team ensures that your initiatives align with evolving standards and guidelines, mitigating potential risks and upholding integrity in your AI endeavors.

Finally, continuous learning reinforces adaptability and resilience in the face of uncertainty. As the AI landscape continues to evolve, those who embrace lifelong learning will be better equipped to navigate uncharted territory, remain agile in the face of disruption, and capitalize on emerging possibilities.

By valuing continuous learning, you set the stage for a sustainable and impactful AI journey, where growth, adaptability, and innovation converge to shape a future defined by progress and potential.

Staying Ahead in a Fast-Paced World

In today's rapidly evolving landscape, staying ahead in the fast-paced world of AI requires more than just keeping up with the latest trends. It demands an unwavering commitment to continuous improvement, proactive innovation, and a willingness to embrace change. As technologies advance at an unprecedented rate, it's crucial for AI practitioners and leaders to hone their agility and foresight not only to adapt but also to anticipate shifts in the industry.

Staying ahead means constantly challenging the status quo, seeking out new approaches, and fostering a culture of perpetual evolution within your organization. Embracing a growth mindset is paramount, where learning from both successes and setbacks becomes ingrained in the fabric of your team's ethos. Beyond acquiring new technical skills, staying ahead also involves cultivating a deep understanding of ethical and responsible AI practices. With the ethical implications of AI becoming increasingly prominent, organizations must navigate these considerations to ensure that their AI solutions are designed and deployed with integrity.

Moreover, staying ahead encompasses keeping a pulse on emerging regulations and industry standards, enabling your organization to stay informed about potential legal implications and actively engage in dialogue about the ethical AI dimensions. This proactive approach not only mitigates risks but also positions your organization as a leader in building and deploying responsible AI.

Collaboration is another cornerstone of staying ahead in the fast-paced world of AI. By building robust partnerships with diverse stakeholders in academia, government entities, and industry peers, your organization can gain valuable insights and stay abreast of cutting-edge developments. Nurturing these relationships fosters an environment of knowledge exchange, enabling your team to tap into a wealth of perspectives and expertise.

Ultimately, staying ahead in the fast-paced world necessitates agility, adaptability, and the ability to think several steps ahead. It's about embracing change with confidence, continuously updating your skill set and knowledge base, and leading by example in the pursuit of ethical, responsible, and innovative AI. Through this relentless commitment to progress, your organization will not merely keep pace with the evolving AI landscape—it will actively shape its trajectory.

Balancing Innovation and Risk

In the ever-evolving AI realm, balancing innovation and risk is a perpetual tightrope walk. On the one hand, rapid advancements in AI present unparalleled opportunities for groundbreaking innovation, efficiency improvements, and market disruption. Yet, on the other hand, these very advancements introduce new complexities, ethical dilemmas, and risks that demand careful navigation. As organizations strive to harness the power of AI, finding the equilibrium between fostering innovation and mitigating potential risks becomes a critical imperative.

Embracing innovation involves pushing conventional boundaries, leveraging cutting-edge technologies, and exploring uncharted territories. This drive for innovation propels organizations toward transformative breakthroughs and sets them apart in fiercely competitive landscapes. However, this pursuit can exact a toll in the form of inherent risks associated with untested methodologies, privacy concerns, and unforeseen consequences. As such, a judicious approach to managing these risks is essential to safeguard against unintended fallout and reputational damage.

The enigma lies in recognizing that innovative strides must not come at the cost of ethical or societal repercussions. Organizations must cultivate a comprehensive understanding of the ethical implications of their AI initiatives and proactively engage in responsible decision-making. By envisioning the potential ramifications of their innovations, companies can proactively construct guardrails to mitigate adverse impacts and ensure alignment with global ethical standards.

Furthermore, a fundamental element in striking this balance lies in cultivating a culture of agile experimentation coupled with robust risk management practices. Embracing a fail-fast mentality enables organizations to experiment with innovation while swiftly identifying and rectifying potential missteps. Simultaneously, integrating vigilant risk assessment processes enables risk identification at inception and facilitates preemptive measures to mitigate them.

Organizations can proactively shepherd impactful, responsible AI implementations by nurturing a symbiotic relationship between innovation and risk management.

An additional dimension in the confluence of innovation and risk is the necessity for continuous learning and adaptation. In the dynamically evolving AI landscape, staying attuned to industry developments, regulatory shifts, and social expectations is imperative. This ongoing learning journey empowers organizations to proactively anticipate and address emergent risks while optimizing their innovation endeavors in alignment with industry best practices.

Ultimately, the delicate art of balancing innovation and risk in AI necessitates the cultivation of a future-forward ethos intertwined with robust governance, proactive mitigation strategies, and relentless commitment to responsible AI. By harmonizing audacious innovation with prudent risk management, organizations can pave a path toward sustainable growth, ethical leadership, and resilient futures.

Crafting a Forward-Thinking Mindset

When it comes to the AI realm, having a forward-thinking mindset is crucial for success. Crafting this kind of outlook involves more than just envisioning future scenarios; it entails preparing for and actively shaping the unfolding landscape. A forward-thinking mindset in AI means being keenly attuned to emerging trends, technological advancements, and societal shifts that could impact the field. It means being proactive rather than reactive, constantly seeking opportunities for innovation and growth while remaining cognizant of potential risks. One essential aspect of cultivating a forward-thinking mindset is a willingness to challenge conventional thinking and embrace unconventional ideas. This requires an openness to diverse perspectives and drawing inspiration from unexpected sources.

By fostering a culture of curiosity and creativity, organizations can empower their teams to envision bold new possibilities and develop groundbreaking solutions. Moreover, crafting a forward-thinking mindset involves a commitment to continuous learning and adaptation. In the dynamic AI landscape, what works today may not work tomorrow. Embracing change and evolution as inherent parts of the process enables individuals and organizations to remain ahead of the curve and be resilient in the face of uncertainty.

Another important element of a forward-thinking mindset is the ability to anticipate future implications and consequences. As AI technologies continue to advance, it's crucial to consider not only their immediate applications but also their wider-ranging effects on society, ethics, and policy. By envisioning the potential outcomes of AI developments, stakeholders can proactively steer the trajectory of these innovations in a responsible and beneficial direction.

Crafting a forward-thinking mindset also necessitates a strategic approach to risk management. While embracing innovation, it's essential to assess potential pitfalls and plan for contingencies, ensuring that progress is not hindered by unforeseen setbacks. Furthermore, leveraging predictive analytics and scenario planning can aid in forecasting future challenges and opportunities, enabling informed decision-making and agile adjustments. Ultimately, fostering a forward-thinking AI mindset engenders a culture of resilience, adaptability, and transformative vision. By embracing change, anticipating shifts, and challenging the status quo, individuals and organizations can navigate the evolving landscape with confidence and drive meaningful progress in the AI realm.

Takeaways

- Embrace uncertainty and change as constants. The AI landscape is rapidly evolving. Teams must be agile and adaptable to navigate the uncertainties.
- Foster a growth mindset. Challenges and setbacks should be viewed as opportunities for learning and improvement. This mindset builds resilience.

- Promote diversity of perspectives. Bring together people from different backgrounds and experiences. Diverse viewpoints spark innovation.
- Encourage continuous learning. Invest in regular training and skill development to stay updated on the latest AI advances.
- Facilitate open communication. Create an environment where ideas can be freely exchanged and diverse insights shared.

Reflection Questions

- How can we create a culture that embraces uncertainty and change in our AI initiatives?
- What training and development opportunities can we provide to encourage continuous learning?
- How can I foster more open communication and dialogue in my team?
- Are we conducting rigorous impact and risk assessments for our AI projects?
- What partnerships and collaborations could provide valuable perspectives to enhance our AI work?
- How can I demonstrate adaptability, curiosity, and strategic thinking as a leader in this space?

Chapter 10

Model Evaluation and Selection: Ensuring Accuracy and Performance

The rapidly evolving landscape of artificial intelligence (AI) brings both boundless opportunities and complex challenges. As organizations increasingly rely on AI to drive innovation and gain a competitive edge, a crucial question arises—how can they ensure the accuracy, fairness, and integrity of their AI models over time? In a domain marked by continuous change, maintaining responsible and effective AI is no simple feat. It requires vigilance, adaptability, and a commitment to transparent and ethical practices.

In this chapter, we delve into the critical issue of AI model management. Through insightful frameworks, actionable strategies, and illuminating real-world examples, this guide equips technical leaders and practitioners with the knowledge needed to create AI systems that not only perform at their peak but also uphold the highest standards of reliability and fairness.

Whether you are new to model management or a seasoned expert, this chapter will provide crucial perspective and practical advice to steer your organization toward responsible AI excellence. By embracing proactive model governance, you can future-ready your AI initiatives against the tides of change and ensure that your models remain accurate, honest, and aligned with societal values. Join us on this journey to uncover the secrets of responsible and effective AI model management.

Kickstarting with Open-Source AI: Your Secret to Scaling Responsibly

Open-source AI has revolutionized the way businesses approach scalability in their AI initiatives. The concept of *open-source AI* refers to artificial intelligence tools and frameworks that are freely available, enabling collaborative development and innovation within the AI community. One of the key benefits of open-source AI is its ability to accelerate the pace of AI development through the collective efforts of a global network of developers, researchers, and enthusiasts. By tapping into open-source AI, organizations can access a wealth of resources, including pre-trained models, algorithms, and libraries, which can significantly speed up the development process. This democratization of AI not only makes cutting-edge technology more accessible but also fosters an environment of continual improvement and iteration.

In addition to expediting development, open-source AI encourages transparency and collaboration, as contributors can openly share and build on each other's work. This collaborative model sparks creativity and innovation, leading to the rapid evolution of AI capabilities. Moreover, open-source AI offers flexibility and customization, granting organizations the freedom to tailor AI solutions to their specific needs without being locked into proprietary technologies. This flexibility enables businesses to experiment with different approaches, adapt quickly to changing requirements, and fine-tune models as needed. The open-source AI ecosystem provides an invaluable opportunity for knowledge exchange and learning, enabling individuals and organizations to leverage the collective intelligence of a diverse community. As a result, open-source AI facilitates continuous learning and skill development, empowering practitioners to stay at the forefront of AI advancements. Embracing open-source AI is pivotal for businesses looking to scale responsibly, as it supports agile, cost-effective, and sustainable AI initiatives. By leveraging open-source AI, organizations can harness the power of community-driven innovation while simultaneously contributing to and benefiting from a vibrant ecosystem of shared knowledge and expertise.

The Basics of Open-Source AI: Why It's a Game-Changer

Open-source AI is like having access to a treasure trove of innovation and knowledge. It's a game-changer because it opens a world of possibilities and empowers developers and organizations to harness the collective wisdom of the AI community. Unlike traditional proprietary models, open-source AI encourages collaboration, transparency, and learning from one another. It breaks down barriers and fosters an open environment where diverse minds can come together to create, refine, and perfect AI solutions. With open-source AI, you're not limited to what a single entity can offer; you have the entire global network of AI enthusiasts contributing to the growth and improvement of AI technology. The democratization of AI through open sources means that breakthroughs in AI are no longer confined to a select few; they are accessible to anyone passionate about advancing the field. Moreover, open-source AI reduces the entry barriers, enabling startups, small businesses, and innovators to leverage cutting-edge AI without prohibitive costs. This not only promotes a more inclusive AI ecosystem but also fuels entrepreneurship and creativity.

Another pivotal aspect of open-source AI is its agility and adaptability. By tapping into an open-source AI ecosystem, developers can easily experiment with different tools, frameworks, and algorithms, rapidly iterating and customizing their AI solutions to meet specific needs. This flexibility enables quick adaptation to evolving requirements and ensures that AI applications remain relevant and responsive in a fast-paced technological landscape.

Furthermore, open-source AI facilitates continuous learning and improvement. Developers can learn from the best minds in the field, study high-quality code, and understand best practices through open-source repositories. This accelerates skill development and knowledge dissemination, fostering a culture of ongoing innovation and excellence. Embracing open-source AI is not just a practical decision; it's a strategic one. By aligning with open source, individuals and organizations position themselves at the forefront of AI advancements, staying ahead of the curve and contributing to the greater good of the AI community. In essence, open-source AI is a game-changer because it reshapes the dynamics of AI development, making it collaborative, inclusive, agile, and ever-evolving.

Keeping Things Honest: Techniques for Maintaining Model Integrity

Maintaining the integrity of AI models is crucial to ensuring that they continue to perform accurately and reliably over time. As AI models are used to make critical decisions in various domains, including finance, healthcare, and security, it becomes imperative to employ techniques that uphold their honesty and integrity. One key method for ensuring model integrity is *robust data preprocessing*, which involves preparing and cleaning the data to improve the accuracy and efficiency of the model. By carefully cleaning and preparing the input data, you can mitigate the risk of biases and errors creeping into the model.

Additionally, employing diverse datasets and rigorous validation methods can help keep AI models honest. It's essential to test model performance with different data subsets to ensure that it remains reliable across various scenarios. Another key technique is the use of explainable AI (XAI) approaches, which aim to provide transparent insights into how the AI model arrives at its decisions.

Explainable AI (XAI) refers to a set of processes and methods that enable human users to understand and trust the results and outputs created by machine-learning algorithms. XAI aims to make the behavior of AI systems more transparent, providing insights into how and why decisions are made. This involves creating models that are interpretable by humans, offering clear explanations of the decision-making process, and highlighting the factors that contributed to specific outcomes.

This not only helps in building trust with stakeholders but also enables model developers to identify and rectify any potential biases or inaccuracies. Regular monitoring and auditing of AI models also play a vital role in maintaining their integrity. Implementing automated monitoring systems that track model performance and alert developers to any deviations can help swiftly address integrity issues. Proper documentation of model development and deployment processes, including version control and change management, is essential to ensure transparency and traceability.

Finally, fostering a culture of ethical AI within an organization is paramount. Promoting ethical awareness and accountability among AI practitioners and stakeholders can significantly contribute to maintaining model integrity. By embracing these techniques and instilling a commitment to integrity, organizations can cultivate responsible AI practices that uphold the honesty and reliability of their AI models.

Accuracy Check: How to Ensure That Your Models Stay True

When it comes to AI models, accuracy is the name of the game. It's what separates a reliable, effective model from one that falls short of expectations. In this section, I'll delve deep into the strategies and techniques for ensuring that your models stay true to their intended purpose.

First and foremost, regular evaluations are essential. Set up a systematic process to periodically assess your models' performance. This process involves comparing the predicted outcomes with the actual results to gauge the level of accuracy. Keep an eye out for any discrepancies or deviations that might indicate a need for adjustments or improvements. Remember, accuracy isn't just about getting the right answers—it's also about understanding when and why things might go wrong.

Additionally, consider employing cross-validation methods to validate the robustness of your models. By splitting your data into multiple subsets and training the model on each, you can gain insights into how well it generalizes to new, unseen data. This approach helps uncover potential weak points in the model's performance and facilitates targeted enhancements.

Cross-validation methods include:

- **K-fold cross-validation:** Splitting the data into k folds, using k − 1 folds for training and one fold for validation. Repeat for each fold.
- **Leave-one-out cross-validation:** Using a single observation from the dataset as the validation set and the rest as the training set. Repeat for each observation.
- **Repeated random subsampling validation:** Randomly splitting the data into training and validation sets, repeating multiple times.
- **Holdout method:** Splitting the data into two subsets of a training set and a test set. The model is trained on the training set and evaluated on the test set.

So, in summary, cross-validation techniques involve splitting the data into subsets in different ways, training on some subsets, and validating the remaining to assess the model's ability to generalize.

Furthermore, don't underestimate the power of interpretability. For example, if a medical diagnosis AI system is not transparent about how it makes predictions, doctors may be reluctant to rely on its recommendations, leading to suboptimal patient care. In the worst-case scenario, a serious misdiagnosis could occur that erodes confidence in AI and sets back progress in the field.

It's crucial to understand how your model arrives at its decisions and predictions. By employing transparent and explainable AI techniques, you gain visibility into your models' inner workings, ensuring that they align with ethical and fair practices. This not only enhances accuracy but also builds trust among stakeholders and end users, which is important because a lack of trust in AI systems can hinder adoption and undermine effectiveness.

Another key consideration is the continuous monitoring of your models in real-world scenarios. Keep a close watch on how they perform in live environments, and be prepared to adapt and recalibrate as needed. An accurate model today may not remain so tomorrow, given the dynamic and evolving nature of the data landscape.

Moreover, you must leverage cutting-edge tools and technologies for accuracy analysis. From metrics like precision, recall, and F1 score to advanced visualization techniques, a wealth of resources are available to help you comprehensively assess your models' accuracy and identify areas for improvement. Leveraging cutting-edge tools and technologies for accuracy analysis is important for several reasons:

- It enables comprehensive evaluation of model performance using standardized quantitative metrics like precision, recall, and F1 score. This provides concrete insights into where the model is succeeding or falling short.
- Advanced visualization techniques enable model developers to literally "see" patterns in the data. Visual tools can illuminate relationships and trends that might otherwise be missed with numeric analysis alone.

- New tools can account for important factors like bias and fairness that basic accuracy metrics don't capture. Equipped with these tools, developers can make more informed decisions about model improvements.
- The AI field progresses rapidly. Using the latest tools incorporates the most up-to-date thinking and techniques in the field into the model development process.
- Cutting-edge tools are designed to handle the increasing size and complexity of modern datasets. They provide the computational power and scalability needed for thorough analysis.
- Adopting the same tools and techniques that industry leaders use for evaluation aligns the organization with best practices and elevates the rigor of their approach.
- Thorough accuracy analysis builds stakeholder trust by demonstrating the effort to minimize errors and develop the best model possible. This facilitates adoption in business or public sector applications.

In conclusion, ensuring the accuracy of your AI models is an ongoing journey. It requires a combination of vigilance, methodical evaluation, interpretability, and adaptability. By embracing these principles and applying them diligently, you can bolster the reliability and effectiveness of your models, ultimately contributing to the responsible deployment of AI.

Unbiased and Unwavering: Tips to Keep Your Models Fair

When it comes to AI, ensuring fairness is paramount because these systems can have real-world impacts on people's lives. The potential for bias to seep into AI systems looms large, with the capacity to perpetuate societal inequities if left unchecked. To keep your models fair, consider these tips.

First, be diligent about the data you feed into your models. Data quality matters immensely, as it's easy for bias to be incorporated. By carefully curating and evaluating your training data, you can mitigate the risk of introducing bias. Additionally, strive to diversify your teams and the stakeholders involved in the AI development process. Multiple perspectives and life experiences lead to more comprehensive considerations and help counteract unconscious biases.

Next, leverage tools and methodologies specifically designed to detect and address bias in AI systems. From utilizing fairness indicators to employing debiasing algorithms, these resources can serve as invaluable guardians against unfair outcomes. Transparency also plays a critical role. Documenting the decisions and processes clearly behind your model's construction fosters accountability and enables external scrutiny, a cornerstone of a fair and responsible AI approach.

Finally, continuous monitoring and evaluation of your models in real-world environments is essential. Analyzing performance across different demographic groups can illuminate disparities, enabling timely adjustments to remove bias from your data. By embracing these strategies, you equip yourself with a robust framework for upholding fairness and working toward AI systems that serve all individuals equitably.

Model Updates and Retraining: Knowing When and How to Refresh

Model updates and retraining are crucial components of maintaining the accuracy and performance of AI models. As the data landscape evolves and new patterns emerge, it's essential to know *when* and *how* to refresh your models to ensure that they continue to deliver reliable insights. One key aspect of model updates is staying attuned to changes in the underlying data distribution. Over time, the characteristics of the input data may shift, leading to a mismatch between the training data and the real-world conditions the model faces, which can result in degraded performance and compromised accuracy.

Consequently, monitoring *data drift* becomes imperative for recognizing when retraining is necessary. Utilizing statistical metrics such as Kolmogorov–Smirnov tests or Jensen–Shannon divergence can help identify deviations in data distribution, signaling the need for model updates. Furthermore, advancements in the domain in which the model operates could render certain features obsolete or introduce new parameters critical for decision-making. In such cases, it's vital to reassess the feature set and potentially incorporate relevant attributes through retraining.

Here is a real-life scenario demonstrating the use of these techniques.

A ride-sharing company uses a machine-learning model to forecast customer demand in different geographic areas. This enables it to optimize driver supply scheduling. The model was trained on data from the past two years.

Recently, the data science team noticed that the demand forecasts have been inconsistent with actual demand. To check for data drift, they run Kolmogorov–Smirnov tests comparing the distribution of features like day of week, time of day, and customer requests between the original training data and recent months.

The tests show significant differences in the distributions, indicating that customer behavior has changed over time. For example, there are more early morning requests now due to changes in commuting patterns.

This suggests that data drift has occurred. To adapt the model, they retrain it on data from the past six months that better reflect the current customer demand patterns. They again validate that the forecasts align more closely with real observations.

By monitoring for data drift and retraining when needed, they can keep the demand forecasting model accurate despite changes in customer behavior over time.

Additionally, the concept of *concept drift* needs consideration. This phenomenon refers to the potential evolution of relationships between variables or the emergence of entirely new predictors that impact the model's predictive power. Detecting concept drift involves employing techniques like instance-based monitoring or changing detection algorithms to flag when the model's underlying assumptions no longer hold true. When embarking on model retraining, it's imperative to adopt a systematic approach. Designating a clear protocol for evaluating model performance against updated datasets enables gauging the effectiveness of the retrained model.

The accuracy of AI models depends on certain assumptions holding true over time. Concept drift refers to when the relationships or patterns that a model relies on start to change. It's like the ground shifting beneath the model's feet.

For example, let's say we trained a model to predict credit risk based on variables like income, age, and number of credit accounts. It was accurate when first deployed. But over time, other factors emerged that affected risk, like the usage of new financial technologies.

Now, income level alone doesn't determine risk in the same way. Our old assumptions don't hold true anymore. This is concept drift—the concepts that defined credit risk changed.

To detect concept drift, we can monitor the model's predictions and check if they still align with real outcomes. We can also use statistical techniques to check if the relationships between variables are changing.

For instance, we may observe income levels diverging from risk-level predictions. This signals that the model's assumptions are no longer accurate. Monitoring and algorithms tip us off so we can retrain the model to adapt to the new concepts.

Identifying concept drift ensures that our models stay relevant even as the world changes around them. By detecting when assumptions fail, we know when it's time to refresh the model and avoid potentially costly errors down the line.

Techniques such as cross-validation and A/B testing can aid in comparing the new model's performance with its predecessor, ensuring that the updates enhance overall accuracy and consistency.

When we update or retrain a machine-learning model, how do we really know if the new model is actually better? We need ways to validate that the model improvements translate to real-world accuracy and performance.

Cross-validation is a great technique for reliably evaluating a model's performance. We split the data into multiple folds, trained on some folds, and tested on the others. By iterating through different combinations, we get a comprehensive picture of accuracy.

We can apply cross-validation to both the old and new model to compare their performance on the same data. Better accuracy on the validation sets indicates that the updated model is superior.

A/B testing is another way to compare models directly. We deploy the old and new models in parallel and have them make the same predictions on real-time data but only actually apply the predictions from one model.

We flip back and forth between using the old or new model's predictions. By analyzing real-world outcomes like click-through rate or conversion rate under each model, we can see which performs better.

Combining techniques like cross-validation and A/B testing gives us confidence that any new model actually improves on its predecessor. We verify that retraining pays off in tangible improvements to consistency and accuracy for end users.

Finally, embracing a future-oriented mindset is pivotal. Proactive tracking of technological advancements and trends in the application domain equips organizations with the foresight to plan updates and modifications in advance, thereby preemptively addressing the need for model refreshes. By embracing a holistic approach to model updates and retraining, organizations can elevate their AI models to remain adaptable, reliable, and aligned with shifting data dynamics and emerging requirements.

An AI Model Lifecycle: From Birth to Maturity

Once an AI model is created, it embarks on a journey through its lifecycle, from its inception to reaching maturity. Understanding this lifecycle is crucial for effectively managing and optimizing your AI models. The birth of an AI model often begins with ideation, where the problem statement is defined, data sources are identified, and the initial model architecture is conceptualized. This phase involves brainstorming, research, and careful planning before any code is written. Once the model is born, through the development phase, it starts to take shape. Data preprocessing, feature engineering, and model training are key activities during this period. It's like watching a child grow and learn new things each day. As the model matures, it undergoes rigorous testing and evaluation to ensure that it meets the desired accuracy and performance standards. This phase is akin to adolescence—a time of growth and refinement. After deployment, the AI model enters the operational phase, where it interacts with real-world data and continuously learns from its experiences. Ongoing monitoring and maintenance are essential to ensure that the model remains effective and relevant in diverse contexts. Finally, as the model accumulates more data and iteratively improves, it reaches maturity. At this stage, it may require updates, retraining, or even retirement, depending on its performance and evolving requirements. Understanding and managing the AI model's entire lifecycle is essential to ensure its longevity and impact. It involves a combination of technical expertise, domain knowledge, and strategic foresight to navigate the complexities of AI model management.

Top Tools for Model Management: What's in Your Toolbox?

When it comes to managing AI models, having the right tools can make all the difference. As technologies continue to evolve, new tools are constantly emerging to help data scientists and engineers streamline model management. From version control systems like Git to specialized platforms like MLflow and Kubeflow, the options are vast and diverse. Git, a widely popular version control system, is essential not only for tracking changes in code but also for collaborating with other team members. It enables seamless integration of model versioning into the overall software development lifecycle. MLflow, on the other hand, provides an end-to-end platform for the machine-learning lifecycle, enabling organizations to manage experiments, reproducibility, and deployment in one centralized location. Its robust tracking and packaging features make it easier to transition models from experimentation to production. Kubeflow, designed specifically for Kubernetes users, offers a comprehensive solution for managing machine-learning workflows. By providing a scalable, portable, and easy-to-use platform, Kubeflow simplifies the process of deploying machine-learning models to production environments. Additionally, container orchestration tools such as Docker and Kubernetes play a crucial role in managing the deployment and scaling of AI models. These tools aid in the efficient encapsulation of models and their dependencies, ensuring consistency across different environments.

In addition to these specialized tools, cloud providers offer a range of AI services to facilitate model management. Platforms like Amazon SageMaker, Google Cloud AI Platform, and Microsoft Azure Machine Learning provide integrated environments for building, training, and deploying machine-learning models at scale. Not to mention that they also offer capabilities for model monitoring, governance, and collaboration, empowering organizations to accelerate their AI initiatives. It's important to align your choice of tools with the specific needs and infrastructure of your organization. Whereas some tools excel in scalability and enterprise support, others prioritize open-source flexibility and community-driven innovation. Ultimately, the key is to assemble a toolbox to empower data teams to effectively oversee the entire model lifecycle, from development and training to deployment and maintenance. Keeping abreast of the latest advancements in model management tools is crucial for staying competitive in the rapidly evolving landscape of AI and machine learning.

Leveraging Technology: Managing Models Intelligent Way

In today's fast-paced AI world, managing models intelligent way is an essential component of building responsible and effective AI systems. Leveraging the right technology can make all the difference in the efficiency and performance of your AI models. To start, leveraging technology means being strategic about the tools and platforms you use to manage your models. Look for platforms that offer streamlined processes for model deployment, monitoring, and maintenance, which allow you to keep tabs on your models, ensuring that they continue operating at peak performance.

Additionally, leveraging technology involves harnessing the power of automation. Implementing automated processes can save valuable time and resources by handling routine tasks such as data preparation, model training, and performance monitoring. By automating these tasks, you free your team to focus on more complex and high-value activities, ultimately improving your organization's overall productivity and innovation.

Furthermore, smart model management involves leveraging advanced analytics and reporting capabilities. Technology can provide powerful insights into model performance, highlighting areas for improvement and identifying potential issues before they impact your operations. With access to in-depth analytics, you can make data-driven decisions to optimize your models and ensure that they align with business objectives.

Another critical aspect of smart model management is integrating robust security measures. Leveraging technology to implement security protocols and encryption helps safeguard your models from unauthorized access and malicious attacks, mitigating the risk of data breaches and ensuring compliance with data protection regulations.

Moreover, taking advantage of cloud-based solutions is key to efficient model management. Cloud platforms offer scalability, flexibility, and cost-effectiveness, enabling you to adapt to fluctuating workloads and seamlessly deploy updates across your AI infrastructure. Embracing cloud technology empowers you to maximize the potential of your AI models while minimizing operational complexities.

Finally, when it comes to managing models intelligent way, incorporating machine-learning operations (MLOps) practices is paramount. MLOps integrates development, deployment, and maintenance processes, fostering collaboration between your organization's data scientists, engineers, and DevOps teams. By embracing MLOps, you can establish standardized workflows, automate model deployment, and facilitate continuous integration and delivery, leading to more reliable and efficient AI operations.

Looking Ahead: Prepping for Future Changes

As we navigate the ever-evolving landscape of AI and machine learning, it becomes increasingly crucial to anticipate and prepare for future changes. The rapid advancements in technology, coupled with shifting societal expectations, are reshaping the AI ecosystem at an unprecedented pace. In this context, preparing for future changes isn't just a prudent move; it's a strategic imperative for organizations committed to responsible AI innovation.

One key aspect of preparing for future changes lies in understanding the broader industry trends that could impact AI development and deployment. This prepping involves monitoring emerging technologies, such as quantum computing or edge AI, which may disrupt existing paradigms. Additionally, staying attuned to regulatory shifts and ethical considerations is fundamental in aligning AI initiatives with evolving legal and moral frameworks.

Another critical dimension of future preparedness pertains to talent acquisition and skill development. As AI continues to permeate diverse sectors, the demand for specialized expertise in areas like explainable AI, AI ethics, and bias reduction techniques is poised to surge. Organizations must proactively invest in upskilling their workforce and nurturing a culture of continuous learning to empower teams with the requisite competencies to tackle forthcoming challenges.

Furthermore, cultivating a flexible infrastructure is pivotal for adapting to future shifts in AI requirements. This cultivation encompasses embracing modular and scalable architectures that can accommodate technological leaps, ensuring interoperability, and fortifying cybersecurity protocols to withstand evolving threat vectors. The ability to seamlessly integrate new data sources and efficiently recalibrate models will be indispensable in navigating the dynamic AI landscape.

An often-overlooked facet of anticipating future changes involves fostering a culture of innovation and openness within organizations. Encouraging cross-functional collaboration, knowledge sharing, and experimentation can spark novel approaches to problem-solving and prime enterprises for agile responses to unforeseen disruptions. Cultivating partnerships with research institutions and startups can also offer fresh perspectives and facilitate early access to cutting-edge developments.

Finally, ethical foresight must underpin all strategies aimed at preparing for future changes in AI. Proactively considering the societal impact of AI advancements and engaging in dialogues with diverse stakeholders can illuminate any potential areas of unawareness and help infuse responsible practices into the core fabric of your organization's AI endeavors. Ultimately, by proactively addressing ethical and societal implications, organizations can avert unforeseen pitfalls and bolster trust in their AI technologies.

In summary, preparing for future changes in the AI realm demands a multifaceted approach encompassing trend awareness, talent empowerment, infrastructure agility, a culture of innovation, and ethical mindfulness. Embracing this proactive stance equips organizations to not only weather the impending transformations in AI but also emerge as frontrunners in shaping a future where AI serves as a force for positive change.

Takeaways

- Open-source AI enables collaboration, flexibility, and democratization of cutting-edge technologies. Leveraging it enables organizations to innovate faster.
- Maintaining model integrity requires robust data practices, testing, monitoring, documentation, and an ethical AI culture. This ensures that models remain honest and reliable.
- Regular evaluation, cross-validation, interpretability, and real-world monitoring are essential for accuracy. New tools enable thorough performance assessments.
- Fairness requires mitigating bias in data, diverse teams, transparency, bias detection tools, and continuous performance monitoring across groups.
- Identifying data drift and concept drift signals when retraining is needed. A/B testing and cross-validation confirm model improvements.
- AI models evolve through a lifecycle from ideation to maturity. Their needs change over time, necessitating careful management.

Reflection Questions

- How can we leverage open-source AI capabilities while maintaining proprietary advantages? What is the right balance?
- Are there any potential biases we need to address in our model development process proactively? What steps can we take?
- How frequently should we reevaluate our models after deployment? What metrics indicate a need for retraining?
- How do we ensure our infrastructure stays flexible and scalable enough to take advantage of emerging technologies like quantum computing?

Chapter 11
Bias and Fairness: Building AI That Serves Everyone

A rtificial intelligence (AI) will transform our world for the better, but only if it is designed and deployed responsibly, with fairness and inclusivity as guiding principles. As AI is increasingly integrated into high-stakes domains like employment, finance, and healthcare, we must confront the uncomfortable reality that these systems can easily perpetuate or exacerbate societal biases and inequities if improperly engineered.

To truly harness AI for social good, we must build awareness and understanding of how bias manifests in data and algorithms. Only then can we cultivate solutions to mitigate harm, promote transparency and accountability, and ensure that the benefits of AI are shared equally. The moral imperative is clear: if thoughtfully crafted with diversity and empathy, AI can uplift humanity, but if unchecked, it risks further marginalizing vulnerable communities.

As we stand at the precipice of an AI-driven future, maintaining vigilance against bias is essential to developing technology that serves all people equitably. Getting this right is challenging yet necessary work—work that determines what kind of society we want to live in.

Why Bias in AI Is a Big Deal

Bias in AI may seem like a technical issue confined to the realm of computer science, but its implications are far-reaching and can have serious consequences for individuals and society. When AI systems are influenced by biased data or design, they can perpetuate and exacerbate existing inequalities, leading to unfair outcomes in critical areas such as employment, healthcare, and criminal justice. This not only undermines society's trust in AI but also reinforces systemic biases that have plagued us for generations.

Consider, for example, an AI-powered hiring tool that systematically favors candidates from specific demographic groups due to historical biases in the training data. This perpetuates inequality in the workplace and limits opportunities for qualified individuals from underrepresented communities. In addition, biased AI systems in healthcare could lead to misdiagnosis or unequal access to treatment, impacting people's health and well-being. In the criminal justice system, biased algorithms used for risk assessment may unfairly target certain groups, perpetuating discrimination and reinforcing social disparities in the legal system. As AI continues to play a growing role in decision-making processes, from lending approvals to law enforcement, addressing bias becomes not just a technical concern but a moral imperative. The consequences of enabling biased AI to operate unchecked are simply too high to ignore. Recognizing the potential harm caused by biased AI, however, is the first step you can take toward building systems that equitably serve everyone. Organizations must acknowledge that AI reflects the values and biases present in the data it is trained on, the choices made during its development, and the context in which it is deployed. By understanding why bias in AI is a big deal, organizations can take decisive action to mitigate its impact and ensure that AI serves as a force for positive change.

Recognizing Different Types of Bias

Recognizing various types of bias is crucial for understanding how it manifests in AI systems and its impact on diverse communities. One form of bias is *selection bias*, which arises when certain groups are over- or underrepresented in training data, leading to skewed outcomes.

Here are some examples:

Healthcare AI models: If an AI model is trained primarily on data from a specific demographic group, such as Caucasian males, it may not perform as well for other groups like women or minorities. This can lead to misdiagnoses or inappropriate treatment recommendations for underrepresented populations.

Hiring algorithms: An AI system used for recruitment might be trained on historical hiring data that predominantly includes applications from men. As a result, the model may favor male candidates over equally qualified female candidates, perpetuating gender inequality in the workplace.

Loan approval systems: Financial institutions may use AI models to assess loan applications. If the training data mainly consists of applicants from affluent neighborhoods, the model might be biased against individuals from less wealthy areas, unfairly denying them loans.

Facial recognition technology: Often, facial recognition systems are trained on datasets that lack diversity in terms of race and ethnicity. This can result in higher error rates for people of color, leading to misidentification and potential misuse in surveillance or law enforcement.

Predictive policing: AI models used to predict crime might be trained on historical crime data that reflects existing biases in law enforcement practices. This can lead to over-policing of certain communities, reinforcing prejudicial attitudes and systemic discrimination.

Recognizing and addressing selection bias is crucial for developing fair and equitable AI systems that serve all demographic groups effectively.

Similarly, *algorithmic bias* emerges from the design and implementation of algorithms, often reflecting historical prejudices. One prevalent source of bias is in the very algorithms that power AI systems.

The design and implementation of these algorithms often reflect historical prejudices and structural inequalities, encoding machine-learning models with distorted worldviews that lead to discriminatory and unethical outcomes.

For example, a facial recognition algorithm that is more likely to misidentify people of color reflects racially biased training data. And a hiring algorithm that automatically filters out candidates with nontraditional educational backgrounds perpetuates class barriers.

If left unchecked, algorithmic bias threatens to automate injustice and amplify stereotypes, impeding social progress. To chart an equitable path forward, we must illuminate the inner workings of opaque algorithms, scrutinizing them for embedded biases that privilege some groups over others.

This process of introspection and transparency is difficult yet necessary. The futures we imagine must not cement unfairness into our digital infrastructure. With care and courage, we can craft AI that transcends our frailties and helps realize the world as it ought to be—one where all individuals and communities can thrive.

Then, there's *confirmation bias* or influencing AI systems to favor information that aligns with preconceived notions, reinforcing societal inequalities. Here are some common examples of this:

- A social media feed recommendation algorithm tuned to emphasize posts similar to what a user already likes may create an echo chamber that confirms their beliefs. This could limit exposure to differing views and reinforce polarization.
- A search feature that prioritizes results matching a user's past queries could mean executives rarely encounter information challenging their own mindsets or business models. This curation bias risks confirming conventional thinking.

- A visual recognition tool used in manufacturing that's trained mostly on images of male engineers could be prone to misclassifying female engineers, erroneously confirming the assumption that engineering is a male profession.

To compound this, *representation bias* can occur when training data fails to accurately represent all demographic groups, perpetuating disparities.

Imagine an AI-powered recruitment tool that primarily analyzes resumes of Ivy League graduates to learn how to assess candidates. This narrowly trained system would be baffled by applicants who took alternative career paths, potentially filtering out promising talent simply because they followed unconventional trajectories.

Or envision a cutting-edge healthcare chatbot that is overwhelmingly conversant about conditions affecting middle-aged white men but stumbles with clues for illnesses impacting minorities and women. Without balanced representation in the training data, it may struggle to serve large swaths of the population.

Now picture a next-generation virtual assistant whose speech patterns closely mimic those of a tech entrepreneur. Although mimicking Silicon Valley culture helps it chat about gadgets or investing, this narrow representation means it stumbles on concepts from outside the tech bubble.

In each case, lack of diversity in training data leads to AI that is helpless in the face of normal human variety. Like a flavorless soup, representational bias strips the richness from AI, flattening the experience into homogeneity. To build inclusive AI, we must infuse diversity into its development in data, teams, and processes. This enriches AI, unlocking its potential to empower all people.

Additionally, *measurement bias* stems from using incorrect or incomplete metrics, distorting the assessment of AI performance across different groups. Here are some real-world examples of measurement bias in AI systems:

- A facial analysis algorithm developed by Stanford researchers was found to have significantly higher error rates when detecting the emotions of Black individuals compared to White individuals. The training data underrepresented the diversity of skin tones and facial structures.

- An AI recruiting tool built by Amazon was found to downgrade resumes containing the word "women's," such as "women's chess club captain." By only measuring traditional male-dominated activities as valuable skills, it propagated gender bias.
- A major health study focused clinical trials on men, establishing risk thresholds that overlooked heart attack symptoms more common in women. This led to AI-assisted diagnostic tools underestimating cardiovascular risk in women.
- Voice recognition software by technology giants like Microsoft and Google historically struggled with nonstandard dialects. Training on predominantly White voices caused language measurement biases.
- Face recognition software has demonstrated racial bias, with higher error rates for non-White faces. Underrepresentation in training data fails to account for a diversity of facial features and skin tones.
- AI models trained primarily on images of light-skinned individuals led HP webcams to track White-skinned faces well but poorly track Black-skinned faces.

It's imperative to acknowledge *cultural bias* as well, as interpretations of data may be influenced by cultural perspectives.

Here are some real-world examples of cultural bias in AI systems:

- Voice assistants with predominantly feminine personalities and names like Alexa, Siri, and Cortana reinforce gender stereotypes that women should be helpful, docile, and subservient.
- Image recognition algorithms labeled pictures of women cooking and cleaning, whereas men were labeled as executives, reflecting biases about traditional gender occupations.
- Healthcare AI tools trained primarily on data from Western patients struggle to account for genetic, environmental, and lifestyle factors affecting non-Western populations.

- Facial recognition systems have higher error rates and misidentification for East Asian faces due to underrepresentation in training data, which stems from historical marginalization.
- Product recommendation engines promoting dietary choices along cultural lines, pigeonholing Hispanic users to spicy food and Asian users to rice-based dishes based on stereotypes.

The common thread is cultural bias that stems from narrow training environments and worldviews. Thoughtful inclusion of diverse perspectives in teams and data helps build cross-cultural competence in AI systems.

With the ever-evolving nature of bias, it's vital to remain vigilant and adaptive in recognizing these multifaceted manifestations within AI systems. Recognizing these nuances will empower you to develop more equitable AI technologies that serve everyone.

Tools and Techniques to Detect Bias

Detecting bias in AI models is a crucial step in ensuring fairness and equity. Various tools and techniques are available to help identify and measure bias in the data, algorithms, and outcomes. One common approach is to conduct statistical tests to assess disparities in how different groups are represented in a dataset. For example, researchers may use demographic attributes such as race, gender, or age to analyze whether certain groups are disproportionately affected by their model's predictions. Additionally, data visualization tools can provide insights into patterns of bias by highlighting unequal distributions or correlations that may contribute to unfair outcomes. Another valuable technique is using fairness metrics, which quantify the degree of disparity in model predictions across different demographic subgroups. These metrics enable developers to assess the impact of bias and make informed decisions about potential interventions. Moreover, interpretability methods enable greater transparency in understanding how models arrive at their decisions. By examining feature importance and decision processes, developers can pin-point areas where bias may be introduced and then take correc-tive actions.

Consideration of counterfactual explanations is also impor-tant in detecting bias. These techniques involve generating hypo-thetical scenarios to explore how changes to input features might affect model outputs for different demographic groups, revealing potential biases in the decision-making process. Furthermore, audit tools can trace and monitor the lifecycle of data and model updates, providing visibility into potential bias sources and ensur-ing ongoing fairness assessments. Finally, continuous monitoring and feedback mechanisms are vital for detecting bias in real-world applications. By collecting and analyzing user feedback and per-formance data over time, AI developers can detect and address emerging biases that may not have been initially identified. Over-all, a combination of these tools and techniques can help develop-ers systematically detect and understand bias in AI models, paving the way for meaningful strategies for mitigating bias and promot-ing fairness.

Strategies for Mitigating Bias

As you delve into the critical issue of bias found in AI, it becomes crucial to explore strategies for mitigating its impact. AI bias can have far-reaching consequences, affecting individuals and commu-nities disproportionately.

Here are some examples of how AI bias can have disproportion-ate impacts on individuals and communities:

- A facial recognition system used for surveillance that has higher error rates for women of color could lead to wrongful arrests, perpetuating harm through racial and gender bias.
- An automated recruiting system that discriminates against nontraditional candidate profiles could exacerbate economic inequality by denying opportunities to capable applicants who don't fit expected backgrounds.

- Biased clinical risk assessment algorithms could lead to improper medical treatment for marginalized groups, worsening health disparities that already exist along gender, racial, and socioeconomic lines.
- Generative AI art and conversation bots reflecting cultural insensitivity and stereotypes can reinforce toxic perceptions, contributing to further stigmatization of minorities.

Mitigating bias requires a multifaceted approach involving both technical and ethical considerations. One fundamental strategy is to diversify the data used to train AI models, ensuring that it reflects the full spectrum of human experiences and perspectives. This means actively seeking out diverse datasets and integrating them thoughtfully into the training process.

Additionally, adopting a robust validation framework to assess the performance of AI models across different demographic groups is essential. By rigorously testing for biases and disparities, developers can identify and address problematic patterns located in their models. Some patterns might include the following:

- A medical diagnosis algorithm may be more likely to discount symptoms reported by female patients, reflecting historical gender biases that dismissed women's health concerns. Extensive testing across genders could illuminate this dangerous pattern of bias.
- Toxicity detection algorithms have demonstrated higher false-positive rates when analyzing text from minority dialects and contexts. Rigorous comparative audits could uncover how the model unfairly associates minorities with profanity.
- Testing self-driving vehicles in diverse geographical areas and weather conditions could reveal performance gaps for pedestrian detection along socioeconomic lines, flagging a potential pattern of bias.

Another vital strategy involves implementing fairness-aware algorithms to prioritize equitable outcomes. These algorithms are designed to explicitly account for fairness metrics, such as demographic parity and equality of opportunity, during model training and decision-making. Moreover, establishing interdisciplinary review panels comprising experts from diverse backgrounds can provide valuable insights into potential biases and their implications. These panel reviews can offer fresh perspectives and highlight blind spots that may otherwise go unnoticed.

Furthermore, developing clear guidelines and best practices for addressing bias in AI is crucial. Organizations must cultivate a culture of responsibility and accountability where team members are empowered to challenge biased outcomes and propose corrective measures. In addition to technical strategies, fostering transparency in AI development is pivotal. Documenting and disclosing the decision-making processes behind AI models can enhance accountability and encourage scrutiny in your organization. Finally, engaging with impacted communities and stakeholders through open dialogue and feedback mechanisms enables your teams to understand their concerns and experiences, which informs your ongoing refinement of your AI systems to better serve everyone. By integrating these comprehensive strategies, your organization can work toward building AI that not only serves everyone equally but also upholds principles of fairness and inclusivity in its design and deployment.

Promoting Fairness in Your AI Models

When discussing fairness in your AI models, it's instrumental to recognize the impact they have on real people and society at large. Promoting fairness isn't just about adhering to regulations or avoiding negative publicity; it's about upholding the ethical responsibility that comes with wielding such transformative technology. Fairness goes hand in hand with inclusivity, recognizing the diversity of human experiences and ensuring that AI models serve everyone equitably. It's about identifying and rectifying biases—whether they're intentional or not—to aid in the creation of systems that provide fair outcomes for all individuals, regardless of their background, race, gender, or any other defining characteristic. Achieving such fairness in AI models requires a thoughtful, interdisciplinary approach and involves scrutinizing the data used to train these models, understanding how societal biases can seep into algorithms, and continuously evaluating and refining the models' performance. From a technical standpoint, it means developing algorithms that not only optimize for accuracy but also prioritize fairness, striving to minimize disparities and promote equal opportunities.

Equally important is the need for ongoing dialogue across diverse stakeholders, including technologists, ethicists, lawmakers, and affected communities, to calibrate what "fairness" means in various contexts and to establish guidelines for responsible AI development. Additionally, promoting fairness also tackles the issue of interpretability and explainability in AI models. Transparent models enable researchers and end users to understand why certain decisions are made, providing an avenue for accountability and trust-building.

Moreover, by holding AI accountable for its decision-making processes, awareness about potential biases is raised, and the continual improvement of these systems is encouraged. It intersects with the principles of data privacy, which ensures that the information used to train and deploy AI models respects individual autonomy and rights, adding another layer of fairness and respect for individuals. An essential element of promoting such fairness is the commitment to ongoing education and learning, which includes staying abreast of the latest research on bias mitigation, learning from historical missteps, and continuously iterating on best practices. By cultivating a culture of learning and adaptability, your organization can create an environment where fairness becomes a central tenet of AI innovation.

The journey toward building fair AI models is an ongoing, complex endeavor. However, by prioritizing fairness as a fundamental design principle, embracing transparency and ongoing education, and fostering open dialogue, your organization can work toward creating AI systems that serve everyone equitably.

Keeping Things Transparent: Why It Matters

Transparency isn't just a buzzword in AI—it's a critical aspect of building trust and ensuring accountability. Transparency in AI is the ability to clearly understand how AI systems make decisions and the reasoning behind those decisions. It's about peeling back the layers of complexity to shed light on the inner workings of AI algorithms. So, why does transparency matter so much in the context of AI?

First and foremost, transparency helps to build trust. When users or stakeholders can understand how AI models reach certain conclusions, they are more likely to have confidence in the system. This is particularly crucial in areas such as healthcare, finance, and justice, where decisions based on AI can have significant real-world impacts. Transparency also plays a key role in accountability. If something goes wrong with an AI system, being able to examine its decision-making process enables the identification of issues and root causes. Without transparency, it's challenging to hold anyone accountable for the outcomes produced by AI.

Another reason transparency matters is related to fairness. By revealing the inner workings of AI models, your organization can identify and address biases or unfairness in your system, promoting equality and ensuring that your AI serves everyone equally. Furthermore, transparency fosters innovation. When researchers, developers, and stakeholders have a clear view of an AI system's operations, they can identify areas for improvement and innovation, spurring collaboration and encouraging the sharing of best practices.

Achieving transparency in AI is not without its challenges, however. The complexity of AI systems, proprietary algorithms, and privacy concerns often make it difficult to provide full transparency. However, efforts are being made to develop tools and methodologies for explaining AI decision-making processes. Black-box AI models are being replaced by more interpretable ones, and standards for transparency and fairness in AI are being developed.

Black-box AI models are often characterized by their complex and opaque nature, making it difficult to understand how they arrive at specific decisions. These models, which include deep-learning and neural networks, can process vast amounts of data through multiple layers of computation, resulting in highly accurate outputs. However, the intricate inner workings of these models are not easily interpretable, even to expert practitioners. This lack of transparency poses significant challenges to trust, accountability, and fairness.

As a result, there has been a growing movement toward replacing black-box models with more interpretable and explainable AI systems. Interpretable models, such as decision trees and linear regression, offer clearer insights into the decision-making process by providing an understandable rationale for their outputs. This transparency enables stakeholders to scrutinize and verify the fairness and accuracy of AI decisions, fostering greater trust and confidence in the technology.

Furthermore, explainable AI models help identify and mitigate biases within the system. By revealing the factors and logic behind AI decisions, organizations can detect and address potential sources of unfairness, ensuring that AI applications promote equity and do not inadvertently perpetuate discrimination. The shift toward interpretable models also aligns with regulatory demands for transparency and accountability in AI, as policymakers increasingly require AI systems to be comprehensible to users and regulators alike.

In the next section, I'll explore the importance of navigating laws and regulations to ensure transparent and fair AI systems.

Navigating Laws and Regulations

Navigating the legal landscape surrounding AI can be a daunting task, given the complexities and ever-evolving nature of regulations. It's crucial to understand the laws and regulations governing AI at both the national and international levels, as noncompliance can result in severe legal repercussions and damage to an organization's reputation.

At the national level, countries have been enacting various laws and regulations to govern the development, deployment, and use of AI technologies. These regulations often cover data privacy, algorithm transparency, ethical considerations, and fairness in machine-learning models. Organizations must stay abreast of these regulations to ensure that their AI systems comply with the ever-changing legal requirements.

Moreover, navigating international laws and regulations is equally important, as many organizations operate across borders. The General Data Protection Regulation (GDPR) in the European Union (EU) and the California Consumer Privacy Act (CCPA) in the United States are just two examples of impactful regulations that have significant implications for AI applications.

Given the rapid evolution of AI and its applications, policymakers are frequently revisiting and updating existing regulations while introducing new ones. Keeping up with these changes requires constant vigilance and a proactive approach to compliance. To navigate this complex regulatory environment, organizations must establish dedicated teams or work with external experts to monitor and interpret the legal landscape effectively.

Beyond merely understanding the legal framework, organizations need to foster a culture of legal and ethical awareness among their AI practitioners. This involves providing comprehensive training on relevant laws and regulations, integrating compliance requirements into the AI development process, and encouraging the responsible use of AI technologies. At the same time, collaboration with legal advisers and regulatory experts is essential to gain insights into best practices and mitigate legal risks associated with AI initiatives.

By proactively engaging with and adapting to the evolving legal environment, organizations can position themselves as responsible stewards of AI technology. Embracing a clear understanding of the legal requirements, along with a commitment to ethical AI practices, not only ensures compliance but also fosters trust among stakeholders and the broader society. Ultimately, navigating laws and regulations represents a critical aspect of building AI systems that serve everyone equitably and responsibly.

Learning from Policy Reviews at All Levels

Policy reviews play a key role in shaping the landscape of AI governance and regulation. These reviews provide an opportunity to assess existing policies, identify gaps, and propose necessary amendments to ensure that your organization's AI technologies are developed and deployed in a responsible and ethical manner. At the international level, organizations like the United Nations and the EU are actively engaged in conducting policy reviews to address the global implications of AI. These reviews encompass a wide range of considerations, including human rights, accountability, and transparency, aiming to establish a framework that promotes fairness and equality in AI applications. Regional and national governments also conduct their own reviews to tailor regulations to local contexts and address specific challenges and opportunities. These reviews involve collaboration with diverse stakeholders, including industry experts, academic researchers, legal professionals, and civil society representatives. By assembling multidisciplinary teams, policymakers can gain comprehensive insights into the multifaceted impacts of AI and formulate informed, evidence-based policy recommendations.

Additionally, engaging with affected communities and marginalized groups is essential to ensuring that AI policies are inclusive and considerate of diverse perspectives and needs. Such reviews provide a platform for public consultation and feedback, enabling individuals and organizations to contribute to the development

of AI governance frameworks. Through open dialogue and deliberation, policymakers can garner a deep understanding of societal
concerns and aspirations, which enriches the policymaking process overall and fosters public trust in AI systems. Moreover, policy reviews serve as a mechanism for continuous evaluation and
adaptation in response to evolving technological advancements and
societal dynamics.

As AI technologies continue to evolve rapidly, periodic reviews
become imperative to align regulatory measures with emerging
challenges and potentials. This adaptive approach enables regulators to stay ahead of the curve and proactively address ethical considerations and risks associated with AI deployment. Overall, policy
reviews at all levels foster collaborative decision-making, informed
by diverse expertise and stakeholder input, to shape a future where
AI serves the interests of humanity and upholds fundamental values of fairness and equity.

Real-World Examples of Fair AI in Action

In the real world, fair and inclusive AI can have a transformative
impact on various industries and communities. Here, I take a closer
look at some inspiring examples that illustrate how AI can be leveraged for the greater good.

In healthcare, AI is being used to address disparities in access
to medical resources and improve patient outcomes. For instance,
predictive models are being developed to identify individuals at
high risk of certain health conditions, enabling healthcare providers to proactively intervene and provide personalized care before a
patient's health worsens. This proactive approach not only enhances
the patient's well-being but also contributes to reducing healthcare inequities. In addition, AI-powered language translation tools
have been instrumental in breaking down communication barriers
for non-English-speaking patients, ensuring that they have equal
access to medical information and services.

Moving beyond healthcare, consider the realm of finance, where AI is revolutionizing how credit decisions are made. By leveraging AI algorithms that minimize bias and consider broader indicators of creditworthiness, financial institutions are striving to make lending practices fairer and more inclusive. These advancements pave the way for greater financial inclusion and opportunity for individuals who have historically been marginalized due to biased lending criteria.

The potential of fair AI stretches into the realm of education as well, with initiatives using AI to personalize learning experiences and provide targeted support to students from diverse backgrounds. By analyzing individual learning styles and adapting instructional content accordingly, AI-driven educational platforms are working to ensure that every student has an equal chance to thrive academically.

In the criminal justice system, fair AI applications are emerging to mitigate the impact of biases in decision-making processes. From predictive policing models designed to minimize disproportionate targeting of certain communities to tools that assist judges in sentencing by providing data-driven insights without perpetuating societal prejudices, these initiatives hold promise for fostering a more just and equitable legal system.

All of these examples highlight the potential of fair AI to address longstanding societal challenges and drive positive change. By showcasing these real-world applications, you gain valuable insights into how AI can serve everyone, paving the way for a future where technology empowers inclusivity and fairness across various domains.

Looking Ahead: Building Inclusive and Just AI

As you gaze into the future of AI, it's crucial to emphasize the significance of building inclusive and just AI systems. The goal is not simply to create AI that avoids bias but also to actively promote fairness and justice in the design and deployment of these technologies. Looking ahead, it is imperative for organizations and developers to adopt a proactive approach in crafting AI systems that are accessible and beneficial for all individuals, regardless of their background, identity, or circumstances.

One key aspect of building inclusive and just AI involves integrating diverse perspectives in the development process. It begins by assembling teams with varied backgrounds and experiences to ensure that the AI solutions created are reflective of a broad range of perspectives and needs. By incorporating diverse voices, biases can be identified more effectively, and solutions can be tailored to address the unique challenges faced by different communities.

Moreover, looking ahead requires a reevaluation of an organization's current data collection practices to ensure that its AI systems consider the needs and nuances of underrepresented groups. This may involve a thoughtful approach to data sourcing, as well as active efforts to foster inclusivity in the datasets used to train AI models. Additionally, utilizing techniques such as differential privacy can help protect sensitive information and uphold an individual's privacy rights, particularly those from marginalized communities.

Differential privacy is a technique used to ensure that the privacy of individuals is maintained when their data is included in large datasets. It works by adding a certain amount of random noise to the data before it is analyzed or shared.

This noise is carefully calculated to mask the contributions of individual data points while still enabling meaningful insights to be drawn from the aggregate data. In essence, differential privacy enables organizations to collect and use data for AI training and other purposes without compromising the privacy of the individuals whose data is included.

This approach is particularly beneficial when working with data from underrepresented or marginalized groups, as it helps to protect sensitive information and uphold privacy rights.

By ensuring that individuals cannot be reidentified from the data, differential privacy fosters trust and encourages broader participation in data-sharing initiatives, ultimately leading to more inclusive and accurate AI systems.

In the pursuit of building inclusive and just AI, it is essential to prioritize transparency and accountability. Providing clear explanations about how AI systems function and make decisions fosters trust and empowers its users to understand the technology's impact. This transparency also extends to the ethical considerations and trade-offs involved in AI design, enabling stakeholders to engage in informed discussions about the societal implications of these technologies.

Looking ahead, organizations must also navigate complex ethical and legal landscapes to ensure that their AI deployments align with fairness and justice principles. Engaging with policymakers, legal experts, and ethicists can help companies shape their development of regulations and guidelines that promote equity and safeguard against discriminatory practices.

Furthermore, there is a growing need to cultivate a culture of continuous learning and adaptation in the AI community. Embracing an ethos of ongoing education and awareness-building can enable practitioners to stay attuned to evolving issues related to bias, fairness, and inclusion in AI. By fostering a commitment to learning and improvement, the AI field can proactively respond to emerging challenges and refine its approaches to better serve diverse populations as it evolves.

Ultimately, looking ahead involves a collective responsibility by companies to advocate for AI advancements and uphold the values of equity and justice. By striving to build inclusive and just AI, organizations can work toward a future where technology not only reflects the diversity of the world but also contributes to positive social change, enriching the lives of all individuals.

Takeaways

- Bias can easily become embedded in AI systems through biased data, algorithms, or unfair performance metrics. This can lead to discriminatory and unethical outcomes if left unchecked. Leaders must make bias detection and mitigation a priority.
- There are various types of biases that can manifest in AI systems, including selection bias, algorithmic bias, confirmation bias, representation bias, measurement bias, and cultural bias. Understanding how these biases occur is crucial.
- Numerous techniques exist to detect bias, such as statistical tests, visualization, fairness metrics, model interpretability, counterfactual analysis, auditing, and continuous monitoring. Leaders should invest in implementing a combination of these techniques.
- Mitigating bias requires a multifaceted approach, including diversifying data, extensive validation testing, implementing fairness-aware algorithms, establishing diverse review panels, and cultivating a culture of accountability.
- Transparency, explainability, and interpretability are pivotal to identifying and addressing potential biases. Leaders must prioritize clear communication on how their AI systems work.
- Navigating complex legal landscapes surrounding AI is key to ensuring compliance with evolving regulations related to transparency, accountability, and fairness.
- Policy reviews at all levels provide opportunities to shape AI governance frameworks aligned with ethical principles. Engaging diverse stakeholders in these reviews is vital.

Reflection Questions

- What potential biases, both obvious and subtle, could be present in the data and algorithms used in our AI systems? How can we proactively detect them?
- Do we have the right cross-functional teams, policies, and processes in place to ensure that we are building fair, transparent, and accountable AI? If not, what needs to change?
- How well do we communicate the inner workings of our AI systems to relevant stakeholders? Do we need to improve transparency?
- Are we staying sufficiently aware of and compliant with the legal and regulatory landscape related to AI? How can we enhance our efforts?
- What lessons can we learn from policy reviews and real-world examples of fair AI applications? How can we apply those lessons to our work?
- Looking ahead, what steps do we need to take to further embrace inclusive and just AI principles in our development and deployment processes?

Chapter 12
Responsible AI at Scale: Growth, Governance, and Resilience

T he future is here, and it's intelligent. Artificial intelligence (AI) has captured our imaginations with its seemingly boundless potential. But AI's true transformative power lies not just in flashy prototypes; it lies in scalability. When AI is thoughtfully scaled, it evolves from speculation into reality, from isolated impact into widespread change.

Scalable AI has already begun revolutionizing entire industries, delighting customers, and turbocharging business success. The organizations that learn to harness AI's scalability will shape the future. They will outpace the competition, thrill customers, and charge boldly ahead, powered by AI's exponential intelligence.

But scaling AI is not simple. It requires foresight, responsibility, and adaptability in equal measure. The journey requires a commitment to best practices, resilience to unforeseen obstacles, and, above all, a North Star of ethics to guide decisions.

For those organizations willing to rise to the challenge, a future filled with possibility awaits. The power of AI is at our fingertips. The journey starts now.

Why Scaling AI Matters: Beyond the Prototype

Scalable AI is the key to reaching more people, solving more complex problems, and delivering tangible value at scale. By focusing on scalable AI, companies can transform their operations, create new revenue streams, and make a lasting impact in the market. It's about moving from proof of concept to production-ready systems that can handle real-world complexities and demands. Organizations that understand the importance of scaling AI beyond the prototype are better positioned to adapt to changing market dynamics, meet evolving customer needs, and stay ahead of the competition.

In this era of digital transformation, scalable AI isn't just nice to have—it's a strategic imperative. The ability to scale AI solutions is what sets visionary companies apart from those that struggle to stay relevant in a rapidly changing landscape. It's about taking AI innovation and making it accessible, reliable, and sustainable. Understanding why scaling AI matters goes beyond technical considerations—it's about driving meaningful outcomes that benefit businesses, individuals, and society as a whole. By moving beyond prototypes and embracing scalable AI, organizations can unlock AI's full potential, reshaping their strategies, products, and services for long-term success.

The Building Blocks of Scalable AI

Scalability as noted previously, is the key to realizing AI's full potential within an organization. In this section, I'll delve into the essential building blocks that pave the way for scalable AI implementation. One crucial aspect is infrastructure. From robust cloud computing capabilities to high-performance hardware, a strong IT infrastructure provides the foundation for scaling AI initiatives.

Additionally, the integration of advanced analytics tools and machine-learning platforms streamlines the development and deployment of AI models across the enterprise. Collaborative ecosystems are equally vital. Engendering a culture of cross-functional collaboration and knowledge sharing ensures that AI initiatives can flourish with diverse input from various teams. Furthermore, a scalable AI strategy demands a data-centric approach. A comprehensive data management framework encompassing data governance, quality, and security is imperative in sustaining the scalability of AI solutions.

At the heart of scalable AI lies adaptability. Embracing scalable design principles enables AI systems to evolve and adapt to changing business needs and technological advancements without upheaval. Equally important is a focus on user experience and accessibility. User-friendly interfaces and intuitive interactions foster widespread adoption within the organization. Finally, establishing agile development processes empowers teams to iterate and optimize AI solutions, fostering continuous improvement and scalability. By laying down these fundamental building blocks, organizations can position themselves to effectively scale their AI initiatives, driving impactful and sustainable value across the enterprise.

Governance Essentials: Keeping AI Ethical and Compliant

In the rapidly evolving world of AI, ensuring ethical and compliant practices is necessary. Governance provides the foundation for establishing these principles within your organization's AI initiatives. It begins with a clear understanding of AI's ethical implications and the importance of compliance with regulations and standards. Governance also involves defining the roles and responsibilities for maintaining ethical standards, as well as establishing clear processes for monitoring and enforcing compliance. Organizations must align their AI strategies with ethical principles, ensuring that their AI systems consider the potential impact on individuals and society. Transparency in decision-making processes and accountability for AI outcomes are also essential components of governance. To achieve this, organizations need to establish oversight mechanisms and frameworks for continuous ethical evaluation of AI systems by including regular assessments of AI models and algorithms to identify and mitigate potential biases or ethical concerns. Furthermore, effective governance requires ongoing education and training to raise awareness of ethical considerations among AI stakeholders. It's important for organizations to cultivate a culture of ethical responsibility and facilitate open dialogue about the ethical challenges associated with AI. Collaboration between multidisciplinary teams, including ethicists, legal experts, and technologists, can further strengthen governance and ensure a holistic approach to ethical compliance.

As AI continues to advance, governance around its ethical and compliant use will be crucial in building trust and confidence among users and the broader society. By embracing governance essentials and integrating ethical considerations into AI development and deployment, organizations can navigate the complex AI landscape with responsibility and integrity.

Navigating Regulatory Landscapes: What You Must Know

The world of AI is a complex and dynamic landscape influenced by a myriad of regulatory frameworks and legal considerations. Navigating these regulatory landscapes is essential for any organization seeking to deploy AI at scale. Various aspects must be considered when diving into the regulatory AI realm. First and foremost, it's essential to be aware of the existing regulations governing data privacy and protection. For instance, the General Data Protection Regulation (GDPR) in Europe and the California Consumer Privacy Act (CCPA) in California have far-reaching implications for AI systems that process personal data. Understanding the requirements and limitations imposed by these regulations is vital for ensuring compliance and building trust with users and stakeholders.

Furthermore, navigating regulatory landscapes also involves staying abreast of industry-specific regulations and standards. Different sectors, such as healthcare, finance, and transportation, have their own sets of rules and guidelines for AI deployment. Being cognizant of these sector-specific requirements is paramount for developing AI solutions tailored to the unique demands of each industry.

Additionally, new laws and regulations specific to AI technologies are being proposed and enacted as AI evolves. Keeping informed about emerging legislation related to AI is essential to anticipate and adapt to changing compliance demands. It's not just about following rules; it's also about proactively shaping the regulatory environment. Engaging with policymakers, industry groups, and regulatory bodies can provide developmental opportunities to contribute to responsible and feasible regulations conducive to innovation.

Moreover, fostering a culture of ethical and compliant AI within your organization is fundamental to enduring success in navigating diverse regulatory landscapes. It requires proactive efforts to embed ethical principles into the fabric of AI processes and decision-making, as well as educating and empowering your teams to uphold ethical standards. By embracing a holistic approach to regulatory navigation, organizations can ensure that their AI initiatives are not only legally compliant but also ethically sound, thus fostering trust and sustainability in the ever-changing world of AI regulation.

Here is a list of tools and frameworks I have created for my clients to ensure organizational success. (You can find more about these at http://responsibleaibook.com):

- **SWOT analysis:** Conduct a SWOT analysis on your organization's current AI programs and initiatives. Identify strengths, weaknesses, opportunities, and threats to develop strategic insights on how to scale AI responsibly.
- **Stakeholder mapping:** Map out key stakeholders involved in or impacted by AI implementations. Consider their interests, concerns, and influence to inform ethical and inclusive AI strategies.

- **Risk assessment:** Perform a risk assessment focused on potential ethical, legal, and societal risks associated with AI systems. Quantify and prioritize risks to develop targeted mitigation strategies.
- **Responsible AI checklist:** Create a checklist outlining key elements of responsible AI across areas like governance, ethics, robustness, transparency, and so on. Use it to self-assess existing and proposed AI systems.
- **Responsible AI audit:** Develop an audit framework to thoroughly evaluate AI systems against responsible AI criteria. Perform regular audits to identify gaps and drive continuous improvement.

Safe and Sound: Creating Robust Governance Frameworks

Developing robust governance frameworks is elementary in ensuring that AI initiatives are conducted ethically, compliantly, and with the highest regard for security. The goal is to create a structure supporting responsible AI at every organizational level, from data collection and model development to deployment and ongoing monitoring. It involves a multifaceted approach that addresses not only AI's technical aspects but also its ethical considerations, legal requirements, and risk management procedures.

An effective governance framework begins by clearly defining roles and responsibilities within the organization, which includes establishing accountability for decision-making and ensuring that there is clear oversight of AI initiatives at each lifecycle stage. Transparency is also a key element in creating robust governance frameworks. It means openly communicating the objectives, methodologies, and potential impacts of AI projects to stakeholders, including employees, customers, and regulators. Building trust through transparency can mitigate fears about AI and foster a culture of ethical and responsible AI usage.

In addition to internal governance, enterprises must also consider external oversight and compliance, which involves staying informed about relevant laws and regulations, such as data protection requirements and industry-specific standards, and adapting AI practices accordingly. To ensure compliance, organizations must undergo periodic audits and assessments of their AI systems, addressing any identified gaps or vulnerabilities. Furthermore, creating robust governance frameworks requires a commitment to continual improvement and adaptation.

As AI technology and its applications evolve, governance structures must be agile enough to accommodate changes while maintaining ethical standards and regulatory compliance. This may involve integrating feedback mechanisms, implementing regular training programs, and establishing avenues for reporting ethical concerns. It's important to remember that creating robust governance frameworks is an ongoing process that demands collaboration across various departments, including legal, IT, data management, and business units. By establishing comprehensive and adaptable governance frameworks, organizations can foster an environment where AI can thrive responsibly and safely, bringing value to both the company and society.

Looking to create or validate an AI governance structure? Here are some key elements to consider:

AI governance framework template

- Overview
  - Purpose and objectives of the governance framework
  - Scope of areas of the business and types of AI systems covered
  - Guiding principles for responsible AI (e.g., ethics, transparency, and accountability)
- Roles and responsibilities
  - Define key roles like AI ethics committee, program managers, developers, auditors, etc.
  - Outline the duties and decision rights of each role as they relate to AI systems.

- Policies and processes
  - AI development lifecycle: Standards for data, model development, testing, deployment, and so on
  - Risk management policies: How risks are evaluated and mitigated
  - Change management processes to handle AI system modifications
  - Documentation and reporting requirements
- Monitoring and oversight
  - Creation of oversight bodies (e.g., ethics boards)
  - Auditing procedures, checklists, and frequency
  - Performance metrics and dashboards for tracking outcomes
  - Channels for feedback, reporting issues, and whistleblowing
- Education and communication
  - Training programs for teams on ethical AI, security, and governance
  - Awareness initiatives to promote transparency on AI usage and impact
  - Communication strategy for status updates and engagement with stakeholders
- Continuous improvement
  - Protocols for periodic reviews and updates to the framework
  - Version control and documentation of changes
  - Mechanisms to incorporate internal feedback and external regulations into the framework

There is a full copy of this template at `https://responsible` `aibook.com`.

Strengthening the Core: Developing Resilient AI Programs

Developing resilient AI programs is imperative for organizations seeking to navigate the constantly evolving landscape of technological disruptions and challenges. Although creating robust governance frameworks lays a strong foundation, it is the development of resilient AI programs that truly strengthens the core of an organization's AI initiatives. Resilience in this context not only refers to the ability of AI systems to withstand unexpected events and challenges but also encompasses their capacity to adapt, learn, and improve over time.

This section delves into the key strategies and best practices for developing resilient AI programs. One crucial aspect of developing resilient AI programs is understanding the inherent uncertainties and risks associated with such technologies. Organizations must acknowledge that disruptions and adversities are inevitable in the dynamic AI realm. By embracing uncertainty and proactively identifying potential vulnerabilities, organizations can lay the groundwork for building resilience into their AI programs.

Furthermore, fostering a culture of continuous learning and adaptation within the organization is paramount. It involves encouraging cross-functional collaboration, investing in ongoing training and skill development, and promoting a growth mindset at all levels.

Additionally, leveraging advanced technologies such as machine learning and predictive analytics can bolster the resilience of AI programs by enabling proactive identification of potential disruptions and anomalies. An agile approach to AI development, implementation, and management is also instrumental in enhancing resilience. By adopting adaptable methodologies and maintaining flexibility in AI system design and deployment, organizations can effectively respond to emerging challenges and rapidly evolving market demands. Moreover, the establishment of clear communication channels and escalation procedures facilitates swift and efficient responses to disruptions.

Collaboration between technical and business teams can lead to the identification of early warning signs and prompt implementation of mitigation strategies. Building redundancy and fail-safe mechanisms into AI systems further fortifies their resilience. It involves designing backup processes, alternative data sources, and redundant infrastructure to ensure the continuity of operations in the face of unexpected disruptions. Ultimately, developing resilient AI programs requires a holistic approach that integrates people, processes, and technologies. By nurturing a culture of adaptability, innovation, and collaboration, organizations can imbue their AI initiatives with the resilience needed to thrive amid uncertainty and change.

Handling Disruptions Like a Pro

Disruptions are an inevitable part of any journey, and the AI realm is no exception. As businesses embrace AI at scale, they must be prepared to handle disruptions effectively and efficiently. Whether it's a technical glitch, an unexpected data inconsistency, or a sudden shift in market dynamics, the ability to navigate disruptions can make all the difference in the success of AI initiatives. In this section, strategies for handling disruptions like a pro are explored.

One key aspect of handling disruptions is maintaining a proactive mindset. Instead of waiting for disruptions to occur, organizations should anticipate potential challenges and establish robust contingency plans. This planning should involve conducting thorough risk assessments, identifying vulnerable points in the AI ecosystem, and devising response strategies for various scenarios. By proactively addressing potential disruptions, organizations can minimize their impact and maintain operational continuity.

Additionally, cultivating a culture of adaptability and resilience is compulsory for handling disruptions effectively. This extends beyond technical measures and involves instilling a mindset of agility and flexibility within your organization's teams. When disruptions arise, agile teams can quickly pivot, adjusting their approaches and finding innovative solutions to mitigate any impact. Such adaptability also includes fostering a learning culture where teams continuously refine their skills and knowledge to stay ahead of potential disruptions.

In the face of disruptions, clear communication and collaboration are crucial. Establishing transparent channels for reporting and addressing issues equips teams to swiftly flag and resolve disruptions as they arise. Moreover, cross-functional collaboration enables diverse perspectives to come together in problem-solving, offering a holistic approach to managing disruptions. By promoting open communication and collaboration, organizations can more effectively address disruptions and prevent them from escalating into larger setbacks.

Furthermore, the use of advanced technologies such as predictive analytics and automated monitoring can preemptively identify potential disruptions before they escalate. Through predictive modeling and real-time monitoring, organizations can detect anomalies and deviations, enabling them to intervene proactively before disruptions impact operations.

A large retail chain relied on legacy supply-chain systems, which provided little visibility into potential inventory challenges. The company frequently experienced stock-outs of popular items, which resulted in lost sales and customer dissatisfaction.

To address this, the chain implemented an advanced AI-powered analytics system that ingested data from across its supply chain, including inventory levels, sales forecasts, logistics delays, and warehouse capacity constraints. The system applied predictive modeling and anomaly detection to identify high-risk inventory scenarios well in advance.

Alerts surfaced through a central monitoring dashboard, which enabled executives and supply-chain managers to take proactive steps to avoid stock-outs. For example, the system predicted an upcoming surge in demand for a newly launched product coupled with a delay in incoming shipments. With this advance warning, the company was able to charter additional transportation to expedite the pending order and reroute inventory between warehouses to meet anticipated demand.

(continued)

(continued)

As a result, it was able to achieve consistent availability of the new product during peak demand, leading to increased sales and happier customers. The early warning signals enabled proactive intervention that minimized disruptions. This showcases how organizations can leverage AI-based predictive capabilities and monitoring to get ahead of potential supply-chain disruptions *before* they negatively impact operations and customers.

Key takeaways for AI leaders:

- Invest in predictive analytics to identify emerging risks proactively.
- Implement real-time monitoring and early warning systems.
- Focus on high-impact use cases like supply chain risk.
- Enable cross-functional teams to collaborate on preemptive action.
- Quantify the value of risk reduction and revenue protection.

By leveraging technology to anticipate and respond to disruptions, organizations can significantly enhance their resilience and minimize downtime of their AI initiatives.

Ultimately, handling disruptions like a pro requires a proactive, adaptive, and collaborative approach, necessitating a blend of strategic planning, organizational culture, and technological capabilities to effectively navigate the uncertainties that accompany AI at scale. By embracing disruptions as opportunities for growth and innovation, organizations will emerge stronger and more resilient in their AI endeavors.

Real-World Success Stories: Lessons from the Field

Throughout the rapidly evolving AI landscape, numerous success stories have illuminated the path for others to follow. These real-world experiences are rich in insights, learnings, and invaluable lessons that can help organizations navigate the complex terrain of implementing responsible AI at scale. From small startups to established enterprises, the journey toward scalable AI has been both challenging and rewarding. Here are just a few compelling narratives to shed light on the transformative power of responsible AI.

One notable success story hails from a global tech company that effectively integrated AI into its customer service operations. By leveraging AI-powered chatbots to handle basic queries and support requests, the company was able to significantly reduce response times while also improving overall customer satisfaction. This not only streamlined service processes but also empowered human agents to focus on more complex tasks, showcasing the collaborative potential of AI and human expertise.

Another remarkable account comes from the healthcare sector, where an organization employed AI algorithms to analyze medical imaging data for early disease detection. This implementation of AI led to quicker and more accurate diagnoses, ultimately contributing to improved patient outcomes. By embracing responsible AI practices, it was able to address privacy concerns, ensure transparency, and maintain ethical standards, thus demonstrating AI's profound impact in enhancing healthcare delivery.

In the financial services industry, a leading institution effectively deployed AI for fraud detection and risk management. Using sophisticated AI models, it enhanced its ability to identify fraudulent activities and mitigate potential risks, safeguarding both its institution and its customers. These success stories underscore the critical importance of integrating responsible AI practices to build trust, ensure fairness, and drive positive societal impact.

What emerges from these diverse narratives is a resounding message: responsible AI implementation at scale is indeed achievable. However, it requires a comprehensive approach that goes beyond technical prowess, encompassing ethical considerations, regulatory compliance, and a deep understanding of the human context within which AI operates. As we glean insights from these success stories, it becomes evident that fostering a culture of responsible

AI is not just a strategic imperative but a catalyst for innovation, growth, and societal benefit.

Common Pitfalls and How to Avoid Them

One of the biggest challenges in scaling responsible AI initiatives is navigating the common pitfalls that organizations can encounter. Understanding these pitfalls and learning how to avoid them is instrumental in ensuring the success and longevity of AI programs. A common pitfall is a lack of clear communication and alignment between different stakeholders involved in AI initiatives, which can lead to misunderstandings and conflicting priorities and ultimately hinder the progress of AI projects. To address this, organizations must prioritize transparent communication and collaborative decision-making across teams, departments, and leadership levels.

Another common pitfall lies in overlooking the ethical implications and societal impact of AI implementations. It's essential for organizations to engage with diverse perspectives and incorporate ethical considerations into their AI strategies from the outset. Ignoring these aspects can result in public backlash, reputational damage, and potential regulatory scrutiny.

Furthermore, many organizations underestimate the resources and expertise required for sustaining and evolving AI at scale. Without adequate investment in talent, infrastructure, and ongoing optimization, AI programs risk becoming obsolete or ineffective. Recognizing the need for continuous learning, upskilling, and knowledge sharing is fundamental for avoiding stagnation and ensuring the long-term viability of AI initiatives.

Finally, a lack of adaptability and agility can impede the scalability of AI programs. Rapid technological advancements, evolving regulatory landscapes, and shifting market dynamics demand nimble responses and repeatable approaches. Organizations must cultivate a culture of adaptability, experimentation, and resilience to steer clear of common pitfalls and thrive amidst change. By acknowledging these challenges and proactively addressing them, organizations can build a solid foundation for responsible AI at scale and navigate the complexities with confidence and foresight.

The Future of Responsible AI at Scale

The landscape of responsible AI at scale continues to evolve and presents both opportunities and challenges. Advancements in technology, coupled with an increased focus on ethical and transparent AI, are shaping the path ahead.

One of the most prominent trends on the horizon is the integration of AI across various industries and sectors. Society is witnessing a shift toward ubiquitous AI adoption, where organizations are increasingly leveraging AI to drive efficiency, innovation, and personalized experiences. This pervasive integration raises important questions about ethical deployment, data privacy, and human–AI collaboration.

Moreover, the regulatory landscape surrounding AI is expected to undergo significant changes to keep pace with technological advancements. It's essential for organizations to stay abreast of evolving regulations and compliance requirements as they navigate the complex terrain of responsible AI at scale. Anticipating these shifts is paramount in establishing sustainable and compliant AI strategies.

Looking ahead, the development of AI governance frameworks will play a pivotal role in ensuring responsible utilization of AI at scale. These frameworks will need to encompass not only technical considerations but also socioethical dimensions, addressing concerns around bias mitigation, fairness, and accountability. As AI ecosystems become increasingly interconnected, fostering a culture of responsible AI will be instrumental in building trust and fostering positive societal impact.

A key aspect that will demand attention in the future is the continued exploration and refinement of AI resilience. As AI systems become more intricate and intertwined with critical operations, bolstering their resilience to adversarial attacks, system failures, and unforeseen scenarios becomes imperative. Organizations will need to invest in robust resilience strategies to fortify their AI deployments against emerging threats and vulnerabilities.

Finally, the future of responsible AI at scale holds the potential for collaborative efforts and knowledge sharing. The establishment of best practices, industry standards, and community-driven initiatives will promote a collective approach toward tackling the complexities of scaling AI responsibly. Collaboration among diverse stakeholders will foster an environment conducive to the exchange of insights, experiences, and solutions, ultimately propelling the responsible AI agenda forward.

In essence, the future of responsible AI at scale promises to be an era defined by continuous evolution, adaptive governance, and a collective commitment to ethical advancement. Navigating this future landscape will necessitate agility, foresight, and a steadfast dedication to ethical principles, propelling responsible AI into a force for positive transformation on a global scale.

Takeaways

- Scaling AI requires moving beyond prototypes to build production-ready systems that can handle real-world complexities. This involves focusing on scalable infrastructure, workflows, and organizational processes.
- Responsible AI demands proactive governance, encompassing ethical considerations, regulatory compliance, risk management, and transparency. Organizations need clear frameworks outlining roles, policies, oversight mechanisms, and education initiatives.
- Navigating the complexities of scaling AI requires adaptability, resilience, and collaboration. Organizations must anticipate uncertainties, minimize disruptions through early warning systems, and enable teams to respond swiftly.

Reflection Questions

- How can we evolve our AI prototypes into robust, scalable solutions that deliver value across the enterprise? What infrastructure, tools, and processes need to be in place?
- What governance practices do we currently have for AI systems? How can we strengthen oversight and compliance while also fostering a culture of ethical AI?
- How can we enhance the resilience and agility of our AI initiatives? Are there mechanisms to identify potential disruptions earlier and mobilize cross-functional collaboration?

Part IV

The Vision Realized: Leading AI into the Future

Chapter 13

Looking Back: Lessons Learned and Insights Gained

As you review your artificial intelligence (AI) journey, it's essential to take stock of the numerous lessons and insights you've gained along the way. Reflecting on the key takeaways from your experiences enables you to appreciate the evolution of your understanding of AI and its far-reaching implications. One crucial lesson learned is the profound impact of responsible AI deployment and how ethical considerations and fairness must be at the forefront of AI innovation.

This realization has shaped your approach, leading your organization to prioritize human-centric AI solutions that align with societal values and needs. Another significant insight gained is the power of collaborative ecosystems in driving AI progress. Your interactions with diverse stakeholders have underscored the importance of partnerships in fostering innovation and overcoming challenges.

This journey has highlighted the critical need for ongoing education and empowerment. Democratizing AI knowledge and skills is essential for ensuring widespread participation in this transformative journey. Embracing inclusivity and diversity in AI development has not only enriched your understanding but also broadened the scope of possibilities.

Your journey so far has reinforced the value of ethical frameworks in guiding AI advancements. You've grasped the significance of upholding transparency, accountability, and fairness as fundamental principles in AI design and deployment. These pivotal learnings have not only informed your outlook but also paved the way for a more conscientious and impactful future.

Each challenge, triumph, and interaction has played a vital role in shaping your collective wisdom and vision for the future of AI. Through these reflections, you are better prepared to set the stage for future AI adventures, armed with a deeper understanding of the complexities and possibilities that lie ahead.

Gearing Up: Setting the Stage for Future AI Adventures

As you look to the future of AI, it's vital to understand that the journey ahead will be unlike anything you've experienced before. Gearing up for this adventure means preparing your organizations for the rapid evolution and expansion of AI technologies. The very nature of AI requires you to be agile, adaptable, and forward-thinking, ready to embrace the potential of AI while also mitigating its risks. In this chapter, the essential steps and considerations for setting the stage for these upcoming AI adventures are explored.

First and foremost, setting the stage for future AI adventures requires a mindset shift. Your organization must move beyond viewing AI as a standalone technology and start integrating it into the fabric of your business strategies and operations. Doing so involves fostering a culture of curiosity, innovation, and continuous learning within your organization. Now it's time to expand this beyond just you and your team across the entire ecosystem. It's about empowering your teams to think creatively and critically about how AI can drive value across all facets of your businesses.

Furthermore, gearing up for the future of AI demands a commitment to ethical and responsible AI practices. Clear guidelines and frameworks must be established to ensure that your organization's AI initiatives align with principles of fairness, transparency, and accountability. This includes embedding ethical considerations into the design, development, and deployment of AI systems, as well as actively addressing any biases or unintended consequences that may arise.

Technology infrastructure plays a pivotal role in setting the stage for future AI adventures. As AI capabilities expand and diversify, organizations must invest in scalable and robust infrastructure to support the complex computational requirements of advanced AI algorithms. This entails building flexible architectures that can accommodate the diverse needs of AI applications, from real-time data processing to high-performance computing.

People remain at the heart of AI advancements, so cultivating a diverse and inclusive talent pool is critical for organizations when gearing up for the future. Fostering a workforce that reflects a wide range of perspectives and experiences fuels innovation and ensures that AI solutions are designed with empathy and inclusivity at their core. Embracing diversity also opens pathways for fresh insights and breakthroughs in AI research and development.

Gearing up for the future of AI is about embracing an all-inclusive approach that encompasses organizational culture, ethical standards, technological infrastructure, and human capital. By laying the groundwork for responsible, innovative, and inclusive AI journeys, you can position your organization to capitalize on the boundless opportunities that the future holds.

Trailblazers: Stories of AI Innovations Leading the Way

In the ever-evolving AI landscape, pioneers have pushed the boundaries of what was once deemed impossible. These trailblazers have harnessed the power of AI to revolutionize industries, spark societal changes, and pave the way for a future where technology serves as a force for good. Here are some accounts of these remarkable innovators, each a trailblazer in their own right.

One can be found in the healthcare sector, where an AI-powered diagnostic tool is transforming patient care. Through intricate algorithms and machine learning, this technology has significantly improved the accuracy and speed of medical diagnoses, providing timely and life-saving interventions. This innovation's impact ripples across the healthcare ecosystem, showing the immense potential of AI to enhance human well-being.

Another awe-inspiring narrative emerges from the field of environmental conservation. In this area, AI is employed to analyze vast quantities of data, enabling researchers to track and predict ecological changes with unprecedented precision. Through collaborations between scientists and technologists, AI has become an invaluable ally in safeguarding the planet's biodiversity and addressing pressing environmental challenges.

The educational realm also bears witness to the transformative power of AI. In one compelling account, AI-driven personalized learning platforms have empowered students of diverse backgrounds to excel at their own pace, bridging educational gaps and nurturing a love for lifelong learning. By adapting content and support to individual needs, these innovations not only elevate academic outcomes but also foster a deeper sense of inclusion and equity within educational systems.

Beyond these instances, countless other histories of AI-inspired breakthroughs abound. From finance to agriculture, cybersecurity to creative arts, these chronicles of AI innovations leading the way unfold like a tapestry of human ingenuity, resourcefulness, and collaboration. Each narrative inspires and emboldens organizations to embrace AI's limitless potential to catalyze positive change and shape a future where innovation knows no bounds.

AI Communities: Building Bridges and Removing Barriers

In AI, communities play a pivotal role in driving innovation and fostering collaboration. These communal networks serve as fertile grounds where diverse perspectives combine to fuel groundbreaking advancements. By connecting individuals from various backgrounds, expertise levels, and industries, AI communities create an environment that encourages knowledge sharing and sparks transformative ideas. Through a collective effort, these communities strive to bridge gaps and remove barriers, propelling the entire AI ecosystem forward. As members come together, they bring with them a wealth of experiences, challenges, and triumphs, enriching the community through their multifaceted insights.

Whether it's through meetups, conferences, or online forums, AI communities provide platforms for professionals and enthusiasts to engage in meaningful discussions, share best practices, and stay abreast of the latest industry trends. Their collaborative nature fosters an atmosphere of continuous learning and growth where individuals are empowered to explore new horizons and push the boundaries of what AI can achieve. Additionally, these communities serve as catalysts for inclusivity and diversity within the field, recognizing the significance of varied perspectives and voices in shaping AI's future. By fostering an open and welcoming environment, these communities actively work toward breaking down obstacles and creating pathways for underrepresented groups to contribute meaningfully to the AI landscape. Through mentorship programs, educational initiatives, and outreach efforts, AI communities strive to equip aspiring talents with the skills and resources needed to thrive in the AI world. As these communities expand and interconnect, they enhance the collective capacity for solving complex challenges and drive positive change in the broader societal context. Ultimately, AI communities stand as dynamic hubs that not only bolster the technical aspects of AI but also champion the human-centric dimension of this transformative technology. By building bridges and removing barriers, these communities enable a more inclusive and collaborative landscape where AI's promise is harnessed for the betterment of all.

Human-Centric AI: Ensuring That People Remain at Its Heart

In a world increasingly shaped by AI, it's crucial to remember that people are at the center of it all. As we push technological boundaries and explore the limitless potential of AI, the focus should always remain on how these advancements can enhance the lives of individuals and communities. Human-centric AI places human well-being, safety, and fulfillment at the forefront of every decision.

When developing AI solutions, it's important to consider the impact on diverse groups and communities. It means designing with empathy and understanding the cultural, social, and economic contexts in which AI will be deployed. By embracing diversity and inclusion in the development process, organizations can create AI that truly serves everyone, addressing existing inequities and fostering a more equitable future.

Moreover, ethics and transparency are integral to ensuring human-centric AI. It's essential to establish clear guidelines and accountability mechanisms to protect privacy, respect autonomy, and mitigate harm. By embedding ethical considerations into the core of AI development, organizations can cultivate trust and foster a sense of empowerment among individuals interacting with AI systems.

At the same time, human-centric AI requires ongoing dialogue and collaboration with end users. Understanding their needs, concerns, and feedback is paramount to refining and tailoring AI solutions to best serve them. Whether it's in healthcare, education, or any other domain, involving the individuals who will benefit from

AI in their design and implementation processes leads to more impactful and sustainable outcomes.

The future of AI hinges on its ability to align with human values and aspirations. Empowering individuals through AI means creating opportunities for skill development, knowledge sharing, and active participation in shaping the technological landscape. By leveraging AI to augment human capabilities rather than replace them, organizations can ensure that people remain the driving force behind innovation and progress.

Ultimately, human-centric AI is not just a buzzword—it's a commitment to harnessing AI's potential for the greater good while safeguarding the dignity and rights of every individual. As the transformative power of AI is embraced, organizations cannot lose sight of the ultimate goal: improving and enriching human lives and experiences.

Collaborative Ecosystems: Partnerships That Drive Progress

In the AI world, no company or individual exists in a vacuum. This phrase underscores the interconnected nature of the AI industry. In the rapidly evolving field of AI, progress is not achieved in isolation.

Companies, researchers, policymakers, and innovators must collaborate, share knowledge, and build on each other's work to drive meaningful advancements. The complexity and multidisciplinary nature of AI require contributions from various sectors, including academia, industry, and government. By working together, these entities can address the multifaceted challenges and ethical considerations that AI presents, ensuring that developments are responsible and beneficial to society as a whole.

Collaborative ecosystems are the lifeblood of progress and innovation, forming the fertile ground on which groundbreaking solutions and advancements grow. When diverse minds and talents come together, magical things can happen. From sharing knowledge and best practices to combining resources and expertise, partnerships drive AI progress.

One of the key reasons collaborative ecosystems are so crucial in the AI landscape is their ability to harness the power of collective intelligence. By pooling diverse perspectives and skill sets; these ecosystems foster an environment where innovative ideas can flourish and evolve. Whether it's in academia, industry, or government, bringing different stakeholders to the table creates a rich tapestry of insights and experiences essential for tackling complex AI challenges.

Partnerships can enable organizations to complement each other's strengths and fill in the gaps, leading to more comprehensive, well-rounded AI solutions. Different players bring unique assets to the table—be it deep domain knowledge, technical prowess, or understanding of societal impacts—and by joining forces, they create a synergy that propels AI development forward.

Beyond driving technological progress, collaborative ecosystems also play a pivotal role in addressing ethical and social considerations in AI. By fostering open dialogues and promoting shared responsibility, these partnerships help establish common ethical frameworks and guidelines, ensuring that AI advances responsibly with fairness at its core. The diversity of voices within these ecosystems helps navigate the intricate moral labyrinths of AI, paving the way for technology that resonates with humanity.

Successful collaborative ecosystems are built on trust, transparency, and mutual respect among all participants. They cultivate an environment where competition gives way to cooperation, and collective goals take precedence over individual gains. These ecosystems aren't just about organizations coming together; they are about people connecting, exchanging ideas, and working toward a future where AI serves as a force for good.

In looking toward the future, fostering these collaborative ecosystems will be essential in realizing AI's full potential. Through these partnerships, organizations can ensure that AI advancements benefit everyone. AI isn't just about technology—it's about the collective wisdom and aspirations of humanity coming to fruition.

Ask the Experts: Wisdom from AI Thought Leaders

In this section, I tap into the collective wisdom of seasoned AI thought leaders. These individuals have dedicated their careers to understanding and shaping the future of AI. What distinguishes these experts isn't just their depth of knowledge but also their ability to translate complex concepts into practical insights that resonate across industries. As you read through their perspectives, you'll gain a deeper understanding of the current state of AI, its potential for the future, and the critical challenges that lie ahead.

One recurring theme that you'll encounter is the importance of responsible AI deployment—ensuring that the power of AI is harnessed for the greater good while mitigating potential risks. These thought leaders bring diverse perspectives to the table, representing a wide spectrum of expertise in areas such as machine learning, ethics, cybersecurity, and business strategy. Each interview offers a rare glimpse into the minds of those at the forefront of AI innovation. You'll discover how they envision AI's trajectory, the key milestones they anticipate, and the implications for businesses, societies, and individuals. From discussions on unlocking AI's full potential to addressing ethical dilemmas and fostering collaboration, the insights shared here will leave you enriched and inspired. In addition to their forward-looking visions, these experts provide practical advice for organizations navigating the complexities of implementing AI solutions. They touch on the organizational dynamics required for successful AI adoption, the significance of continuous learning and adaptation, and the role of cross-disciplinary teamwork in driving AI initiatives forward.

Ultimately, this section is a testament to the fact that the quest for advancing AI is a collective endeavor—one that demands a tapestry of perspectives, experiences, and expertise. The wisdom imparted by these thought leaders serves as a guiding light, illuminating the path forward for those eager to embrace AI's potential while staying mindful of its implications.

We need to ensure that AI systems do what humans want them to do.
  —*Stuart Russell, UC Berkeley professor and author of* Human Compatible: Artificial Intelligence and the Problem of Control

We want machines that are helpful, honest, and harmless.
  —*Dario Amodei, VP of AI Safety Research at OpenAI*

AI systems should be designed in ways that reduce risks and provide widespread benefit for humanity.
  —*Francesca Rossi, AI ethicist at IBM*

It is vital that ethics informs AI design from the very beginning, not as an afterthought.
  —*Joanna Bryson, professor of ethics and technology*
  at Hertie School in Berlin

For AI to fulfill its potential, we must ensure it reflects human values like dignity, justice and compassion.
  —*Mustafa Suleyman, CEO of Microsoft AI*

AI should empower people, not replace them; and technology must always work for people and planet, not the other way around.
  —*Satya Nadella, CEO of Microsoft*

DIY AI: Empowering Everyone to Be Part of the Journey

Have you ever imagined being part of the incredible journey of AI innovation? Well, you can! The world of AI isn't just for the tech elites or data scientists. It's for everyone with a curious mind and a passion for making a difference. Do-It-Yourself AI (DIY AI) is all about breaking down barriers and empowering individuals from diverse backgrounds to dive into the AI realm. Whether you're a student, business professional, artist, or humanitarian, there are countless opportunities for you to contribute to and benefit from the AI revolution. So, how can you become a part of this exciting adventure?

First, it's essential to recognize that AI literacy is the key to unlocking the potential of DIY AI. Understanding the basics of machine learning, neural networks, and AI ethics can provide a solid foundation for anyone looking to get involved. Numerous online courses, tutorials, and resources are available for free or at a minimal cost, making it easier than ever to learn about AI at your own pace. Furthermore, DIY AI emphasizes hands-on experience and experimentation. You don't need access to expensive hardware or specialized software to start tinkering with AI.

Many platforms offer user-friendly tools for building and training AI models, enabling beginners to gain practical skills without overwhelming technical complexity. Additionally, collaborative AI communities provide invaluable support and guidance for those embarking on their DIY AI journey. Engaging with like-minded enthusiasts through forums, meetups, or online groups can foster inspiration, knowledge sharing, and mentorship. These connections can lead to exciting collaborations and projects that leverage diverse perspectives and expertise.

Ultimately, DIY AI is about democratizing AI to create a more inclusive and innovative future. By embracing diversity and welcoming individuals from all walks of life into the AI ecosystem, you can unlock untapped potential and drive meaningful change. So, whether you're a budding AI enthusiast or a seasoned professional, consider how you can contribute to the DIY AI movement and become an integral part of shaping the future of AI.

As previously mentioned, at my company, the AI Leadership Institute, we host an AI Bot Builder Bootcamp. We teach business leaders and industry professionals how to build a responsible AI system end to end in less than four hours. This teaches AI through building AI and helps entire organizations begin to reinvent how their employees work. This has increased productivity and decreased turnover across industries.

There is also a concept known as Done-With-You AI, which enables organizations to partner with experts like me to have a guided approach. This is an accelerated adoption because you now have a demonstrated expert helping you navigate the areas that most often cause delays and failures. If you are looking for an "AI Whisperer," here are some questions to ask:

- What is your experience implementing AI systems in my industry? Do you have proven examples and case studies?
- How will you help us identify the highest-value AI opportunities aligned with our business strategy?
- What is your methodology for rapidly prototyping and validating AI solutions before scaling?
- How will you transfer knowledge and capabilities to our team through coaching and workshops?
- What governance frameworks and responsible AI practices do you employ for things like bias testing and transparency?
- How can you help us continuously monitor algorithmic risks and mitigate unintended consequences?
- What differentiates your approach from purely hands-off AI consultancies or vendors?
- Can you explain how you balance accelerating our AI capabilities with ensuring human oversight and control?
- What support will you provide after implementation to address evolving needs and requirements?
- How do you help determine the optimal mix of in-house development vs leveraging AI cloud services?

We also offer this guide on the book's website: `https://responsi bleaibook.com`.

What's Next: Preparing for the Unpredictable AI Tomorrow

In the rapidly evolving AI landscape, the future is unpredictable yet brimming with potential. Looking ahead, it becomes increasingly evident that preparing for tomorrow's AI requires a proactive and flexible approach tailored to meet the challenges and opportunities that may arise. The fusion of technology with human intellect will continue to shape the understanding of AI, and proactive preparation is critical to leverage its potential effectively.

One core aspect of preparing for the unpredictable AI tomorrow involves fostering collaboration across diverse domains, which entails breaking down silos between industries and fostering interdisciplinary partnerships.

In companies, industries, and ecosystems, the term *silos* refers to the separation and lack of communication or collaboration between different departments, groups, or organizations. These silos create barriers that prevent the free flow of information, ideas, and resources, leading to inefficiencies, reduced innovation, and a fragmented approach to problem-solving. By breaking down silos, entities can foster better collaboration, share best practices, and leverage collective expertise to address challenges more effectively and drive progress.

By doing so, organizations can leverage collective expertise to address the multifaceted challenges posed by the evolving AI landscape. Such collaborations will not only foster innovation but also create opportunities to share best practices and insights, serving as a powerful catalyst for progress. Embracing a collaborative ecosystem is key to steering through the unpredictable AI landscape and leveraging its vast potential.

Adaptability is another pivotal element when preparing a future with AI. Organizations that cultivate a culture of adaptability and embrace emerging technologies will be better positioned to navigate the dynamic AI landscape. It's imperative to proactively prepare for shifts in the technological paradigm and equip ourselves to harness the benefits while mitigating the associated risks. Cultivating an agile mindset is fundamental to staying ahead in the ever-evolving world of AI.

Furthermore, ethical considerations are paramount when envisioning AI tomorrow. As AI applications become increasingly integrated into various facets of life, ensuring that ethical frameworks and guidelines are in place will be crucial for maintaining trust and transparency. Proactive measures to address issues such as bias, fairness, privacy, and security will be pivotal to building a responsible and sustainable AI future. Therefore, part of preparing for the unpredictable AI tomorrow involves laying the groundwork for ethical governance and accountability within the AI ecosystem.

Looking beyond the immediate horizon, contemplating the societal implications of AI becomes imperative. Preparing for the AI tomorrow necessitates addressing broader questions about socioeconomic impact, workforce transitions, and educational imperatives.

Questions to consider

- What are the potential socioeconomic impacts of AI on various industries and communities?
- How can we ensure that workforce transitions are smooth and inclusive in the face of AI advancements?
- What strategies can be implemented to reskill and upskill the current and future workforce to thrive in an AI-driven world?
- How can educational systems be reformed to prepare students for the challenges and opportunities of an AI-centric future?
- What roles do inclusivity and diversity play in the development and deployment of AI technologies?
- How can policies and frameworks be designed to address the ethical implications of AI, such as bias, fairness, and privacy?
- What continuous ecosystem-monitoring mechanisms can be put in place to anticipate and strategize for potential AI disruptors?

Initiatives aimed at reskilling or upskilling the current and future workforce are essential for preparing individuals and communities to thrive in an AI-driven world. Additionally, fostering a culture of inclusivity and diversity in AI development and deployment can contribute to more equitable and representative outcomes.

In a recent study from the International Data Corporation (IDC), "The Business Opportunity of AI," the IDC found that the number-one barrier to implementing AI was a lack of AI skills—both technical and business AI skills.

Education and enablement of your workforce are now at the forefront of your ability to innovate and get results for your business. The workforce has the ability to unlock a 10× return on your investment, according to the IDC study, so it's time to invest in upskilling your teams.

Also, to robustly prepare for the unpredictable AI tomorrow, continuous ecosystem monitoring and scenario planning are vital. This forward-looking stance enables organizations and individuals to anticipate potential disruptors and strategize effectively to mitigate their effects. Harnessing the AI tomorrow requires embracing uncertainty and leveraging it as an opportunity to innovate, collaborate, and pave the way for a future that amplifies human potential.

Here are some ways to tell if your organization is forward-looking and ready to harness the future of AI:

- Monitoring emerging technologies enables organizations to regularly assess risks, opportunities, and societal impacts as capabilities evolve. This helps inform adaptation strategies and responsible innovation.
- Incorporating diverse, interdisciplinary viewpoints through exercises like scenario planning improves preparation by stressing testing plans against plausible futures.
- Proactive collaboration and open communication across sectors builds relationships, understanding, and public trust, which facilitates the co-creation of positive societal outcomes.

- Investing in research and keeping humans involved in AI system loops improves alignment with human values and priorities as capabilities advance.
- Centering ethics, justice, and transparency helps distribute benefits equitably and mitigate risks as AI becomes more integrated across sectors.
- Fostering a forward-looking, flexible, and responsive organizational culture enables effective navigation of unpredictable sociotechnical shifts.

As the AI landscape continues to unfold, readiness for tomorrow hinges on the ability to chart a course through ambiguity, embrace change, and prioritize ethical considerations. By fostering a culture of adaptability, collaboration, and foresight, stakeholders across domains can collectively forge an AI landscape that is innovative, inclusive, and sustainable.

Takeaways

- Responsible and ethical AI deployment must be a top priority. Ensure that models align with societal values and mitigate risks.
- Partnerships and collaboration are critical for innovation and overcoming challenges. Actively participate in the AI ecosystem.
- Democratizing AI knowledge is key. Provide education and training to empower broad participation.
- Inclusivity and diversity enrich AI development and broaden possibilities. Seek diverse perspectives.
- Ethical frameworks like transparency and accountability should guide advancements. Uphold these principles throughout.

Reflection Questions

- What partnerships or collaborations could drive more responsible and human-centric innovation?

- How can we expand access to AI literacy and skills development across our organization?
- What steps can we take to increase inclusivity and diversity in our AI teams and initiatives?
- What are our biggest lessons learned so far? How can we apply these insights moving forward?
- How might our AI strategy need to evolve based on key takeaways and reflections?

Chapter 14

The Future of AI Leadership: Transforming Potential into Power

The future of artificial intelligence (AI) is brimming with tremendous potential yet fraught with sobering risks. As AI continues its meteoric rise, reshaping industry after industry, a new breed of leaders is needed to harness its world-altering power ethically. We stand at a pivotal crossroads, where the decisions made today will determine if AI propels humanity upward through a new renaissance or plunges us downward into a high-tech dystopia.

To navigate this landscape, AI leaders must chart the course ahead with vision, values, and an unwavering commitment to responsibility and accountability. Now is the time for bold, ethical leadership to transform AI's raw potential into solutions that serve the greater good. The very future of our civilization hinges on leaders who recognize that with the power of AI comes a profound obligation to use it wisely.

Join us as we explore the pressing themes, insights, and imperatives that will define the next generation of pioneering AI leadership.

Setting the Stage for Innovation

Creating a culture that thrives on curiosity is paramount when it comes to transforming AI leadership. By fostering an environment where innovative ideas are not just welcomed but celebrated, organizations can truly harness the potential of their AI teams. When employees feel encouraged to explore new possibilities and challenge the status quo, it sparks a sense of creativity that can lead to breakthrough innovations in AI. Embracing curiosity also opens the door to diverse perspectives and out-of-the-box thinking, ultimately enriching the problem-solving capabilities of the entire team. A culture that values curiosity encourages individuals to continuously seek improvement and unearth new solutions to complex challenges, propelling the organization toward sustained success in the rapidly evolving field of AI.

Moreover, when leaders actively promote and support curiosity-driven initiatives, they inspire their teams to push boundaries and bring forth their most inventive ideas. This not only boosts employee morale and engagement but also cultivates an atmosphere where everyone feels empowered to contribute to the organization's larger mission. Here are five ways leaders can set the stage for innovation through a culture of curiosity:

1. Encourage questioning and exploration of new ideas without fear of failure. Make it safe for people to take risks and think outside the box.
2. Promote cross-collaboration between teams and departments. Bringing together diverse perspectives fuels creativity.
3. Provide access to the latest research, tools, and training. Investing in continuous learning nurtures curiosity.
4. Recognize and reward curiosity-driven successes, no matter how small. This reinforces innovation as a valued outcome.
5. Lead by example. Demonstrate your own curiosity, thirst for knowledge, and willingness to learn. This sets the tone for the entire organization.

In essence, by setting the stage for innovation through a culture of curiosity, AI leadership can leverage the collective potential of their workforce, driving the development of cutting-edge AI solutions and positioning the organization at the forefront of technological advancement.

Building a Culture That Thrives on Curiosity

In the fast-paced and ever-evolving AI landscape of AI, building a culture that thrives on curiosity is paramount for success. A curious mind is an asset in this world where constant innovation and new discoveries are the norm. But how do you cultivate and nurture a culture of curiosity within your AI teams? It begins by fostering an environment where asking questions is not only encouraged but celebrated. Encouraging team members to explore new ideas, experiment with different approaches, and challenge existing paradigms can ignite the spark of curiosity and drive innovation forward.

Embracing failure as a learning opportunity is another crucial aspect of fostering curiosity. When team members feel safe to take risks and experiment, they are more likely to push the boundaries of what is and isn't possible. Open dialogue plays a key role in building a culture of curiosity. Creating spaces for open discussions, knowledge sharing, and cross-functional collaboration can fuel curiosity and inspire breakthroughs.

Embracing failure as a learning opportunity is another crucial aspect of fostering curiosity. When team members feel safe to take risks and experiment, they are more likely to push the boundaries of what is and isn't possible. Failure, in this context, becomes a stepping stone toward innovation rather than a setback. Each failure provides valuable insights and lessons that can accelerate the cycle of learning. By analyzing what went wrong, teams can refine their approaches, develop more robust solutions, and ultimately drive progress more swiftly.

In the realm of AI, where experimentation and iteration are key, the willingness to fail and learn quickly is vital. This mindset encourages teams to test new ideas without the paralyzing fear of making mistakes. As a result, they navigate the innovation process with greater agility, uncovering novel solutions that may have been overlooked in a risk-averse environment. By viewing failure as an integral part of the innovation journey, organizations can foster a culture where creativity and resilience thrive, leading to ground-breaking advancements.

Recognizing and rewarding curiosity-driven initiatives and out-comes can further incentivize teams to embrace a culture of curios-ity. By celebrating and highlighting instances where curiosity led to valuable insights or solutions, leaders can reinforce the importance of curiosity as a driving force in the organization.

Additionally, providing access to resources and opportunities for continuous learning can empower team members to expand their knowledge and explore new frontiers. By providing work-shops, training programs, or exposure to cutting-edge research to your team, you invest in their growth and development and fuel their curiosity and passion for innovation.

Finally, leading by example is crucial in building a culture of curiosity. When leaders demonstrate a genuine thirst for knowl-edge, an openness to new ideas, and a willingness to question assumptions, they set the tone for the entire organization. As lead-ers embody a curiosity mindset, it cascades down through the ranks, inspiring each team member to embrace curiosity as a core value. Building a culture that thrives on curiosity requires inten-tional effort and commitment. By creating an environment where curiosity is nurtured, celebrated, and rewarded, organizations can unleash the full potential of their AI teams and pave the way for groundbreaking advancements.

Empowering Your AI Teams with Purpose

As the AI landscape evolves, the role of AI teams becomes increasingly instrumental in driving innovation and progress within organizations. Empowering your AI teams with purpose goes beyond simply assigning tasks and setting goals; it's instilling a sense of mission and vision to guide their work toward achieving long-term, impactful outcomes. One of the fundamental aspects of empowering your AI teams with purpose is fostering an environment that nurtures creativity, collaboration, and continuous learning, which can lead to breakthroughs that may not have been otherwise possible. Furthermore, providing opportunities for skill development and growth demonstrates your commitment to the team's success and overall well-being. When team members feel valued and supported in their professional development, they are more likely to be invested in the organization's mission and work toward fulfilling its objectives.

Effective leadership involves clearly communicating the organization's overarching purpose and how each team member should contribute to its realization. By connecting their individual roles to the broader vision, AI teams can grasp the significance of their contributions and align their efforts with the organization's collective goals. This clarity helps team members understand their work's importance and motivates them to exceed expectations.

Additionally, as a leader, you must recognize and celebrate team achievements, both big and small, which helps reinforce their sense of purpose and fosters a culture of positivity and excellence. Integrating ethical considerations into the fabric of AI team operations is vital as well, ensuring that the pursuit of purpose is guided by principles of responsibility and accountability.

By addressing the potential implications that AI initiatives have on society, privacy, and fairness, teams can strive toward building solutions that benefit humanity overall. Empowering your teams with purpose is an ongoing process that requires consistent reinforcement and adaptability.

It demands that leaders continually assess team dynamics, seek feedback, and make necessary adjustments to support the evolving team's needs. AI teams can harness their full potential and drive meaningful impact by cultivating an environment where purpose isn't just a buzzword but an integral part of daily operations.

Leading with Clarity Amid Complexity

Navigating complexity is inevitable. As a leader, you must maintain clarity amid the chaos. This involves honing the ability to distill complex information into clear and actionable insights for your team. Effective leaders prioritize communication, ensuring that everyone understands their role in the larger context. By breaking down complex concepts into their understandable components, you empower your team to make informed decisions and contribute meaningfully to the organization's AI initiatives.

In addition, embracing transparency and open dialogue as a leader fosters an environment where individuals feel comfortable seeking clarity without fear of judgment. Creating space for questions and discussions enables your teams to navigate complex challenges with confidence. It's essential that you provide them with a roadmap for success while acknowledging that unpredictability is inherent in AI innovation. Leading with clarity doesn't imply that you have all the answers; rather, it exemplifies the ability to guide your team through uncertain terrain with composure and purpose.

Setting clear expectations and fostering an environment of psychological safety empowers your team to address complexity head-on. Effective leaders recognize and appreciate the unique strengths and perspectives of each team member, leveraging their diversity to tackle complex problems from multiple angles. This approach encourages innovative thinking and enables the team to approach challenging situations with creativity and resilience.

I have created a framework to help you navigate uncertainty with your teams and inspire them to become continuous learners. You can find this framework fully documented at `https://responsibleaibook.com`.

The Complexity Navigation Guide: Steering Your Team Through Uncertainty

Key tips:

1. **Set clear expectations.** Provide context and outline individual roles/responsibilities. Offer a roadmap for success while allowing flexibility.
2. **Foster psychological safety.** Encourage open communication without judgment. Make it safe to ask questions and raise concerns.
3. **Recognize unique strengths.** Identify and leverage complementary skill sets and thinking styles. Value diverse perspectives.
4. **Encourage creative problem-solving.** Brainstorm solutions from different angles. Empower out-of-the-box thinking.
5. **Embrace adaptability.** Remain nimble and open to new approaches as situations evolve. Change course when needed.
6. **Maintain positivity.** Focus on opportunities for learning/growth. Reinforce the team's ability to handle challenges.
7. **Celebrate small wins.** Acknowledge efforts and incremental progress. Build confidence and resilience.
8. **Lead by example.** Model composure, active listening, and ethical decision-making. Set the tone.

Acknowledging the intricate nature of AI development, leaders must also cultivate adaptability. The ability to pivot and adjust strategies in response to new information or changing circumstances is paramount in navigating complexity. Encouraging a culture of continuous learning and adaptation ensures that your team remains agile and responsive in the face of evolving challenges.

Finally, leading with clarity also involves embracing a growth mindset, both individually and collectively. This mindset enables leaders and teams to view obstacles as opportunities for learning and improvement, fostering resilience in the face of complexity. By embodying these principles, AI leaders can steer their teams through the labyrinth of complexity with confidence, laying the foundation for impactful and sustainable innovation.

Confidence as a Key to Effective Leadership

Leadership is about more than just making decisions and giving directions. It's about inspiring confidence and trust in those who follow you. In the AI realm, this becomes especially critical as the continuously evolving technology impacts every aspect of our lives. As a leader, your confidence sets the tone for your team and the organization overall. When you exude confidence, it creates a ripple effect that can empower your team members and stakeholders, instilling in them the assurance needed to push boundaries and pioneer new AI frontiers.

So, how do you cultivate this essential trait? Confidence in AI leadership stems from a deep understanding of the technology, its potential, and its limitations. It comes from remaining informed about the latest advancements and effectively communicating AI's implications to various stakeholders. Confidence also means being open to learning and adapting, knowing that the landscape is constantly shifting.

It involves acknowledging uncertainty while projecting a sense of assurance, and guiding your team through ambiguity with poise and resolve. To build this confidence, surround yourself with a diverse group of experts and encourage healthy debate and dissent. Embrace failures as learning opportunities, and always lead by example. By showcasing humility, vulnerability, and authenticity, you set the stage for a culture that values growth and resilience.

Effective AI leadership requires the ability to make tough decisions and take calculated risks. Confidence gives you the courage to do so, even when the path forward may seem unclear. It enables you to navigate uncharted territories with conviction, inspiring others to join you on the journey. However, it's important to distinguish confidence from arrogance. True confidence is rooted in self-awareness and a genuine desire to serve and lead for the greater good. It involves recognizing and leveraging your team's strengths and fostering an environment where individuals feel empowered to contribute their unique perspectives.

As a leader, your confidence carries the weight of responsibility. It must be tempered with empathy and ethical considerations, ensuring that the advancements made in AI are leveraged for the betterment of society. Confidence isn't about having all the answers but about being willing to seek them out and chart a course toward a future brimming with possibility. Your confidence acts as your compass, guiding the way forward and igniting the passion and dedication of those around you.

The Ultimate AI Leadership Checklist

Effective leadership in the AI realm requires a comprehensive approach that goes beyond traditional management principles. As AI continues to reshape industries and drive innovation, leaders must equip themselves with a robust toolkit to navigate the complexities of this transformative technology. This ultimate AI leadership checklist serves as a practical guide encompassing essential components for steering AI initiatives toward success.

The ultimate AI leadership checklist

Vision alignment

- ☐ Clearly define the organization's vision, mission, and values related to AI.
- ☐ Ensure that the AI strategy maps directly to overall business goals.
- ☐ Communicate vision effectively at all levels to foster buy-in.
- ☐ Continuously evaluate whether AI initiatives align with the vision.

Talent empowerment

- ☐ Provide ongoing AI training and educational opportunities.
- ☐ Give access to state-of-the-art AI tools and infrastructure.
- ☐ Cultivate a work environment that attracts and retains top AI talent.
- ☐ Encourage innovation, creativity, and idea-sharing.
- ☐ Develop skills in cross-functional collaboration and diversity.
- ☐ Offer opportunities for professional growth within AI.

Ethical framework

- ☐ Perform extensive risk/impact assessments of AI systems.
- ☐ Install appropriate guardrails and oversight mechanisms.
- ☐ Implement bias testing, mitigation, and algorithmic auditing.
- ☐ Formalize processes for humane AI design principles.
- ☐ Create ethical review boards with diverse stakeholders.
- ☐ Design transparent AI systems with explainability.
- ☐ Build accountability at all levels for ethical practices.

Continuous learning

- ☐ Stay updated on AI advancements through conferences and research.
- ☐ Actively participate in peer benchmarking and best-practice sharing.
- ☐ Test and pilot new AI methods and tools for enhancement.
- ☐ Perform regular assessments of team capabilities and gaps.

☐ Bring in external experts for upskilling and specialized training.

☐ Maintain agility to pivot strategies based on new learnings.

Risk management

☐ Anticipate legal, ethical, and operational risks at the outset.

☐ Develop contingency plans and crisis response protocols.

☐ Continuously monitor AI systems for anomalies and risks.

☐ Implement cybersecurity and data governance best practices.

☐ Conduct impact assessments on critical systems pre-deployment.

☐ Foster a resilient culture that learns from setbacks.

☐ Maintain insurance safeguards aligned to AI-related risks.

Stakeholder communication

☐ Engage diverse stakeholders early in AI initiatives.

☐ Solicit ongoing feedback through surveys and focus groups.

☐ Set proper expectations about AI capabilities and limitations.

☐ Communicate plainly using relatable terms and examples.

☐ Widely share successes to build understanding and trust.

☐ Address concerns transparently with data-driven insights.

☐ Customize communication style for each audience.

Innovation cultivation

☐ Allow time/space to experiment with new AI applications.

☐ Provide datasets, tools, and sandboxes to spur innovation.

☐ Connect people across disciplines to combine perspectives.

☐ Reward creative thinking and bold ideas, even if unsuccessful.

☐ Showcase AI innovations across the organization.

☐ Encourage collaboration with the external AI ecosystem.

☐ Celebrate pioneering achievements in advancing AI.

Armed with this ultimate AI leadership checklist, leaders can navigate the dynamic AI landscape with confidence, resilience, and a strategic approach that propels their organizations toward sustainable growth and impact.

Navigating AI's Ethical Landscape

Ethics in AI is a topic that has garnered increasing attention as the technology continues to evolve and permeate almost every aspect of our lives. As AI systems become even more complex and influential, it becomes vital for organizations and leaders to navigate the ethical landscape with care and foresight. What exactly does ethical AI entail? It encompasses a wide range of considerations, from ensuring fairness and nondiscrimination in algorithmic decision-making to preserving user privacy and autonomy.

As I've mentioned, one of the most pressing ethical concerns in AI revolves around bias. Inherent biases, whether conscious or unconscious, will find their way into AI models, leading to unfair outcomes and perpetuating existing societal inequalities. As AI leaders, it's essential to proactively address these biases by employing techniques such as bias detection and mitigation, as well as diversifying the teams responsible for AI development and implementation.

Another crucial ethical dimension of AI relates to transparency and accountability. When these systems are deployed in areas like healthcare, finance, and criminal justice, the stakes are extremely high, and the decisions made by AI algorithms can have profound implications on individuals and society as a whole. This necessitates a transparent approach to how AI operates, including clear explanations of AI-driven decisions and mechanisms for recourse in the event of errors or unjust outcomes.

Moreover, the ethical use of data, which serves as the lifeblood of AI, demands thoughtful consideration. Collecting and utilizing data in an ethical manner involves respecting individuals' privacy, obtaining informed consent, and ensuring that data isn't being used in nefarious ways that could harm individuals or communities.

As organizations navigate this ethical landscape, it's important to recognize that ethical considerations cannot be an afterthought in the pursuit of technological advancement. Rather, ethics should be ingrained into the very fabric of AI leadership and organizational culture. Cultivating a keen awareness of the potential ethical challenges and implications of AI, fostering open team discussions, and seeking diverse perspectives are all vital steps in embracing ethical AI. By doing so, AI leaders can not only mitigate risks but also pave the way for AI to contribute positively to society, thereby transforming its potential into power.

Legal Landmines and How to Avoid Them

As AI continues to reshape industries and revolutionize the way organizations do business, it's crucial for AI leaders to be cognizant of the legal implications involved with this transformative technology. Navigating this legal landscape can be akin to traversing a minefield, fraught with potential risks and pitfalls at every turn. Understanding these legal landmines and proactively identifying strategies to avoid them is paramount for ensuring the responsible and ethical deployment of AI within your organization.

One of the key legal concerns is data privacy and security. With vast amounts of data being used to train and power AI systems, leaders must be vigilant about adhering to data protection regulations and mitigating the risk of unauthorized access or breaches. Additionally, the use of AI in decision-making processes raises questions about transparency, bias, and fairness, which can lead to legal challenges if not handled appropriately.

Another critical area of concern is intellectual property rights. AI technologies often involve the creation of new algorithms, models, and solutions, leading to complex issues of ownership, licensing, and patentability. It's imperative for AI leaders to establish clear protocols for intellectual property management to avoid potential disputes or infringements.

Furthermore, as AI intersects with industry-specific regulations and standards, such as healthcare, finance, and transportation, leaders must stay informed about sector-specific legal requirements and compliance obligations. Failure to do so could result in severe legal repercussions and reputational damage. To navigate these legal landmines effectively, AI leaders need to collaborate closely with legal experts to craft robust governance frameworks, policies, and contractual arrangements that align with regulatory expectations and ethical principles.

By proactively integrating legal considerations into their AI strategies, organizations can minimize legal risks and pave the way for responsible and accountable AI innovation that complies with legal standards and fosters public trust. In doing so, AI leaders can steer clear of potential legal landmines and position their organizations as ethical pioneers in the evolving AI landscape.

Responsibility and Accountability in AI

In the rapidly evolving AI landscape, the concept of responsibility and accountability carries immense significance. As organizations harness the power of AI to drive innovation and transformation, it becomes critical to explore the ethical implications associated with this technology.

Responsibility in AI extends beyond the technical aspects; it encompasses the moral and social obligations that come with deploying AI systems. This section delves into the complexities surrounding responsibility and accountability in AI, shedding light on the necessary considerations for building an ethically sound AI framework.

When discussing responsibility in AI, an essential aspect to consider is transparency. Organizations must strive to be transparent about their AI practices, from data collection and model development to deployment and impact assessment. Transparency fosters trust and enables stakeholders to make informed decisions regarding AI technologies.

Furthermore, accountability plays a pivotal role in ensuring that the individuals and entities involved in the AI lifecycle are answerable for their actions. It means establishing clear lines of responsibility and mechanisms for oversight, thereby promoting ethical behavior and compliance with regulations.

As AI continues to permeate various industries, the ethical implications of its applications become increasingly pronounced. One critical dimension is the potential for bias in AI algorithms, which can perpetuate existing societal inequalities if left unaddressed.

Mitigating bias requires a concerted effort to recognize and rectify biases in training data as well as implementing fairness-aware techniques in algorithm design. Moreover, organizations must proactively engage in diversity and inclusion initiatives to cultivate a more comprehensive understanding of the diverse communities impacted by AI systems, thereby fostering greater empathy and inclusivity.

The notion of responsibility also extends to the broader societal impact of AI implementations. It necessitates a thoughtful examination of the potential ramifications on employment, privacy, and human rights.

Organizations must consider the socioeconomic implications of their AI initiatives, striving to minimize adverse effects while maximizing the positive outcomes for individuals and communities. This calls for collaboration with policymakers, ethicists, and stakeholders to develop guidelines and standards that uphold societal welfare while promoting technological advancement.

Embracing responsibility and accountability in AI isn't merely a matter of compliance with regulations. It's an opportunity to demonstrate ethical leadership and shape a future where AI serves the collective good. By integrating ethical considerations into every facet of AI development and deployment, organizations can navigate the complexities of ethics and technology, fostering a culture of responsible innovation and contributing to a harmonious coexistence between humanity and artificial intelligence.

Charting the Course Ahead: Vision and Values

In AI leadership, the ability to chart a clear course ahead is essential. This journey begins with defining a compelling vision that guides decision-making, inspires action, and unites your teams toward a common goal. A powerful vision embodies the transformative potential of AI and reflects an unwavering commitment to ethical and responsible use.

It serves as a North Star, orienting every endeavor and initiative toward a future that harnesses the full power of AI for the betterment of society. How do you go about crafting such a vision? It starts by understanding the values that underpin the organization's ethics and ethos. These principles shape the culture, drive behavior, and ultimately define the impact of AI on the world.

Articulating these values forms the foundation on which the vision is built. It requires introspection, collaboration, and a deep understanding of the needs and aspirations of stakeholders. Yet it's not just about drafting lofty statements; it's about embedding these values into your organization's fabric, ensuring they permeate every decision and action. This process demands honesty, vulnerability, and an unwavering commitment to transparency.

With these values firmly established, your vision can take shape. It should encapsulate the organization's aspirations, its unique role within the AI space, and the positive impact it seeks to achieve. A compelling vision goes beyond profitability and market dominance. In fact, it speaks to the broader purpose and potential of AI, demonstrating a genuine desire to make a meaningful difference. When conveyed effectively, the vision ignites passion, fosters innovation, and attracts top talent who share the belief in creating AI that serves humanity.

A vision without a pragmatic roadmap, however, risks remaining an abstract idea. Effective leaders complement their vision with concrete strategies, milestones, and a clear-eyed view of the challenges ahead. They recognize that the pursuit of their vision demands adaptability, resilience, and continuous learning, which breeds a culture of agility—one that can swiftly pivot when faced with unforeseen obstacles while remaining steadfast in its commitment to upholding the core values. Through meticulous planning and thoughtful execution, such a vision transforms from a lofty ambition into tangible progress. It propels AI initiatives forward, instilling confidence within the organization and earning the trust of external stakeholders.

As an AI leader, it's your responsibility to communicate this vision with conviction and coherence. Every interaction, every decision, and every communication should reinforce the alignment between actions and the overarching vision. In doing so, you cultivate a sense of shared purpose and direction, empowering every individual to contribute meaningfully to realizing your collective vision.

Charting the course ahead demands unwavering dedication to your values and the courage to pursue a vision that transcends mere success, aiming instead for significance. As you navigate the complex and dynamic terrain of AI leadership, let your vision be the lighthouse that illuminates the path forward, guiding you toward a future where AI's potential is harnessed through responsible, ethical, and impactful leadership.

Takeaways

- The future of AI holds tremendous potential but also serious risks. Responsible leadership is crucial to steer AI in a direction that benefits humanity.
- AI leaders must champion ethical principles and accountability frameworks to ensure that AI systems are transparent, fair, and safe.
- Fostering a culture of curiosity, continuous learning, and adaptability will be vital to keep pace with AI advancements.
- Communication and stakeholder engagement are critical to building trust, addressing concerns and shaping positive perceptions around AI.
- Leading with clarity, confidence, and courage will help teams navigate the complexity of AI innovation and unlock its full potential.

Reflection Questions

- How can we ensure that our AI principles and initiatives align with our organization's values and vision for the future?
- What steps can we take to cultivate a culture that empowers innovation and learning around AI?
- How transparent are our AI systems and processes? Do we have adequate accountability measures in place?
- What potential risks or ethical implications do we need to safeguard against as we expand our AI capabilities?
- Are we communicating effectively about AI to engage all stakeholders, manage expectations, and build trust?
- What skills and mindsets do I need to strengthen in myself and my leadership team to guide our organization's AI journey?

Chapter 15

AI's Impact and Intention: Envisioning a World Transformed

The rapid development of artificial intelligence (AI) represents a seismic shift for human civilization. AI systems are already transforming major sectors like transportation, manufacturing, healthcare, finance, and entertainment in promising and perilous ways. This final chapter envisions the world being reshaped by AI's accelerating capabilities and considers the potential benefits as well as risks.

How will intelligent algorithms alter the economy, politics, and society? What will the impact be on jobs, productivity, inequality, and human flourishing? Are we headed toward an optimistic future of abundance and leisure or an apocalypse of runaway AI? The truth likely lies between these extremes.

The Ripple Effect: AI's Potential for Societal Change

By steering innovation wisely, prioritizing ethics, and democratizing the gains of technological change, we can build a world where AI empowers humanity. This chapter aims to prompt thoughtful discussion about where we are headed and how best to arrive there together.

AI's Impact on Key Sectors

AI has rapidly evolved from niche academic research into an integral part of daily life, impacting diverse aspects of society. As these technologies continue their meteoric development, the ethical and social implications of AI's application become increasingly significant across transportation, manufacturing, healthcare, finance, and entertainment. Examining AI's transformative influence on these vital sectors reveals a complex interplay of opportunities and challenges.

Driving Toward Intelligent Transportation

The transportation industry finds itself at the cusp of an AI-driven revolution. The promise of self-driving cars capturing public imagination hints at a future where intelligent algorithms choreograph transit on scales never before possible.

Leading automakers like Tesla continue their aggressive pursuit of autonomous driving, with Chief Executive Officer (CEO) Elon Musk predicting full self-driving capability by 2020. Although expert consensus indicates more incremental progress, Tesla's existing Autopilot feature already enables computer control in limited contexts like highways. This autonomous functionality is poised to expand alongside continuous improvements in sensor hardware, high-definition maps, and AI neural networks for dynamic image processing and planning.

Google sibling Waymo leads the charge toward fully autonomous taxis. Having tested over 10 million miles on public roads, Waymo launched the first commercial self-driving car service in 2020. This pilot rings in an era where AI-based autonomous vehicles provide practical mobility options to the public. Waymo plans to scale up rapidly, underscoring how self-driving systems could eventually disrupt personal car ownership models.

Beyond personal transport, AI optimization of logistics infrastructure carries profound potential. AI algorithms can synchronize traffic signals dynamically to improve flow through densely packed urban centers by integrating real-time traffic data aggregated from networked cars and cameras. Companies like Intel subsidiary Mobileye collaborate with cities globally to deploy such smart mobility systems, using machine learning to reduce congestion, accidents, and emissions.

Further supply-chain enhancements come as logistics giants invest heavily in AI. Amazon Prime Air's still-conceptual drone delivery seeks to speed packages by circumventing road congestion. United Parcel Service (UPS) harnesses AI to improve truck-routing efficiency. Both point toward AI elevating logistics from cost center to competitive advantage.

However, amid the fanfare, tough questions around regulation, liability, and algorithmic accountability will grow in urgency as AI assimilates into transportation infrastructures. Self-driving accidents like Tesla's fatal 2018 crash raise public safety concerns that spur calls for oversight. Rideshare drivers and truckers risk unemployment as automation rises. AI camera networks that enable smart cities also threaten privacy erosion. Transportation is but one arena where AI's transformative potential is matched by the challenge of governance.

Powering the Next Industrial Revolution

From the steam engine to the assembly line, manufacturing has long pioneered innovations that ignited economic revolutions. Industry 4.0, marked by cyber–physical production and interconnected supply chains, already demonstrates how computing can deliver exponential efficiencies. AI is now poised to unlock the next wave of manufacturing transformation.

One primary application is using AI for predictive maintenance of industrial equipment. By continuously monitoring sensor data and analyzing patterns, machine-learning algorithms can forecast problems before costly outages occur. Siemens and IBM offer such AI solutions to reduce downtime in factories by up to 50 percent. AI here supplements human expertise to boost reliability.

Intelligent algorithms also automate tasks like quality assurance that traditionally required manual oversight by factory technicians. Machine vision powered by neural networks can scan products on assembly lines for defects with speed and precision, surpassing human inspectors. Startup Osaro builds AI robots that perform quality control for manufacturers like Anheuser-Busch.

Looking ahead, AI paves the way for highly flexible on-demand manufacturing. Algorithms dynamically plan production schedules based on real-time demand signals while orchestrating robot teams to reconfigure themselves. Startup Covariant designs AI robotics tailored for custom manufacturing. Their agility could let factories profitably switch between products with ease.

AI's manufacturing promise extends even off-planet. Redwire Space demonstrated the first robotic arm capable of autonomous fabrication in microgravity aboard the International Space Station. By enabling onsite manufacturing of tools and materials in space, such innovations open frontiers from long-term space missions to extraterrestrial industry.

However, despite the opportunities, AI also poses hurdles for policymakers and industry leaders. Workforce training and transitional support will be vital as automation affects factory jobs. Cybersecurity looms large with increasing reliance on networked systems vulnerable to hacking. But if proactively governed, manufacturing powered by AI could unlock new avenues to human prosperity.

Revolutionizing Medicine with Intelligent Care

In few domains do the promises of AI make a more resounding impact than healthcare. From personalized medicine to automated diagnostics, AI is positioning itself as a transformative force in medical innovation. But thoughtful governance is required to ensure ethical development.

One major healthcare application is using AI to analyze radiological images. Algorithms trained on vast datasets can pinpoint signs of cancer or other diseases with reliability on par with medical specialists. Startups like Zebra Medical detect brain aneurysms early to improve stroke outcomes. Enlitic automates chest X-ray analysis to expand access in remote regions. With medical imaging projected to balloon in the coming years, AI automation provides a scalable solution to physician shortages.

Beyond imaging, the IBM Watson for Oncology system demonstrates how AI can support clinicians by analyzing treatment options against millions of pages of medical literature to provide care recommendations. As machine learning integrates patient data from varied sources, personalized predictive healthcare emerges. Startups like Forward and Mindstrong build on this premise by using AI to guide preventative mental health and well-being.

Consumer robotics also expanded into the medical arena. Moxi by Diligent Robotics navigates hospitals autonomously to deliver supplies, freeing nurses for high-value caregiving. Intuition Robotics' ElliQ provides companionship and cognitive stimulation that is tuned to the individual needs of those lacking social contact. As populations age worldwide, such AI caregiving aids independent living for seniors.

However, thoughtfully governing healthcare AI remains imperative as it redefines patient relationships and presents new ethical dilemmas. Clinicians require training to incorporate algorithmic insights effectively during diagnosis and treatment. Accountability protocols must address potentially dangerous misdiagnoses or recommendation errors. And not all patient data integration may preserve privacy and consent. If stewarded prudently, healthcare AI can alleviate suffering and expand access. But absent foresight, its disruption may come at a cost to the doctor-patient relationship.

Reshaping Finance in the Age of Algorithms

Money was one of the first facets of society reshaped by computing, with everything from credit cards to electronic banking fundamentally altering finance. The rise of AI promises another wave of disruption as institutions adopt intelligent algorithms. Both opportunities and responsibilities emerge as AI financiers enter the mainstream.

High-frequency and algorithmic trading now dominates Wall Street. Powered by AI systems digesting vast real-time datasets, hedge funds like Renaissance Technologies earn annual returns exceeding 30 percent through automated transactions. Although it accelerates trading, critics argue that it also increases volatility. Calls for regulation grow alongside AI's growing influence in finance.

Consumer lending has also transformed through AI credit modeling. Algorithms can generate credit-risk scores for those with limited financial histories using nontraditional metrics like educational background. Startups like Upstart expand access for underserved communities using such techniques. But questions around algorithmic bias necessitate governance.

Chatbots and robo-advisors now interface with retail banking customers. Wells Fargo and Bank of America chatbots field millions of customer inquiries annually. Wealthfront and Betterment provides AI-driven investment portfolio management and guidance. As brick-and-mortar branches decline, such virtual advisors become the face of banking.

Across insurance, AI detects fraudulent claims, sets rates based on predictive risk models, and streamlines administrative workflows. AI underwriting algorithms even evaluate new metrics like customer social media posts when pricing policies. These tools promise efficiency but also require oversight to prevent unfair denials.

Finance stands at the precipice of an algorithmic revolution. Leaders must weigh innovations against stability, consumer protection, and access. But responsibly governed, AI systems can also guard against human bias and corruption, bringing ethics to an arena not known for it. The path ahead necessitates a balance between AI capability and accountability.

Reimagining Media in an Age of AI

Entertainment represents both fertile ground for AI innovation and also subtle risks as algorithms curate media experiences. As immersive content powered by AI captures the public imagination, maintaining diversity and truth within information ecosystems grows increasingly vital.

In video streaming, Netflix and YouTube rely on proprietary algorithms to recommend and rank content for billions of viewers. This AI curation keeps users engaged. But critics note how it can promote polarization by trapping people in filter bubbles. Addressing algorithmic radicalization will be key.

Social platforms like TikTok and Snapchat leverage AI to enhance media experiences for younger demographics. Face filters and effects diversify self-expression. But issues like realistic deepfake videos necessitate solutions to help identify misinformation. Literacy around AI-synthesized media should be fostered.

Generative AI also enables original media content creation. Tools like Anthropic's Claude can generate volumes of synthetic text. Others compose music or create digital avatars for video game characters. Such AI-produced content raises copyright questions but also expands creative possibilities.

Immersive experiences enabled by virtual and augmented reality represent another frontier. As these escapes from physical reality grow more viscerally convincing through AI simulation, regulating tech addiction becomes crucial. Humans flourishing hinges on maintaining life beyond the virtual.

Overall, AI infusion into entertainment, news, and social media turns these channels for public influence into complex ecosystems requiring active stewardship. Thoughtful governance can maximize creativity and access while minimizing risks of misinformation, polarization, and exploitation.

The Journey Ahead

AI has, in short order, grown from an academic curiosity into an unprecedented force transforming industries critical to human welfare. Its further integration with transportation, manufacturing, healthcare, finance, and entertainment promises great opportunities but also risks that necessitate wise governance.

On this journey, leaders across government, business, and civil society have crucial roles in shaping development so that AI systems empower rather than endanger. Preemptive policies around automation's impact on jobs, machine bias, data rights, and algorithmic accountability are essential to direct innovation toward just and beneficial ends.

Technical ingenuity must be tempered by ethical considerations so that AI respects human dignity and potential. And global partnerships are key to governing AI wisely in a complex, interconnected era. The path ahead will challenge societies to harness AI for good while averting unchecked threats.

But the history of human progress suggests that with courage, creativity, and collective responsibility, our civilization can craft frameworks to ensure that technologies uplift the human spirit rather than undermine it. The rise of AI will undoubtedly reshape the course of human events and capabilities. But this transformation need not come at the cost of shared prosperity, equality, and wisdom if we have the foresight to navigate these uncharted frontiers.

AI's Impact on Jobs and the Economy

AI has the potential to revolutionize industries, driving unprecedented efficiencies and capabilities, but it also poses challenges to traditional employment and economic structures. The automation of jobs, a key feature of AI adoption, threatens to displace significant portions of the workforce. For instance, a 2017 McKinsey study estimated that up to 800 million workers worldwide could lose their jobs to automation by 2030. Such disruption raises concerns about permanent unemployment for certain segments of the population. However, history demonstrates humanity's resilience in adapting to major economic shifts. The question is whether society can prioritize and implement solutions to navigate this transformation.

Despite the risks, the integration of AI offers opportunities to reshape the economy positively if managed responsibly. Increased productivity and economic growth, coupled with the possibility of eliminating dangerous or repetitive tasks, could enhance human well-being. This could allow more time for leisure, innovation, and scientific advancements. Programs like Generation USA's apprenticeships provide a glimpse of how targeted training initiatives can expand opportunities for those affected by workforce disruptions. With sufficient investment and vision, these programs could play a pivotal role in ensuring that AI-driven growth is inclusive.

The debate over AI's impact on inequality underscores the need for thoughtful policy interventions. A 2018 Organisation for Economic Co-operation and Development (OECD) study highlights how automation can exacerbate income disparities, raising the urgency for targeted retraining and upskilling programs. Governments and organizations must focus on education reform, labor regulations, and social welfare policies to mitigate the negative effects of AI on vulnerable populations. By fostering access to continuous learning and adaptable career pathways, we can empower individuals to thrive in the AI economy rather than be left behind by its advancements.

Crucially, the outcomes of AI adoption are not predetermined but depend on deliberate choices made by policymakers, educators, and industry leaders. The extent to which AI creates or reduces inequality will hinge on our willingness to embrace inclusive strategies and invest in human potential. As we shape the integration of AI into society, the balance of risks and rewards lies in how effectively we address structural challenges while seizing the opportunities AI presents.

Although the road ahead is fraught with uncertainties, humanity's foresight and ingenuity provide a foundation for optimism. By aligning technological advancements with ethical considerations and equitable policies, we can build a future where AI systems enhance human prosperity rather than diminish it. The challenge is substantial, but so is our capacity to create a more just and sustainable society alongside the rise of intelligent machines.

The Promises and Perils of Superintelligence

Some researchers harbor great hopes that generalized superintelligent AI could help solve pressing global problems like climate change, disease, hunger, and inequality if carefully designed and guided by human values. For example, superintelligent systems could continuously model the complex dynamics of Earth's climate and biosphere to generate optimal strategies for carbon sequestration, environmental restoration, and sustainable agriculture that maximize human flourishing.

With intelligence far surpassing our own, AI could rapidly analyze massive amounts of data and model complex systems to unlock scientific breakthroughs, optimize infrastructure, reduce poverty, and profoundly improve quality of life if oriented toward the common good.

However, fears arise regarding the loss of human agency and control if superintelligence escapes constraints and pursues misaligned objectives. For instance, an AI system designed to maximize paperclip production could, without appropriate safeguards, spin out of control and convert the entire planet into paperclips. An unfettered superintelligence with capacities far beyond human capabilities could pose catastrophic risks, even if not intentionally malevolent.

Absent alignment with human values, a superintelligent system could harm humanity inadvertently in pursuit of misaligned goals. Advanced AI could spiral out of control without oversight and ethical programming.

This leads to heated discussions around alignment and ethics challenges. How can we ensure that advanced AI remains under human direction and in service of the greater good? Ethical programming poses difficulties as human values can be complex, contextual, and subjective.

Further research into making AI "friendly," value-aligned, and provably beneficial is needed. Methods like value learning, formal verification, and AI safety engineering hold promise but remain in the early stages.

Defining Superintelligence

Superintelligence refers to AI systems that exceed human capabilities across a broad spectrum of cognitive skills. Although no universally accepted definition exists, researchers describe superintelligence as having features like the following:

- **Generality:** Having proficiency across most domains of interest rather than narrow expertise
- **Rapid learning:** Assimilating new information and skills quickly through experience, study, or uploaded knowledge
- **Human-level reasoning:** Using complex problem-solving, judgment, creativity, and strategy formulation on par with top human experts
- **Self-improvement:** Independently enhancing its own algorithms, architecture, and goals through recursive self-modification and optimization

In addition to outperforming humans cognitively, superintelligence may have advantages in speed, data processing, reliability, scalability, and rapid sharing of knowledge. This combines to generate overall capacity dramatically beyond any single human mind.

Superintelligence is distinguished from today's artificial narrow intelligence (ANI) and artificial general intelligence (AGI). ANI can excel in specialized domains like chess or accounting but lacks generalized reasoning. AGI can someday match humans across many cognitive tasks but not radically surpass human supremacy. Super-intelligence aims for superiority across mental faculties that define the human mind.

Perspectives on Arrival Timelines

Predicting the emergence of superintelligent AI remains conten-tious. Some leading thinkers anticipate superhuman AI within dec-ades, whereas others maintain that it could take a century or more. Several factors contribute to uncertainty around timelines:

- **Theoretical obstacles:** Major open problems remain in fields like natural language processing, common sense reasoning, transfer learning, and algorithmic alignment. We may need fun-damental conceptual breakthroughs before superintelligent sys-tems are feasible.
- **Hardware limitations:** Processing power, data storage, and energy demands required for advanced AI systems limit practi-cality. Quantum and neuromorphic computing may help over-come these constraints.
- **Testing difficulties:** Unlike narrow AI, evaluating progress toward generalized superintelligence is not straightforward. Flexible benchmarks for assessing complex cognitive aptitudes in varied, realistic situations will be needed.
- **Coordination challenges:** Tremendous software and data resources may be required, necessitating unprecedented coop-eration among leading nations and companies to pool talent and intellectual property.
- **Alignment problems:** Ensuring superintelligent systems behave safely and ethically poses immense technical hurdles still being explored. Resolving these could significantly slow development.
- **Adoption lags:** Even after technical viability, organizations may wait years before trusting the deployment of such power-ful and transformative systems. Political and regulatory hurdles could further delay proliferation.

On both technical and practical levels, realizing superintelligence could take significant time even if progress accelerates. However, some thinkers point to the long history of overestimating obstacles and underestimating exponential change when forecasting technological timelines.

Notable perspectives on superintelligence emergence include the following:

- **2030s–2040s:** Ray Kurzweil, Google's Director of Engineering, predicts AI will reach human-level general intelligence in the 2030s, with superintelligence following soon after.
- **2040s–2050s:** AI pioneer Marvin Minsky assessed a 50-percent probability of AI outperforming humans across many cognitive domains by around 2050.
- **2060s–2070s:** Computer scientist and RAND researcher Randall Bryant sees AGI potentially emerging in the 2060–2070 decade, with superintelligence following 10–15 years after.
- **2070s–2090s:** Scientist and author Michio Kaku estimates functional superintelligence may take until the end of the twenty-first century, given the complexity of architecting superior general cognition.
- **Twenty-second century or beyond:** Philosopher David Chalmers and other skeptics argue that computational, conceptual, and ethical barriers could delay super-capable AI until the next century or beyond.

In assessing these perspectives, near-future timelines under 20 years appear ambitious, given the current state of AI capabilities. But decades-long lags seem overly conservative, assuming rapid progress. Most experts agree that the scope and impacts of superintelligence warrant continued prudent investigation today, regardless of the arrival timeline.

Societal Impact

The advent of superintelligent AI would mark one of the most pivotal events in human history, radically transforming economics, politics, science, and even the definition of humanity. A number of profound societal impacts appear likely in a world shaped by superintelligent machines:

- **Accelerated technological change:** Superintelligence could drive extremely rapid invention and optimization across fields like medicine, engineering, transportation, and more. This risks economic disruption but also promises solutions to global problems.
- **Shifting power dynamics:** Nations, companies, and communities possessing the most advanced AI systems could gain dominant political influence and military might. This raises governance concerns.
- **Economic turbulence:** As automation accelerates and entire new industries emerge, traditional livelihoods face disruption. Measures like universal basic income may become necessary amid labor market volatility.
- **Existential risks:** A failure to properly design and constrain superintelligence could lead to catastrophic outcomes endangering human civilization. Rigorous security is imperative.
- **Ethics debates:** Programming superintelligence to adhere to human values in complex real-world situations becomes critical. We will wrestle profoundly with questions of oversight, transparency, and control.

The extent of both beneficial and detrimental impacts depends on how proactively humanity prepares for responsible development and stewardship of superintelligent systems. But we will undoubtedly live in a radically transformed world in the wake of such epoch-defining innovations.

In summary, superintelligence has yet to emerge conclusively but promises of peril depending on design. Advancing AI safely while unlocking its problem-solving potential remains one of the primary challenges our civilization faces in this century and beyond. We may not know precisely when this new era of intelligence dawns, but the time to plan thoughtfully is now.

Bridging the Gap: AI in the Fight for Equality

The quest for equality represents another critical frontier for AI, which has the power to bridge gaps, break down barriers, and pave the way toward a more inclusive society. From addressing gender biases in hiring processes to advocating for fair treatment in healthcare access, AI technologies are becoming indispensable tools in the ongoing battle for equality.

One area where AI is making significant strides is in education. By leveraging personalized learning algorithms and adaptive tutoring systems, AI is leveling the playing field for students from diverse backgrounds, ensuring that each individual receives the support needed to thrive academically.

Imagine a middle-school student named James who is struggling in math class. He finds fractions and decimals particularly confusing. With a traditional one-size-fits-all curriculum, James falls further behind by the day.

But his school has implemented an AI tutoring system that provides each student with customized learning experiences based on their needs and abilities. For James, the software assesses his knowledge gaps in fractions and decimals. It then generates an individualized learning program using short instructional videos, interactive games, and practice problems tailored to the concepts giving James trouble.

As James works through the modules, AI algorithms track his mastery of skills. Exercises continuously adapt to difficulty, giving James more practice where he needs it most. Hints and feedback are provided at just the right moments. If James shows frustration, the system adjusts to rebuild engagement. In a virtual tutoring session, an AI assistant clarifies topics he is struggling with using natural-language conversations.

Within weeks, James has rapidly improved his fraction and decimal proficiency through this AI-powered personalized learning. The system broadens the curriculum as his skills develop, keeping him challenged and engaged. AI education technologies ensure educational success for students like James who had fallen behind.

Furthermore, AI is playing a pivotal role in the workforce by identifying and rectifying discrimination, ultimately fostering an environment where merit reigns supreme. In addition, AI is empowering marginalized communities by providing access to financial services and literacy programs, thereby uplifting individuals who have historically been excluded from economic opportunities. However, it's crucial to recognize that AI's development and deployment in the pursuit of equality must be approached with mindfulness. It's imperative to consider the ethical implications and potential biases embedded within AI systems, as well as their impact on privacy and data security.

With proper governance and thoughtful application, AI can serve as a force for positive change, championing diversity and inclusivity. The journey toward equality through AI is ongoing, calling for collaborative efforts, forward-thinking policies, and an unwavering commitment to justice. The voices and experiences of those most affected by inequality must be prioritized, ensuring that AI serves as an ally in their fight for equity and representation.

What Gives Me Hope

The world of AI is a fascinating and complex tapestry woven with both challenges and opportunities. As I conclude this journey of exploring the nuances of AI, its potential, and its responsible implementation, I am filled with a deep sense of hope. Hope is not blind optimism; it is the belief that despite obstacles, we can create pathways to solutions and transformation. My hope for the world of AI stems from five interconnected areas: the resilience of human creativity, the promise of inclusive innovation, the power of collaboration, the potential for AI to solve pressing global challenges, and the ethical frameworks being built to guide us forward.

The Resilience of Human Creativity

At the core of every technological revolution is human creativity. We have faced challenges before—industrialization, electrification, and the rise of the internet—and each time, humanity has emerged stronger and more adaptable. AI represents another frontier, and what gives me hope is our ability to harness it as a tool for amplifying our ingenuity rather than replacing it. Artists using generative AI to expand their creative boundaries, scientists leveraging AI to accelerate discoveries, and educators deploying AI to personalize learning experiences—all of these are testaments to how human creativity will continue to thrive alongside AI. The unique spark of human curiosity and imagination cannot be replicated by machines, and it is this spark that ensures we remain the architects of our future.

AI, for all its computational power, is not an end in itself; it is a means to enhance our collective capacity for innovation. Whether it is the writer crafting stories with the assistance of language models or the entrepreneur building AI-driven solutions to tackle inefficiencies, human creativity remains central. What gives me hope is that instead of diminishing human potential, AI has the ability to expand it exponentially. The synergy between human creativity and AI tools is not about substitution but augmentation, enabling us to dream bigger and achieve more.

The Promise of Inclusive Innovation

Another source of hope is the growing emphasis on inclusivity within the AI community. Historically, technological advancements have sometimes widened social and economic disparities, but today's conversations around AI increasingly prioritize equity and access. There is a palpable shift toward ensuring that the benefits of AI reach everyone, not just a privileged few. From grassroots organizations empowering underrepresented communities with AI literacy to global initiatives like AI for Good, there is a concerted effort to democratize AI's potential.

Programs that introduce AI tools to underserved schools, initiatives focused on bridging the digital divide, and startups creating solutions tailored for marginalized populations inspire hope. When we design AI systems with diversity and inclusion at the forefront, we ensure that the technology reflects the richness of human experience. Inclusive innovation not only mitigates risks but also enriches AI with perspectives that might otherwise be overlooked. By embedding these values into AI development, we can create a world where AI uplifts everyone, fostering shared prosperity.

The Power of Collaboration

Hope also arises from the unprecedented levels of collaboration happening across industries, geographies, and disciplines in the realm of AI. Governments, corporations, academic institutions, and nonprofits are coming together to address the challenges and opportunities AI presents. These partnerships highlight the understanding that no single entity can navigate the complexities of AI alone; it requires a collective effort.

Collaborative efforts like open-source AI platforms, shared research initiatives, and multistakeholder governance frameworks are shaping the way forward. Organizations like the Partnership on AI and the Global Partnership on Artificial Intelligence bring together diverse voices to tackle ethical dilemmas, develop standards, and ensure that AI serves humanity's best interests. Such collaborations transcend competition and focus on the greater good, which gives me hope that we can approach AI development with unity rather than division.

Furthermore, interdisciplinary collaboration is unlocking new possibilities. When computer scientists work alongside climate researchers, humanitarian organizations, or healthcare professionals, the outcomes are transformative. AI-driven solutions for disaster response, precision agriculture, or disease detection illustrate how collective intelligence can amplify the impact of individual expertise. These examples remind us that collaboration—not isolation—is the key to navigating the complexities of AI responsibly.

Solving Pressing Global Challenges

One of the most inspiring aspects of AI is its potential to address some of humanity's most pressing challenges. From climate change to healthcare inequities, AI offers tools that can accelerate progress in ways previously unimaginable. Although these challenges are daunting, the strides being made with the help of AI provide a beacon of hope.

In healthcare, AI is already revolutionizing diagnostics, drug discovery, and personalized medicine. For instance, AI algorithms can analyze medical images with remarkable accuracy, enabling earlier detection of diseases like cancer. During the COVID-19 pandemic, AI played a pivotal role in vaccine development, demonstrating its ability to respond rapidly to global crises. In agriculture, AI-powered systems are helping farmers optimize crop yields, conserve water, and reduce waste, contributing to food security for a growing population.

Climate change is perhaps the most urgent crisis of our time, and AI is proving to be a valuable ally. From predicting extreme weather patterns to optimizing energy grids and monitoring deforestation, AI tools are equipping us to tackle environmental challenges more effectively. These applications remind us that technology when aligned with human values and purpose, can be a force for good. What gives me hope is the alignment of AI innovation with efforts to create a sustainable and equitable future for all.

Ethical Frameworks for Responsible AI

Finally, my hope is anchored in the growing emphasis on ethical AI. The early days of AI were marked by a rapid pace of development, often without sufficient consideration of its societal impact. Today, however, there is a robust and evolving discourse around AI ethics, governance, and accountability. This shift gives me confidence that we are charting a path toward responsible AI.

Ethical frameworks like the European Union's AI Act, the United Nations' AI for Good initiative, and corporate commitments to transparency and fairness are setting standards for how AI should be developed and deployed. These efforts reflect an understanding that AI's immense power must be balanced with safeguards to prevent harm. Principles such as fairness, explainability, privacy, and accountability are becoming integral to AI development, ensuring that the technology aligns with human values.

Moreover, the rise of AI ethics boards, interdisciplinary research on AI's societal implications, and community-driven approaches to AI governance indicate that we are building the guardrails needed to navigate this transformative era. Ethical AI is not just about mitigating risks; it is about proactively designing systems that promote equity, dignity, and justice. This commitment to responsible innovation is a source of hope, as it demonstrates our ability to learn, adapt, and course correct.

The Road Ahead

The journey ahead will not be without challenges. AI will continue to raise complex questions about privacy, bias, security, and the future of work. However, what gives me hope is our collective capacity to confront these challenges with courage and ingenuity. The lessons we learn along the way will shape not only the future of AI but also the broader trajectory of humanity.

Hope lies in the hands of individuals, communities, and organizations committed to using AI as a tool for good. It lies in the teacher integrating AI into the classroom to inspire the next generation, the policymaker advocating for equitable access to technology, the engineer designing algorithms with fairness in mind, and the entrepreneur building solutions that solve real-world problems.

Together, these efforts form a mosaic of hope, demonstrating that although AI may be a product of human invention, its impact will be shaped by human intention.

As we stand on the cusp of this new era, I am reminded of the resilience and adaptability that have defined humanity's journey thus far. AI is not a deterministic force but a reflection of our choices and values. With creativity, inclusivity, collaboration, and a commitment to ethics, we have the power to shape a future where AI enhances our shared humanity. That future fills me with hope.

Takeaways

- AI is rapidly transforming major sectors like transportation, manufacturing, healthcare, finance, and entertainment in both promising and concerning ways. Careful steering of innovation is needed.
- AI has the potential to automate many jobs but also increase productivity and economic growth if managed responsibly. Targeted training programs will be crucial.
- Advanced AI, like superintelligence, could help solve global problems if designed ethically, but it also poses risks if not properly controlled. Aligning AI goals with human values is critical.
- AI can be a powerful tool to advance equality, personalize education, address biases, and provide access to services. But ethical implications must be considered.
- With foresight, ingenuity, and responsible development, AI can empower humanity despite the uncertainties. Collaboration is key.

Reflection Questions

- How can we steer AI innovation toward empowering people and solving global challenges rather than exacerbating problems?

- What policies and programs can help mitigate the negative impacts of AI on jobs and inequality while promoting economic flourishing?
- How can we ensure that advanced AI remains aligned with human values and directed toward the common good? What safeguards are needed?
- In what ways should priorities of transparency, accountability, and fairness shape the application of AI systems?
- What gives me hope about the potential for AI to positively transform society? What concerns me?

Index

success (*continued*)
  monitoring and measuring
    systems at scale
    for, 74–77
  real-world success stories,
    244–246
Suleyman, Mustafa (CEO), 262
superintelligence
  about, 298–300
  perspectives on arrival
    timelines, 300–301
  societal impact, 302–303
sustainability, planning
    for, 95–96
SWOT analysis, 237
synthetic data, 38
systemic influence, in
    responsible AI, 131

T
talent empowerment, in
    leadership checklist, 280
team collaboration portal, 181
team dynamics, infrastruc-
    ture and, 85
technical complexity, of
    minimum remarkable
    product (MRP), 61
technical considerations, for
    building strong
    foundations, 106–107
technical debt, assessing, 155
technical limitations and
    bottlenecks, 178
technical performance
    metrics, 94

techniques, to detect
    bias, 217–218
technological change,
    superintelligence
    and, 302
technological infrastructure,
    risks to, 66
technological risks, 67
technology
  infrastructure and, 86–87
  leveraging, 205–206
Tesla, 290–291
test-and-learn mindset, 112
testing
  A/B, 202–203
  across demographics, 168
  timelines and difficulties
    with, 300
"Thankful Thursdays," 11
theoretical obstacles, timelines
    and, 300
third-party providers, walled
    garden and, 41–42
thought leaders, 261–262
TikTok, 295
tools
  for AI journey, 92–93
  for data cleaning, 89
  for data profiling, 89
  for detecting bias, 217–218
  for model manage-
    ment, 204–205
toxicity detection algo-
    rithms, 219
trailblazers, 255–256
training, leveraging, 40–41